*Palgrave Macmillan Studies in Family and Intimate Life*

Series Editors: **David Morgan**, University of Manchester, UK, **Lynn Jamieson**, University of Edinburgh, UK and **Graham Allan**, Keele University, UK.

*Titles Include*:

Graham Allan, Graham Crow and Sheila Hawker
STEPFAMILIES

Harry Blatterer
EVERYDAY FRIENDSHIPS
Intimacy and Freedom in a Complex World

Julie Brownlie
ORDINARY RELATIONSHIPS
A Sociological Study of Emotions, Reflexivity and Culture

Ann Buchanan and Anna Rotkirch
FERTILITY RATES AND POPULATION DECLINE
No Time for Children?

Emma Casey and Yvette Taylor (*editors*)
INTIMACIES, CRITICAL CONSUMPTION AND DIVERSE ECONOMIES

Deborah Chambers
SOCIAL MEDIA AND PERSONAL RELATIONSHIPS
Online Intimacies and Networked Friendship

Robbie Duschinsky and Leon Antonio Rocha (*editors*)
FOUCAULT, THE FAMILY AND POLITICS

Jacqui Gabb
RESEARCHING INTIMACY IN FAMILIES

Jacqui Gabb and Janet Fink
COUPLE RELATIONSHIPS IN THE 21ST CENTURY

Dimitra Hartas
PARENTING, FAMILY POLICY AND CHILDREN'S WELL-BEING IN AN UNEQUAL SOCIETY
A New Culture War for Parents

Stephen Hicks
LESBIAN, GAY AND QUEER PARENTING
Families, Intimacies, Genealogies

Clare Holdsworth
FAMILY AND INTIMATE MOBILITIES

Janet Holland and Rosalind Edwards (*editors*)
UNDERSTANDING FAMILIES OVER TIME
Research and Policy

Mary Holmes
DISTANCE RELATIONSHIPS
Intimacy and Emotions Amongst Academics and Their Partners in Dual-Locations

Rachel Hurdley
HOME, MATERIALITY, MEMORY AND BELONGING
Keeping Culture

Lynn Jamieson and Roona Simpson
LIVING ALONE
Globalization, Identity and Belonging

Lynn Jamieson, Ruth Lewis and Roona Simpson (*editors*)
RESEARCHING FAMILIES AND RELATIONSHIPS
Reflections on Process

Carmen Lau Clayton
BRITISH CHINESE FAMILIES
Parenting, Relationships and Childhoods

Lara McKenzie
AGE-DISSIMILAR COUPLES AND ROMANTIC RELATIONSHIPS
Ageless Love?

David Morgan
RETHINKING FAMILY PRACTICES

Petra Nordqvist, Carol Smart
RELATIVE STRANGERS
Family Life, Genes and Donor Conception

Julie M. Parsons
GENDER, CLASS AND FOOD
Families, Bodies and Health

Róisín Ryan-Flood
LESBIAN MOTHERHOOD
Gender, Families and Sexual Citizenship

Sally Sales
ADOPTION, FAMILY AND THE PARADOX OF ORIGINS
A Foucauldian History

**Palgrave Macmillan Studies in Family and Intimate Life**
**Series Standing Order ISBN 978–0–230–51748–6 (hardback)**
**978–0–230–24924–0 (paperback)**
(*outside North America only*)

You can receive future titles in this series as they are published by placing a standing order. Please contact your bookseller or, in case of difficulty, write to us at the address below with your name and address, the title of the series and one of the ISBNs quoted above.

Customer Services Department, Macmillan Distribution Ltd, Houndmills, Basingstoke, Hampshire RG21 6XS, England

# Intimacies, Critical Consumption and Diverse Economies

Edited by

**Emma Casey**
*Kingston University, UK*

and

**Yvette Taylor**
*London South Bank University, UK*

First published 2015 by
PALGRAVE MACMILLAN

Palgrave Macmillan in the UK is an imprint of Macmillan Publishers Limited,
registered in England, company number 785998, of Houndmills, Basingstoke,
Hampshire RG21 6XS.

Palgrave Macmillan in the US is a division of St Martin's Press LLC,
175 Fifth Avenue, New York, NY 10010.

Palgrave Macmillan is the global academic imprint of the above companies
and has companies and representatives throughout the world.

Palgrave® and Macmillan® are registered trademarks in the United States,
the United Kingdom, Europe and other countries.

ISBN: 978–1–137–42907–0

This book is printed on paper suitable for recycling and made from fully
managed and sustained forest sources. Logging, pulping and manufacturing
processes are expected to conform to the environmental regulations of the
country of origin.

A catalogue record for this book is available from the British Library.

Library of Congress Cataloging-in-Publication Data

Intimacies, critical consumption and diverse economies / [edited by] Emma
Casey, Yvette Taylor.
    pages cm.—(Palgrave Macmillan studies in family and intimate life)
ISBN 978–1–137–42907–0 (hardback)
    1. Consumption (Economics) – Social aspects. 2. Households – Economic
aspects. 3. Families. 4. Consumer behavior. 5. Intimacy (Psychology) I. Casey,
Emma. II. Taylor, Yvette, 1978-

HC79.C6I575 2015
339.4'7—dc23                                                    2015019841

# Contents

List of Figures                                                    vii

Acknowledgements                                                   viii

Notes on Contributors                                               ix

Also by Emma Casey and Yvette Taylor                                xii

Introduction                                                         1
*Emma Casey and Yvette Taylor*

### Part I    Expanding the Field: Conceptualising Intimate Consumption

1   Collective Action and Domestic Practices: England in
    the 1830s and 1840s                                             13
    *Colin Creighton*

2   Buying the Ties That Bind: Consumption, Care and
    Intimate Investment among Transnational Households in
    Highland Ecuador                                                36
    *Emma-Jayne Abbots*

3   Interconnectivities and Material Agencies:
    Consumption, Fashion, and Intimacy in Zhu Tianwen's
    'Fin-de-Siècle Splendor'                                        60
    *C. Laura Lovin*

### Part II    'Sticky' and Shifting Sites of Intimate Consumption

4   'My Bedroom Is Me': Young People, Private Space,
    Consumption and the Family Home                                 87
    *Siân Lincoln*

5   The Transgressive Potential of Families in Commercial Homes     107
    *Julie Seymour*

6   Belonging in Difficult Family Circumstances: Emotions,
    Intimacies and Consumption                                    126
    *Sarah Wilson*

7   'You're Not Going Out Dressed Like That!': Lessons in
    Fashion Consumption, Taste and Class                          145
    *Katherine Appleford*

**Part III   The Intimate Social Life of Commodities**

8   Pretty Pants and Office Pants: Making Home, Identity
    and Belonging in a Workplace                                  173
    *Rachel Hurdley*

9   Buying for Baby: How Middle-Class Mothers Negotiate
    Risk with Second-Hand Goods                                   197
    *Emma Waight*

10  The Hidden Lives of Domestic Things: Accumulations in
    Cupboards, Lofts, and Shelves                                 216
    *Sophie Woodward*

*Index*                                                          233

# List of Figures

| | | |
|---|---|---|
| 8.1a | [Mike Biddulph (copyright 2013)] | 174 |
| 8.1b | | 175 |
| 8.2a | | 180 |
| 8.2b | | 181 |
| 8.3a | | 192 |
| 8.3b | | 193 |

# Acknowledgements

The impetus behind this collection was a one-day meeting of the British Sociological Association Families and Relationships study group in early 2013 on the theme of intimacies, families and practices of consumption. Thanks are due to the BSA for supporting the event, to all our contributors for meeting the various deadlines with such efficiency and to Tam Sanger for preparing the Index.

# Notes on Contributors

**Emma-Jayne Abbots** is Senior Lecturer in Anthropology and Heritage at the University of Wales Trinity Saint David. Her research and teaching interests centre on the cultural politics, the materialities and the visceralities of consumption. She is broadly concerned with theorising embodied engagements with objects, particularly food and domestic items, care and intimacies, and kinship and gender relations. Abbots has written widely on these topics and is the co-editor of *Why We Eat, How We Eat: Contemporary Encounters between Foods and Bodies* (2013, with A. Lavis) and *Careful Eating: Embodied Entanglements between Food and Care* (in press, with A. Lavis and L. Attala).

**Katherine Appleford** is Senior Lecturer in Sociology at Kingston University. Her doctoral research, conducted at the London College of Fashion, University of the Arts London, examined the links between fashion and class, and explored the ways in which class is mobilised in British women's fashion practices and discourse. Her more recent work continues to question the relationships between fashion and identity, and considers distinctions in women's understandings of looking 'good', and attitudes towards body shape and size.

**Emma Casey** is Senior Lecturer in Sociology at Kingston University. Her books include *Women, Pleasure and the Gambling Experience* (2008) which was shortlisted for the BSA Philips Abrams Memorial Prize and *Gender and Consumption: Domestic Cultures and the Commercialisation of Everyday Life* (edited with Lydia Martens, 2007). Her articles have appeared in a range of journals including *European Journal of Cultural Studies, Sociological Research Online, Feminist Theory, Journal of Consumer Culture, International Journal of Sociology* and *Social Policy and Leisure Studies*. Casey is currently working with Mass Observation Archive on an ESRC funded project on the theme of gambling and households (RES-000–22–4314).

**Colin Creighton** is a fellow in the Department of Social Sciences, University of Hull. His main research interests lie in the historical sociology of the family in Britain and in family and gender issues in sub-Saharan Africa.

**Rachel Hurdley** is a research fellow in the School of Social Sciences, Cardiff University. Her work focuses on the small practices, spaces and things of everyday life. An ethnography of organisational culture funded by the Leverhulme Trust is the basis for her chapter, developing earlier work on 'the power of corridors' and 'dismantling mantelpieces'. Hurdley's particular interest is methodology: what do we do and how do we do it, to make knowledge?

**Siân Lincoln** is Senior Lecturer in Sociology at Liverpool John Moores University. Her research interests are around contemporary youth culture, young people and private space and young people and social media. She published her first book, *Youth Culture and Private Space* (Palgrave Macmillan), in 2012. Her work has also appeared in journals including *Leisure Studies, YOUNG: Journal of Nordic Youth Research, Space and Culture, Continuum: Journal of Media and Cultural Studies, Journal of Sociology, Information Technology and People, Film, Fashion and Consumption* and *New Media and Society*.

**C. Laura Lovin** is a researcher at the Weeks Centre for Social and Policy Research, London South Bank University, where she studies the transnational journeys and quests for employment of immigrant workers from Romania in two major sites of global capitalism, the cities of London and New York. She holds a PhD in Women's and Gender Studies from Rutgers University. Her areas of specialisation include contemporary feminist theories, transnational mobilities, critical consumption studies, cultural politics and policy, and Eastern European feminisms. Her articles and reviews have appeared in anthologies and journals published in the US and Europe. She taught Women's and Gender Studies courses at Rutgers-New Brunswick and Rutgers-Newark.

**Julie Seymour** is Senior Lecturer in Medical Sociology at the Hull York Medical School (HYMS). Her research interests focus on family and childhood practices in relation to domestic labour, health and illness, emotional labour, work–life balance and body donation. Her recent works include Dermott, E. and Seymour, J. (eds) (2011) *Displaying Families: A New Concept for the Sociology of Family Life*, and Juozeliuniene, I. and Seymour, J. (eds) (2015) *Family Change in Times of the De-bordering of Europe and Global Mobility: Resources, Processes and Practices*.

**Yvette Taylor** is Professor of Social and Policy Studies and Head of the Weeks Centre for Social and Policy Research, London South Bank University. She has held a Fulbright Scholarship at Rutgers University (2010–11) and a British Academy Mid-Career grant (2013–14). Her books include *Fitting into Place? Class and Gender Geographies and Temporalities* (2012), *Lesbian and Gay Parenting: Securing Social and Educational*

*Capitals* (Palgrave Macmillan, 2009) and *Working-Class Lesbian Life: Classed Outsiders* (Palgrave Macmillan, 2007). Edited collections include *Educational Diversity* (Palgrave Macmillan, 2012), *Sexualities: Reflections and Futures* (2012), *Theorizing Intersectionality and Sexuality* (Palgrave Macmillan, 2010) and *Classed Intersections: Spaces, Selves, Knowledges* (2010). Yvette is currently working on an ESRC standard grant 'Making space for queer identifying religious youth'.

**Emma Waight** is Research Fellow in Design at the University of Southampton where she completed a PhD in Human Geography in 2015. Increasingly inspired by writings on new materialisms, her main research interests are retail and consumption and the way they relate to identity, practice and ethics in daily life. Her thesis funded by ESRC and the parenting charity NCT investigated mothers' second-hand consumption practices. Waight also holds an MPhil in Design with a focus on ethical fashion and continues to work closely with the fashion industry.

**Sarah Wilson** is Senior Lecturer in Sociology in the School of Applied Social Science at the University of Stirling. Her research has explored chronic illness and young people's experience of parental substance use. Her most recent work has focused on the construction and experience of (non) belonging, however positive, negative or ambivalent, among 'looked after' young people. This work has employed visual, audial and artistic methods.

**Sophie Woodward** carries out research in the fields of material culture, consumption and feminist theory. Her research into material culture has been focused primarily upon clothing, through an ethnography of women's wardrobes and through research into denim as the co-founder of the Global Denim Project (with Daniel Miller); her current project into dormant things (http://projects.socialsciences.manchester.ac.uk/dormant-things/) focuses upon things that have accumulated in the home but are no longer used. She has a continuing interest in the methodological challenges of understanding material culture and has explored this through ethnographic and interdisciplinary approaches. She is the author of several books including *Why Women Wear What They Wear* (2007), *Blue Jeans: The Art of the Ordinary* (with Daniel Miller, 2012) and *Why Feminism Matters* (with Kath Woodward, Palgrave Macmillan, 2009).

# Also by Emma Casey and Yvette Taylor

## Emma Casey

Casey, E. (2008) *Women, Pleasure and the Gambling Experience*. Hampshire: Ashgate.

Casey, E. and Martens, L. (eds) (2007) *Gender and Consumption: Material Culture and the Commercialisation of Everyday Life*. Hampshire: Ashgate.

## Yvette Taylor

### Book Series:

Critical Diversities: Policies, Practices and Perspectives, Routledge
Gender and Education, Palgrave Macmillan

Taylor, Y. (2007) *Working-Class Lesbian Life: Classed Outsiders*. New York: Palgrave Macmillan.

Taylor, Y. (2009) *Lesbian and Gay Parenting: Securing Social and Educational Capital*. Basingstoke: Palgrave Macmillan.

Taylor, Y. (ed.) (2010) *Classed Intersections: Spaces, Selves, Knowledges*. Farnham: Ashgate.

Taylor, Y., Hines, S. and Casey, M. (eds) (2010) *Theorizing Intersectionality and Sexuality*. Basingstoke: Palgrave Macmillan.

Taylor, Y. (2012) *Fitting into Place? Class and Gender Geographies and Temporalities*. Abingdon, Oxon: Ashgate.

Taylor, Y. (ed.) (2012) *Educational Diversity: The Subject of Difference and Different Subjects*. Basingstoke: Palgrave Macmillan.

Hines, S. and Taylor, Y. (eds) (2012) *Sexualities: Reflections and Future Directions*. Basingstoke: Palgrave Macmillan.

Taylor, Y. and Addison, M. (eds) (2013) *Queer Presences and Absences*. Basingstoke: Palgrave Macmillan.

Taylor, Y. and Sanger, T. (eds) (2013) *Mapping Intimacies: Relations, Exchanges, Affects*. Basingstoke: Palgrave Macmillan.

Taylor, Y. (ed.) (2014) *The Entrepreneurial University: Public Engagements, Intersecting Impacts*. Basingstoke: Palgrave Macmillan.

Taylor, Y. and Snowdon, R. (eds) (2014) *Queering Religion, Religious Queers*. New York: Routledge.

Taylor, Y., Stella, F., Reynolds, T. and Rogers, A. (2015) *Sexual Citizenship and the New Europe*. London: Routledge.

# Introduction

*Emma Casey and Yvette Taylor*

Our aims in producing this new collection are twofold. The first aim responds to a call to rebalance theoretical emphasis of large-scale global economies characterized by, for example, structural risk, crisis and recession (Beck, 1992; Giddens, 1992; Bauman, 2007; Featherstone, 1990; Slater, 1997) alongside attention towards small scale, critically diverse and everyday 'intimate' consumer economies (Casey and Martens, 2007; Clarke, 2004; Jackson and Moores, 1995; Sanger and Taylor, 2013). Secondly the collection aims to offer detailed empirical accounts of diverse intimacies, domestic economies and family lives. It attempts to relocate forms of 'critical consumption' in and through a range of 'diverse economies' and 'diverse methods' across time and place. How do we understand underrepresented social realities within consumer culture, such as non-consumption, mundane consumer choices, the choice not to consume, and alternative forms of consumption?

Sensibilities of austerity and 'responsible' consumerism idealize middle-class forms of personhood based on deferred gratification, restraint and modesty (Armstrong, 2010; Atkinson et al., 2012; Allen and Taylor, 2013; Skeggs, 2004). In contrast, admonishing statements about 'inappropriate' material desires litter the statements of politicians who locate the poor as being resistant to work and too dependent on state 'hand-outs'. In the context of growing European inequality under austerity agendas – rising unemployment, benefit cuts, growing numbers of families dependent on food banks – these discourses work to mask the presence of severe cuts and injustices by holding the poor morally responsible for their plight. Such divisions also heighten a process of consumer distinction, in the deliberate selection and rejection of consumption choices by 'us' and 'them' (Bourdieu, 1985). Consumption might be reframed not only as a form of expression, pleasure and choice,

1

but also of vilification, inequality and social exclusion (see for example, Casey, 2013). Understandings of 'critical consumption' reflected in the chapters in this collection suggest that the proliferation of global consumer and neo-liberal economies has far reaching consequences for the everyday lives of individuals and their ability to actively participate in social life.

In many ways, these aims draw from previous attempts to develop the dedicated study of gendered domestic consumption practices. Historically, sociological research has tended to overlook both the complexities and diversities inherent in intimate life and also the particular role of material cultural practices in providing sociological understandings of familial and household life. There have of course, been some notable exceptions to this and some innovative attempts to collate feminist accounts of domestic consumption practices. For example, Jackson and Moores's writing in the introduction to their 1995 collection of inter-disciplinary essays *The Politics of Domestic Consumption,* called for a dedicated study of the creative and active appropriation of domestic consumption (p. 1) which would simultaneously be attuned to the gendered, classed and ethnic cultures and structures of power and constraint underpinning domestic relations. Jackson and Moores describe this twofold approach to domestic consumption as a 'dialectic of creativity and constraint', which unpicks the interconnections between structure and agency. More recently, Casey and Martens' collection *Gender and Consumption,* published a decade after Jackson and Moores, argued for the need for gendered approaches to the study of consumption (2007).

The collection expanded on previous work by illuminating the commercialization of domestic space and also examining the everyday production and reproduction of socio-economic relations. It revealed consumption to be integral to the broader cultural practices interwoven into women's everyday, intimate lives. Here, this collection expands on these ideas some eight years later by moving on from discourses of market forces of consumption and instead, shifting its focus to incorporate an account of some of the effects that recent dramatic economic austerity measures have had on intimate consumer practices. Recently, researchers have questioned some of the consequences of the burgeoning inclusiveness of consumption as a concept, as well as the ideological effects of academic accounts in which more and more arenas of social life and action are analysed within a discourse of market shaped consumption (see e.g. Gabb, 2009; O'Hagan, 2014; Taylor, 2012; Reynolds, 2012; Edwards and Weller, Slater and Miller, 2007; Thompson, 2011; Williams, 2004).

Sociologists have increasingly explored the home as space for the display of goods which might signify value (Skeggs, 1997) yet relatively little has been made of ways in which emotions, relations and domestic intimacies, intersect with cultural and economic forms of exchange (Reay, 2008; Gillies, 2007). Drawing on earlier work unpicking the relationships between domestic life and consumption (e.g. Casey and Martens, 2007) and everyday spaces for the pursuit of intersections of class, gender and sexualities (e.g. Taylor, 2010), this collection provides a space for the dedicated study not only of at-home consumption, but also of other types of consumption which might connect to the domestic without actually taking place at home, a comprehensive study of which we argue necessitates an examination of the fluid and interconnected roles of emotions, feelings and in short the intimate practices of diverse forms of consumption.

Here, we seek to dwell on the relationships between feelings and things, between the emotional and the material, by presenting studies that engage with contemporary debates about, for example, meaningful material objects (Finch, 2007; Miller, 2008; Thrift, 1997; Taylor and Falconer, 2014) – or the lack thereof – and multiple constructions and constitutions of 'the domestic' (and when the 'domestic' is not owned or rented but still 'held' in, for example, accounts of young homeless people's consumption, see Wilson, this collection). Chapters connect with and develop debates surrounding the emotional and material labour involved in producing and reproducing domestic, work and intimate spaces (Gregg, 2013), encouraging different ways of thinking about consumption patterns, including some of the perceived impacts on domestic life within the context of the 'work-life' balance.

The chapters demonstrate the particular pertinence of this especially for women in late modernity as they experience specific pressures to manage the work-life balance as part of a broader project of neo-liberal selfhood and subject making. Empirical chapters illustrate varied domestic inferences and the affective and symbolic materiality of a variety of domestic environments. New understandings of critical diversities are offered in presenting new and diverse accounts of the ways in which bodies and objects move in and out of domestic spaces. The focus is not always on adult consumers and residents. As chapters on spaces of home demonstrate, children and young people occupy and move within domestic spaces of consumption in very particular ways. The chapters also pinpoint the transgressive potential of intimate consumption and debates surrounding the delicate borders between diverse tastes and 'disgust' and the relationship between these debates and wider contemporary issues to do with inclusion and exclusion, which is central to our understanding of critical consumption (Gorman-Murray, 2013). Within this collection, shifting geographies of intimate consumption are presented alongside broader genres of material culture and diverse methods including visual web-based narratives.

By placing emphasis on everyday life and mundane forms of leisure and consumption such as fashion, second-hand shopping, storing objects and appropriation of everyday spaces for the display of objects, the chapters propose an alternative to mainstream accounts of spectacular, public consumption (see also Casey, 2013). The chapters in this collection are written at a very particular point in history – one defined by dramatic economic uncertainties and against the backdrop of a post-welfare, austerity climate. As others have argued, consumption offers an avenue into exploring the impact that these wider social and political shifts might have as individuals live out their everyday lives within an increasingly intensified consumer economy. We hope to get closer to specific scene spaces, providing an analysis of intimate, sensual and affective encounters with the tangible materiality of place and space, including *things* within those spaces such as food drink, décor, furniture and so on (taste), along with *sensual and affective* articulations of light, dark, dirt, and *atmospheric* environment (smell) (see Taylor and Falconer, 2014). The chapters interrogate the various ways in which types of consumption might hold value and capital, and explore the potential risks underpinning 'at home' consumption (including the role of new digital technologies). They provide methodological insights into researching diverse intimacies of everyday life by looking at how the home facilitates pleasure, value and status. The collection offers new advances in terms of how different domesticities, enable, restrain and control consumption, impacting on the subjective and material wellbeing of families, residents, individual within – and beyond – the 'domestic'. It examines geographies and spaces of consumption in international and local-global spheres, asking what might constitute forms of 'critical consumption' in and through 'diverse economies'.

Chapters are from a diverse range of empirical and theoretical locations brought together initially as a joint venture between the British Sociological Association Families and Relationships and Leisure study groups, convened by the editors. Chapters variously offer historical reflection, critical examination of intersectionalities of class, gender and ethnicities and explore the social and intimate lives of objects. Chapters engage with contemporary debates surrounding austerity and thrift (Allen et al., 2013; Jensen, 2012; Taylor, 2012) by pointing to new ways of exploring socio-spatial inequalities within the context of consumption and its relationship to value. Authors offer novel perspectives on consumption and studies of intimacy by focusing on studies of everyday routine and practice of consumption and particularly the taken-for-granted-ness of everyday life. They examine some of the everyday, intimate cultural implications of financial crisis, austerity and concerns around production and consumption, by demonstrating through a range of novel empirical case studies how consumption experiences connect with a variety of lived experiences of. The collection also draws on contemporary theoretical accounts of intersectionalities (e.g. Berger, M.T and Guidroz, 2010; Crenshaw, 1989; Taylor, 2012; Skeggs, 1997) by insisting on the importance of embedding consumption within broader identity formations of for example class, gender and race. To this end, the chapters in the collection are international in focus, drawing on research from the UK, US, Ecuador and East Asia and contribute to current understandings of a diverse range of consumer practices as they connect to everyday practices of e.g. mothering, caring and pleasure seeking.

The collection is divided into three key sections, each intended to further advance the concept of critical consumption. In Part I *Expanding the Field: Conceptualising Intimate Consumption* we present papers that demonstrate the historical context of intimate consumption practices and demonstrate recent advances in sociological accounts of intimate consumption. Colin Creighton's chapter *Collective Action and Domestic Practices: England in the 1830s and 1840s* for example, offers a historical perspective on domestic consumption and intimacies. Focusing on shifts in the nineteenth century to employment laws restricting working hours Creighton examines the impact of these changes on the development of the 'nuclear' family. Importantly, these legislative and philosophical shifts are framed in the paper as being part of a wider, often religious, political and moral concern for the sanctity of domestic and familial care and bonds. Interestingly, this perspective shifts from more conventional explorations of transformations to the workplace which have tended to focus on legislative changes as influenced by a growing empathy for the plight of the working classes. Emma-Jayne Abbots' chapter, *Buying the Ties that Bind: Consumption, Care and Intimate Investment Among Transnational Households in Highland Ecuador* offers novel empirical research into inter-generational mobility and its relationship to consumption. Focusing on households in a rural community of Jima in Highland Ecuador, Abbots explores the ways in which consumption reproduces inter-personal relationships and reshape family life and enact affective relationships. Specifically, it examines how the wives of migrants invest in the long-term reproduction of their household and maintain intimate relations with their geographically distant husbands through their everyday material engagements with commodities. C. Laura Lovin's chapter offers an account of Zhu Tianwen's volume of short stories *Fin-de-Siècle Splendour*. Lovin considers the contemporary feminist contribution to consumerism and materialism that emerges within the volume and examines the 'sensorial-affective' processes of consumption.

Part II of the collection *'Sticky' and Shifting Sites of Intimate Consumption* considers how families facilitate, control, (re)configure and (re)produce spaces for the pursuit of consumption. The chapters in this section explore a range of domestic settings for consumption, including young people's bedrooms, family life in 'commercial homes', mother and daughter relationships and consumption in difficult family scenarios. Sian Lincoln's chapter *'My Bedroom is Me': Young People, Private Space, Consumption and the Family Home* presents original empirical research into young people, space and bedrooms. Exploring the bedroom as a significant youth cultural domain, Lincoln describes the 'layers' of regulation from both inside and outside the home that interrogate the boundaries of public and private space. The chapter demonstrates how a young person's bedroom can be shaped by a series of complex negotiations and intersections both with public and private domains, and how bedrooms operate as space for carving out and reproducing identities. Julie Seymour's chapter *The Transgressive Potential of Families in Commercial Homes* presents research into families who work in the hospitality industry, specifically in family-run hotels, pubs and boarding houses, collectively known as 'commercial homes'. Seymour focuses on the emotional labour provided by such family members, particularly children, as part of the economic imperative of the business. As such, there is considerable clarity about the intersection of emotions and economic forms of exchange although the production of such labour is best performed invisibly. Drawing on recent conceptual developments in family sociology, it considers the ways in which the host family is 'displayed' as an economic process and the curious mix of 'hypervisibility' and 'displayed reticence' which constitutes the labour of servicing other families' leisure in such establishments. The chapter highlights the role that host families play in facilitating the leisure and consumption of other families 'at play' and contributes to the interrogation of the diversity of domestic spaces of consumption by showing how these can include spaces of public consumption.

In *Belonging in Difficult Family Circumstances: Emotions, Intimacies and Consumption* Sarah Wilson draws on research findings exploring practices of consumption and belonging among looked after children. Wilson's chapter considers how material consumer goods are often used by young people as tools to provide a temporal escape from troubled thoughts or as a means of exploring difficult past experiences and associated current or past emotions, as well as troubling issues of identity and possibilities for the future. At the same time, the young people's access to such resources was often contingent, as a result of their limited financial and fragile relational resources. The chapter is situated in relation to wider literature on children and young people's 'ordinary' and 'conspicuous' practices of consumption including in less affluent circumstances such as Pugh (2009), Lareau (2011) and Buckingham (2011). Katherine Appleford's chapter *'You're Not Going out Dressed Like That!' Lessons in Fashion Consumption, Taste and Class* continues the theme of familial and inter-personal relationships in facilitating space for the pursuit of consumption. Appleford explores in her chapter the significance of the mother-daughter relationship in academic discourse on fashion consumption. She notes that the ways in which mothers shape their daughters' fashion tastes differs significantly with social class and the chapter focuses in particular on the various ways in which middle class and working class mothers influence their daughters fashion tastes.

The third and final part to the collection is entitled *The Intimate Social Life of Commodities*. Here we present chapters that address sociological research examining the relational qualities of commodities within domestic, intimate settings. Chapters address for example the appropriation of material objects in domestic settings and provide novel accounts of everyday objects in the enactment of intimacies and everyday life. In this section, Rachel Hurdley's chapter *Pretty Pants and Office Pants: Making Home, Identity and Belonging in a Workplace* draws on ethnographic research conducted on a British university campus in order to examine patterns of making home, identity and intimacy at work. Hurdley develops themes of homely/personal spaces and intimacies and considers the processual, contingent character of relations between people and things. Emma Waight's chapter explores the emotional contexts of second-hand consumption practices amongst mothers, and echoing earlier studies examining parenthood as dual site for celebration and anxiety (for example Martens, 2010), points to the classed and gendered context of second-hand consumption. Focusing on discourses of thrift, safety and 'nurture' at NCT nearly-new sales, Waight points to the risky construction of motherhood which is always assessed against a wider duty of care. In *The Hidden Lives of Domestic Things: Accumulations in Cupboards, Lofts and Shelves* Sophie Woodward draws on previous research that has highlighted the ways in which relationships are enshrined and constituted through everyday practices (Morgan, 1996) by examining the enactment of everyday life, culture and relationships within unused and rarely used or 'dormant' objects'. The chapter considers the possibilities and potentials for extending this approach to wider genres of material culture that are in stored within the home to explore this in relation to Gregson's notion of 'accommodating' (2007) relationships to others.

In short, the chapters in this collection offer novel perspectives on consumption and studies of intimacy by focusing on studies of everyday routines and practices of consumption within family life and as part of the reproduction of inter-personal relationships. Chapters differently illuminate some of the intimate, everyday, cultural implications of for example, austerity measures, welfare, and related neo-liberal discourses of production and consumption by demonstrating through a variety of novel case studies how intimate, familial consumption patterns intersect with, reflect and sometimes reproduce structural inequalities and inter-sectionalities (see also Taylor, 2012; Skeggs, 1997). They demonstrate some of the ways in which families restrain and control consumption practices and how particular forms of consumption affect the wellbeing of families and other inter-personal relationships. Excitingly, authors offer new insights into the ways in which we can understand how the home facilitates – or indeed impedes – pleasure, value and status.

# References

Allen, A., Hollingworth, S., Mansaray, A. and Taylor, Y. (eds) (2013) 'Collisions, Coalitions and Riotous Subjects: Reflections and Repercussions' *Sociological Research Online,* 18(4) 1 <http://www.socresonline.org.uk/ 18/4/1.html>.

Allen, K. and Taylor, Y. (2013) 'Failed Femininities and Troubled Mothers: Gender and the Riots' *Studies in the Maternal,* Special Issue on Austerity Parenting, 4(2).

Armstrong, J. (2010) 'Class and Gender at the Intersection: Working-Class Women's Dispositions towards Employment and Motherhood'. pp. 235–253 in Taylor Y (ed.) *Classed Intersections:Spaces, Selves, Knowledges.* Aldershot: Ashgate.

Atkinson, W., Roberts, S. and Savage, M. (2012) *Class Inequality in Austerity Britain.* Basingstoke: Palgrave MacMillan.

Bauman, Z. (2007) *Consuming life.* Cambridge: Polity.

Berger, M.T. and Guidroz, K. (eds) (2010) *The Intersectional Approach. Transforming the Academy Through Race, Class and Gender.* Chapel Hill: The University of North Carolina Press.

Crenshaw, K.W. (1989) 'Demarginalizing the Intersection of Race and Sex: A Black Feminist Critique of Antidiscrimination Doctrine, Feminist Theory, and Antiracist Politics' in University of Chicago Legal Forum 1989:139–67.

Edwards, R. and Weller, S. (2014) *Families, Relationships and Societies*, 3(2), (July 2014) 185–199.

Featherstone, M. (1990) Perspectives on Consumer Culture, *Sociology* 24(1): 5–22.

Featherstone, M. (1991) *Consumer Culture and Postmodernism*. London: Sage.

Gabb, J. (2012) 'The Affects of Method' in Taylor, Y., Hines, S. and Casey, M. (eds) (2010) *Theorizing Intersectionality and Sexuality*. Basingstoke: Palgrave Macmillan.

Gorman-Murray (2013) 'Liminal Subjects, Marginal Spaces and Material Legacies: Older Gay Men, Home and Belonging' in Taylor, Y. and Addison, M. (eds) *Queer Presences and Absences*. London: Palgrave Macmillan.

Gregg, M. (2013) *Work's Intimacy*. Hoboken, NJ: Wiley.

O'Hagan, C. (2014) *Families, Relationships and Societies*, 3(2), (July 2014), 201–217

Skeggs, B. (1997) *Formations of Class and Gender*. London: Sage.

Skeggs, B. (2004) *Class, Self, Culture*. London: Routledge.

Slater, D. (1997) *Consumer Culture and Modernity*. Oxford: Polity Press.

Taylor, Y. (2012) *Fitting into Place? Class and Gender Geographies and Temporalities*. Farnham: Ashgate.

Taylor, Y. and Gillies, V. (eds) (2014) 'Intersecting Family Lives, Labours, Locales', *Families, Relationships & Societies*, 3(2), 163–165.

Taylor, Y. and Falconer, E. (2014) "Seedy Bars and Grotty Pints': Close encounters in queer leisure spaces '*Social and Cultural Geography*, 16(1): 43–57.

Thompson, C.J. (2011) Understanding Consumption as Political and Moral Practice: Introduction to the Special Issue. *Journal of Consumer Culture*, 11(2): 139–144

Williams, C.C. (2004) The Myth of Marketization: An Evaluation of the Persistence of Non-Market Activities in Advanced Economies. *International Sociology*, 19(4): 437–449.

# Part I

# Expanding the Field: Conceptualising Intimate Consumption

# 1
# Collective Action and Domestic Practices: England in the 1830s and 1840s

*Colin Creighton*

In recent years our understanding of domestic practices and relations of intimacy have made enormous advances (Giddens, 1992; Jamieson, 1998; Gillies, 2003; Gabb, 2008; Morgan, 2011). However, our grasp of the broader social and economic processes within which intimate relations are constructed, and the interplay between the two, has not kept pace. In this chapter I argue, through an historical case study, that in exploring this interaction we need to pay more attention to social movements because of the important part they play in mediating between macro socio-economic change and the practices of individual families. To date, studies of family practices have paid little attention to the role of social movements (Staggenborg, 1998) while scholarship on social movements has, with a few notable exceptions, paid scant attention to movements directed towards family change (Della Porta and Diani, 2006; Snow et al., 2004).[1]

Through this case study I seek to explore two major ways in which collective struggles influence the formation of domestic practices.[2] The first is by acting to change the structural conditions which shape domestic practices. The second is through the meaning-making processes (Snow and Benford, 1992) of articulating a persuasive alternative to existing practices and convincing relevant audiences that this cannot be realised through individual efforts but only through a modification of situational constraints.

Under examination are the decades of the 1830s and 1840s, when social conflict over the dramatic economic and social changes brought about by the industrial revolution reached a peak of intensity. Population increase, technological advances, the spread of factory production with its associated discipline, large-scale migration into the overcrowded and insanitary manufacturing towns, the decline of many domestic indus- tries and the abandonment of older legislative controls over economic activity had a profound impact upon people's lives, the nature and extent of which is still debated today (Berg, 1980, part 5; Brown, 1991; Hilton, 2006, chap. 9; Humphries, 2007). Moreover, the indus- trial revolution involved cultural as well as economic transformation (Gray, 1996, pp. 1–3) and was accompanied by a clash of contrasting philosophies and social ideals, with criticism of the direction and effects of economic change becoming more acute from the late 1820s (Perkin, 1969, pp. 218–339; Hilton, 2006, chaps. 5 and 7).

This provides the context for the emergence of the Ten Hours Movement (THM) for the 1830s and 1840s were the years in which indus- trial workers in the northern factory towns first started to grapple, collec- tively, with the issue of what kind of domestic practices they wanted to create, and how they could do so, in their new and harsh environment. The challenge was not only one of adjusting to new conditions; it was more profound than this, for workers were confronting what they saw as threats to the very possibility of meaningful family life. The combi- nation of downward pressure on wages, high rates of unemployment, the insecurity associated with the fluctuations of the trade cycle, long (and in some trades lengthening) hours of work, and excessive reliance upon the labour of young children, together with grossly overcrowded housing conditions, all seemed to threaten the ability of the working- class family to reproduce itself, let alone enjoy emotionally satisfying family relationships. These problems gave rise to sustained collective action and ambitious political demands. In this period, workers in a wide range of trades and industries voiced dissatisfaction with the mate- rial and emotional pressures on the family. It was the textile towns of the north of England, however, that generated the most vocal protests and the most sustained campaign to ameliorate conditions.

The Ten Hours Movement, which provides the main focus of this chapter, struggled for reduced hours of work across two and a half decades, from 1830–1855, and compelled generally unwilling govern- ments to make concession after concession until the tenhour day was finally conceded. This campaign marked an important historical turning- point in the formation of domestic practices among the working-class in England, for it constituted the first collective effort of modern times to confront the impact of the factory system and the unregulated market upon family life and to modify the balance between work and home by clawing back time from the rapacious demands of the workplace.

The Ten Hours Movement emerged in 1831 from the alliance between the trade union-backed Short-time Committees in Lancashire, where the cotton spinners had struggled intermittently during the 1820s on behalf of child workers, and the Yorkshire-based campaign, led by the radical Tory land agent and philanthropist, Richard Oastler, for restrictions on child labour.[3] Its main objective was to persuade Parliament to ban the employment of children under nine years of age in the cotton and woollen textile industries, and reduce the hours of children under 18 to a maximum of ten a day (not including meal times). Because governing circles were in thrall to the belief that nothing should interfere with free contracts between employers and adult workers, the proposed legislation related, initially, solely to children and young persons, but in the 1840s protection of adult women was also demanded, and first incorporated into the Factory Act of 1844. However, the movement was determined, throughout, to shorten the working day for all adults, and it was assumed, correctly, by supporters and opponents alike, that since the labours of children and adults were inextricably linked, legislation for children would also cut the working hours of adult men.

The movement drew support from a variety of groups of workers, including mule-spinners, power-loom weavers and card-room hands in the Lancashire cotton towns, weavers, wool-combers and other skilled workers in the woollen and worsted industries of the West Riding, artisans from both counties and the declining handloom weavers. Additional support came from some sympathetic clergy, medical men and ultra-Tories (Ward, 1970a, pp. 60–61; Gray, 1996, p. 23). The movement was well-organised at the grassroots, creating a framework which proved capable of sustained campaigning over two and a half decades. Short-time committees were established in the larger towns in both Yorkshire and Lancashire, with subcommittees in villages and smaller towns. These were coordinated in each county by a central committee which met, respectively, at Leeds and at Manchester. These committees spread their message and put pressure on employers and politicians in a variety of ways. They presented petitions to Parliament, sent deputations to lobby Ministers and MPs, prepared meticulously for the hearings of Sadler's Select Committee, discussed the content of bills with their parliamentary representatives, organised meetings and mass demonstrations across the region, produced handbills, placards, tracts, and pamphlets, campaigned for parliamentary candidates who pledged support for the ten-hour bill[4] and raised subscriptions to support campaigning, although the bulk of the finances came from a sympathetic local employer, John

Wood, Oastler himself and a radical Lancashire mill-owner, John Fielden (Ward, 1970a, pp. 66–70).

While the chief spokesmen for the campaign – Oastler and Bull – were not workingmen, they recognised that they were answerable to the short-time committees (some of which were in existence before Oastler became involved) and policies and tactics were developed through joint consultation. There was a surprisingly high level of agreement between people of differing ideological convictions, but differences did emerge from time to time and these demonstrated that working-class radicals were not deterred from independent action. The most notable example was the formation of the Society for Promoting National Regeneration which proposed to bring the eight-hour day into being through direct action, an initiative from which both Oastler and Bull dissociated themselves (Driver, 1946, pp. 264–268; Ward, 1962, pp. 114–115, 117–118).

One of the features of the textile industries in this period was the heavy reliance upon the labour of children, demand for whose services seems to have peaked in Britain in the 1820s and 1830s and to have been associated with younger ages at starting work (Horrell and Humphries, 1999). The demand for child labour presented parents with very difficult choices and historians have differed, as did contemporaries, in their assessment of how willing they were to send their children to work in the mills (Nardinelli, 1990; Tuttle, 1999). More recently, Jane Humphries has suggested that factory workers in the first half of the nineteenth century were caught in a classic child labour trap. In confronting the choice between seeking early employment for their children or deferring entry in the interest of their education, parents will generally choose the former when their incomes fall below the minimum acceptable level of consumption. The effect of this is to perpetuate the low adult wages, which brought such reliance into being in the first place, and to depress human capital formation, so that it becomes more difficult for child workers, as adults, to break out of the cycle and withhold their own children from early work (Humphries, 2010, pp. 24–37).

The economic arguments of the THM suggest that the campaigners saw the situation confronting families in precisely this way. They maintained consistently that the employment of children was increasing at the expense of adult males and that this process was a conscious strategy of employers; that parents were compelled by poverty to consent to factory labour for their children; and that the effect of widespread early child labour was to pull down the wages of all workers (Creighton, 1992a, pp. 307 and 310–311).

Basu and Vann (1998, discussed in Humphries, 2010, p. 28) have argued that the trap can be sprung either by restricting child labour by law or by effective trade union action. However, trade unions in this period were not sufficiently strong to curb child labour by their own efforts,[5] so workers resorted, as indicated above, to legislative action and through this sought not only to ameliorate the position of children and increase wages and employment prospects throughout the textile industries, but also to raise standards of family life by demanding shorter working hours for all categories of workers (Ward, 1970b, vol. 2, p. 67).

## The Ten Hours Movement's critique of the factory system

The discourse of the THM articulated, clearly and forcefully, both the discontents that workers felt, and a vision of a better family life. It also pointed working-class families towards a different and more preferable strategy than one which involved excessive reliance upon the waged labour of children and acceptance of long hours for all categories of worker.

The Ten Hours Movement voiced three main concerns. The first, shared by many groups of workers both within and beyond the textile regions, was the impact of increasing poverty and insecurity upon family life; this was seen as catastrophic, affecting both material and emotional well-being. One of the foremost of the early tracts of the THM protested that,

> while one part of the community is rolling in the most excessive luxury...see what starvation, yea, destitution in all forms and in almost every degree, are the lot of the Poor; sunk in debt, the landlord, and the shop-keeper quarrelling for the remnants of their furniture, – while straw beds and fireless huts, are their shelter – water-gruel and potatoes their diet – cursing their fate, and almost thrust out of society into the regions of famine; nay, not infrequently dying of hunger! (Hanson, 1831, p. 4).

Material deprivation and the anxieties that this engendered also took their toll on emotional relationships within the household. *The Pioneer* (1833, pp. 81–82) asserted that poverty eroded domestic happiness, making both the overworked artisan, and 'the mother half worn out, her temper chafed', too careworn to give their children the patient attention that they needed. Similarly, William Thompson (1834, p. 8) claimed that because of poverty 'their home is embittered by domestic cares and embarrassments; the fond glow of mutual love is chilled by the frozen breath of adversity; and the parent's love is appalled [*sic*] by the contemplation of the future'.

The second concern was that long hours, a debilitating and dangerous working environment and the intensity of the effort required to keep up with the unremitting pace of the machinery undermined the health and well-being of mill workers, and most particularly of the young. These conditions stunted growth, produced deformities of the spine and legs, weakened constitutions, induced respiratory and skin diseases, wore people out so that they aged prematurely, and contributed to the high rates of mortality of the factory districts. Accidents were common; deaths from unguarded machinery were not unknown. As a result, the overall reproduction of individuals and families was threatened. John Doherty feared the destruction of the rising generation (*Poor Man's Advocate*, p. 70). Oastler (1832, p. 8), similarly, considered that such hours 'WILL FORESTALL THE STRENGTH AND ENERGIES OF UNBORN GENERATIONS' (caps in original).

The third concern, which lies at the heart of this chapter, was that these hours and conditions had a destructive impact on family life. Working days for both children and adults were at least 12 hours long, excluding meal breaks, for six days a week. In busy times yet longer hours were enforced. Presenting his ten-hour bill to Parliament, Michael Sadler averred that, '[n]ot infrequently this labour is extended till eight or nine at night – fifteen hours – having but the same intervals for meals, rest, or recreation' (*Hansard*, 1832, vol. 11, col. 357).

Witnesses to Sadler's Committee of Inquiry gave numerous examples of even more inhumane hours than these. Many reported working, for long periods of time, from five in the morning till eight or nine at night. Hours could be longer in summer than in winter. According to Robert Colton, 'we increased as the days increased, and left off when we could not see; so that in summer we started at half-past three in the morning, and were at it till half-past nine at night' (*Parliamentary Papers*, 1831–1832, XV, para. 325). Such hours left no time for the various activities of family life: no time for housework, no time to create domestic comfort, no time for family conviviality, no time to cultivate ties of parental and filial affection.

One oft-repeated complaint was that opportunities for parents and children to spend time together were minimal. The Reverend George Stringer Bull calculated that a factory child and its parents could only have any interaction for four and a quarter hours per week, and that most of this time was occupied with preparing for, or cleaning after, factory work, or in Sunday school business (Bull, 1832, pp. 9–10). One of the early pamphlets of the THM asked that children be able to come home early enough 'to admit of a little domestic intercourse before retiring to their rest' (*The Factory Bill*, 1833, p. 8). Adults, too, were deprived of family relaxation. As the cloth lappers complained, long hours meant that they were 'debarred from...the heart-cheering pleasure of spending a few hours around their own fireside, amidst their rising families' (*Herald to the Trades' Advocate*, 1830–1831, p. 56).

Oastler denounced the consequences of this situation. Testifying to Sadler's Parliamentary Committee, he bemoaned 'the hopeless absence of domestic joys – the total separation from its parents' smiles, save just at night when exhausted nature seeks repose' and condemned what he said was,

> almost the general system for the little children in these manufacturing villages to know nothing of their parents at all, except that in a morning very early, at five o'clock, very often before four, they are awakened by a human being, that they are told is their father, and are pulled out of bed...and they see no more of their parents, generally speaking, until they go home, and are sent to bed. Now that system must necessarily prevent the growth of filial affection. *(Parliamentary Papers*, 1831–1832, XV, para. 9800)

This situation, Oastler believed, led children 'to consider their parents only as taskmasters', while a parent 'is compelled to treat [a child] as a slave' (*The Ten-Hour Bill*, 1831, p. 12). Coming home earlier in the evening, activists claimed, would 'restore to the children that parental care and influence of which they have almost entirely been deprived' (*The Factory Bill*, 1833, p. 8).

The movement claimed that the weakening of domestic attachments was further exacerbated by the selfishness which the factory system promoted. It 'has succeeded in...*drying up the springs of natural affection,* and *perverting* the very *instincts* of the *human heart*' (*Address*, 1834, p. 4). For Peter McDouall, the factory system

> penetrates like every other iniquity to the cottage. Thus it destroys the best feelings of the human heart, excites a care for self...The mind becomes callous to suffering...the heart becomes hardened to the fate of others...the wife becomes a burden, and the children become curses. (*McDouall's Chartist Journal*, 1841, p. 196)

A further complaint was the destruction of the 'natural' order of relations between parents and children. John Hanson (1831, p. 17) protested that 'with the assistance of machinery, you...have dared to drive the parents out of "the market of labour"; you have hired the infants for your work'. This led to the inversion of proper generational relations as 'our young ones, under this system, instead of being supported by their parents, are themselves compelled to toil for those who gave them birth' (*Proceedings*, 1833, p. 4).

The authority of parents was undermined by this development, as also by the inability to build affectionate relations in the family, with the result that, '[i]t is a very common system, as soon as a child is enabled to earn a little more money than its board wages, for it to strike a bargain with its parent; when it gets to be 13 or 14 years old it will threaten to leave if they will not let it have so much of its wages; and they consider themselves quite free agents and under no control' (*Parliamentary Papers*, 1831–1832, XV, para. 9800).

Shortage of time and the estrangement of children and parents meant that the latter were finding it increasingly difficult to provide education and moral guidance, a task seen as an essential duty of the family. Cavie Richardson (1832, p. 4) expressed his worry that: '[b]eing so little with their Parents, they are under less control; their conduct cannot be watched by them, and there is no check to their evil propensities and sinful courses'. The *Herald to the Trades Advocate* (1831–1832, pp. 57–59) regretted that factory workers could not receive or pass on instruction. *The Crisis* (1833, p. 161) charged that parents (and especially fathers) could not spend enough time with their children when young, 'yet this is the age when they most need education and direction'. Equally deplored was the fact that long hours deprived children of opportunities for formal schooling as they were too tired at the end of the working day to learn effectively.

Long hours of work also undermined home life by precluding time for the domestic duties upon which a comfortable, economical and well-run home depended. As Bull (1833b, p. 3) pointed out, 'if you work eleven hours [rather than ten] this leaves only Ten hours for Reading, Writing, Counting, Sewing, Seaming, Stitching, Basting, Herringboning, Backstitching, Patching, Knitting, Darning stockings, Marking, Baking, Cooking, Cleaning, Play and Sleep'.

Similarly, long hours meant that girls could not learn these essential competencies. 'All that is necessary to cottage economy: the character of a good housewife, it is nearly impossible to acquire: – the needle, the kneading-trough and the laundry are, for the most part, unknown. What time, we ask, have factory children, who are chiefly females, to learn domestic duties?' (*A Brief View*, 1832, p. 18) The need for time thus became the battle-cry of the THM. As (Bull, 1833a, p. 5) put it, 'This, then, Sir, is the battle for an hour; – the mother's hour – the teacher's hour – the minister's hour'.

The deleterious effects of the factory system upon domestic life were intensified by the introduction of the New Poor Law and many THM activists threw themselves whole-heartedly into the prolonged struggle against its introduction into the north of England (Edsall, 1971; Knott, 1986). The Old Poor Law had provided a measure of protection against some of the vicissitudes of life: sickness, accidents, loss of parents, widowhood, old age, lack of work and even, under the Speenhamland system, low wages. Much of this was now to be stripped away under the 1834 Poor Law Amendment Act, which aimed to drastically restrict the support provided to the needy, in their own homes, whether in cash or in kind, and to tie relief, as far as possible, to admission to the work-house. This measure was perceived by its opponents as a cold-blooded onslaught upon the working-class family, a direct attack on living stand-ards, and a denial of the rights of the poor to marry, to bear children, to have a home and to enjoy family independence.

My argument is that the aim of the THM was to transform the situ-ation outlined above and provide suitable conditions for the reproduc-tion of the family and its members by placing the household on a more secure economic footing and providing more time to perform its central activities. This would help to improve the quality of the interpersonal relationships that formed the very purpose of family life. A reduction in working hours was indispensable to this, both directly, through securing time for family duties, and indirectly, through the contribution it could make to reducing pressure on the labour market and thus spreading work, raising wages and stimulating domestic consumption.

## Family aspirations of the Ten Hours Movement

But if the movement expressed profound dissatisfaction with the nature of family ties in the new urban-industrial environment, what was the positive side of their discourse? What practices did the THM try to encourage? What vision of family life did it hold out to its supporters?

Against the miseries of the present, campaigners drew a picture of the family life to which they aspired. It is not surprising, given the threats they perceived to the very possibility of establishing a home, that home and the domestic comforts that home could and should provide were at the core of their thinking. The 'deification of home' which was so prominent in the outlook of respectable working men and women in the second half of the nineteenth century (Kirk, 1998, p. 118) is already apparent in this period. How far this represented the adoption of middle class views of home and how far it emerged more naturally from working-class experiences is difficult to answer. The early development of ideas of home, parenting and domestic responsibility among the working classes has been researched far less extensively than among the middle class (Davidoff and Hall, 1987, esp. chap. 8; Vickery, 2009). There are some indications, however, that whatever their ultimate origins, their roots in popular discourse go back well into the eighteenth century. Joanne Bailey's analysis of pauper letters suggests that active parenting, the desirability of prioritising children's needs and the ability to go without so as to meet these needs, were seen admirable traits by the poor (Bailey, 2010a). Popular literature confirms that labouring men were expected to prioritise their family over expensive forms of leisure and also offers glimpses of idealised and tender fatherhood (Bailey, 2010b). Furthermore, it would appear that in their evocation of the joys of home, family life and children (discussed below), Oastler, Bull and Stephens assumed that their vision was at one with that of their listeners, and the enthusiastic responses from their audiences seem to support this interpretation.[6]

Home was seen as the heart of family life. It had threefold significance: it was a physical place, a setting for domestic practices, and an embodiment of the relationships which constituted family life. It was viewed, in that classic phrase, as a haven in a heartless world; it was a place of comfort and relaxation, a sphere for enjoying the company of spouse and children, a zone of privacy for personal life, and a realm of humanity in contrast to the cash nexus of the world of capitalist employment. It was the foundation and representation of independence and an important source of identity and self-respect. Home symbolised the couple's affection and unity and domesticity provided emotional fulfilment for both husband and wife. Above all, the dream of domestic bliss focused on the relationship of parents and children. As Stephens (1839, p. 23) declaimed, 'Home, sweet home was a man's heaven on earth and the babes God gave were the cherubs that made it ring with joy and gladness'. A well-run home was essential for the welfare of children, providing physical and emotional care, joy and comfort, early education, moral training and happy recollections for later life. Home life, finally, was seen as central to the formation of character – '[d]omestic life is the seminary of the purest affections of our nature', as a contributor to *The Union* expressed it (1842, p. 13) – and the tie between parents and children was a bond of significance which, once created by a happy home, would sustain both the older and younger generations throughout life.

The comfort of the home as haven was often expressed in verse. Mrs J. S's poem praising the enjoyment to be gained from 'our ain fireside' exemplifies this (*Herald*, 1830–1831, pp. 61–62), as does *The Elbow Chair*, a paean to domestic bliss printed in the *Lancashire and Yorkshire Co-operator* (1831–1832, no. 5, p. 7). Annemarie Money (2007) has drawn our attention to the ways in which 'things' act as the embodiment of meaningful social relations and significant connections between family members. The chair, in this poem, is presented in precisely this way. It represents the hopes and fears associated with family life, and is the symbol of relaxation and peace of mind:

When worn with care, how oft, in Thee, I've calmed the anguish of a fever'd mind.: Upon thy arm repos'd my aching head, And my faint heart with Hope's bright visions fed.

Spokesmen of the THM repeatedly stressed that the labouring classes had the right to a decent, comfortable living at home. For Oastler (1835, p. 130), this was 'an inalienable principle of the British constitution'. Stephens (1839, p. 8), declaring that, '[e]very man who is without a home and whose home is not all God meant it to be, IS ROBBED', went on to describe some of the material requirements of a decent home:

And what do I mean by home? I do not mean the tumble-down hovel, containing as many families as rooms, and from seven to a dozen persons in each apartment, of as many feet square. By HOME I do not mean a place where husbands, and wives, and children, are huddled together higgledy-piggledy, like so many swine…but by HOME I mean a place with rooms fit for men to live in – I mean not the poet's home, a place of fancy, but I mean a HAPPY home.

Good food and the sociability of the family meal were further important components of domestic comfort. THM, Anti-Poor Law and Chartist leaders all consistently called attention to the meagreness of the existing diet – 'children are familiar only with potatoes and oatmeal' was a typical complaint (*A Brief View*, 1832, p. 20) – and insisted that workers were entitled to a sufficient amount of good food. John Doherty, a leading trade unionist and prominent factory reformer, argued that wages should be high enough, 'to give the operative and his family four comfortable meals a day' (Kirby and Musson, 1975, p. 457). Furthermore, a well-provisioned meal, as Oastler asserted, epitomised family solidarity as well as comfort and well-being (*The Home*, 1851, p. 81).

The most fundamental requirement for a comfortable home and an adequate diet was sufficient wages, but this needed to be complemented by the skills of a thrifty housewife. The household had to be run efficiently and economically; wages needed to be spent wisely. For (Richardson, 1831, p. 8), lack of competence meant that money was spent but 'it all goes and we've now for it'

Wives needed a wide range of skills. In addition to the ability to shop and budget well, they should be able, in Richardson's words, to 'mak a bit o bread or bake it...o'macking their husbands a shirt' or their sens a shift...how to do tambour work – how to mak a bed – wash a floor or...clean a winder' (1831, p. 10). However, many women no longer possessed the requisite knowledge. According to Oastler (1833, p. 9), young factory women

> did not know how to go a shopping, nor how to make and mend their own clothes: this kind of knowledge was much more necessary to the poor than the rich: to rob the poor of the power of obtaining it was to have a double curse at them: better to have less wages and more domestic economy.

The importance that working class leaders attached to the housewife's abilities can be seen in the objectives of the National Regeneration Society. One of its aims was to teach women 'to wash, bake, brew, make and mend clothes and stockings, and in all other duties pertaining to cottage economy' (*Rights of Industry*, 1833, p. 6). The Owenite journal, *The Union* similarly recommended that women should study the science of Domestic Comfort, which required habits of cleanliness and order, and knowledge of cooking and hygiene and urged that these should early be made part of female education (1842, pp. 321–329).

So highly was the economic contribution of domestic labour valued that when the Ten Hours advocates were told that shorter hours would lead to lower wages, they consistently replied that the value of extra time would be greater, since 'the advantages of family economy would much more than counterbalance any such supposed reduction' (*The Factory Bill*, 1833, pp. 8–9).

In contrast to middle class observers, who saw the lack of competence in domestic matters as a sign of the moral deficiencies of the working class, the Ten Hour spokesmen argued that, for the most part, blame attached to the system, not to individuals and communities. Oastler asserted that the poor had 'been entirely deprived of all chance of knowing' (1835, p. 161). The Ten Hour activists wished to ensure that the working class both possessed the knowledge pertinent to their circumstances and had the power to control its application. They argued that shorter hours of work would allow relevant skills to be learned, and transmitted from one generation to the next.

Domestic comfort was not simply an end in itself. It was also the underpinning for all the relationships which made family life worthwhile. In depictions of the home, the duties and joys of parenthood were particularly strongly emphasised. Parenthood was seen as the main purpose of establishing a family and a home was meaningless if it could not provide children with a secure and happy upbringing.

The presence of children was a delight that parents should rejoice in. These joys were often expressed by working-class poets:

> Then lift the smiling infant on my knee, Whilst elder climb, and seek support from Thee: All cling around and each with rapture glows, To share the kiss a Father's love bestows. (*Lancashire and Yorkshire Co-operator*, 1831–1832, no. 5, p. 7).

Audiences responded enthusiastically to the evocation of these themes in the speeches of JR Stephens, who praised 'the joys of wedlock, the joys of children, and the domestic pleasures' (1839, p. 8) and stated that '[a] wife and children were the greatest blessing a man could have' (p. 23). Joys were complemented by duties. Care of children was one of the great ends of life and the inability to meet parental responsibilities effectively was a major complaint against the factory system.

The THM's discussion of the joys and duties of parenthood was embedded in a wider analysis of the needs of children and the rights of childhood that stemmed from these. The Movement campaigned for children of all classes to have the rights to health and development, physical protection, education and moral instruction, recreation and play, and a caring family life (Creighton, 2012). This insistence upon the rights of children and the necessity of creating conditions which would allow families to meet more adequately the needs which were their responsibility were important in shaping the Movement's vision of desirable practices of consumption in the home.

In this vision the THM can be seen as prioritising what Andrew Sayer (2003), following Alasdair MacIntyre (1981), calls 'internal' as contrasted with 'external' goods. The former are goods and satisfactions which are intrinsic to certain activities and relationships and cannot be achieved separately from them. They have value in their own right and not just through bringing fame, money or social advancement, as do external goods. Applying this distinction to consumption, Sayer (2003, p. 341) has argued that 'much consumption is not primarily a form of status seeking but a means to the development of skills, achievements, commitments, and relationships which have value regardless of whether they bring participants external rewards'.

The THM consistently emphasised the importance of the quality of interpersonal relationships, and most especially the bonds between parents and children. These were the mainspring and purpose of family life, and material comfort was valued not solely for its own sake but for its importance in providing the underpinning for these relationships and the means for realising them. This sentiment was expressed pithily by the placard issued by the Mossley Short-time Committee which advised that some financial sacrifice would be justified in return for a reduction in hours – 'A shilling a week is not to be put in the scale against happiness' (Joyce, 1991, p. 365).

Family consumption practices have a pronounced ethical nature (Hall, 2011) and this is especially true of practices around internal goods. The ethical stance of the THM was part of its conscious rejection of the utilitarian philosophy so widespread in British society at the time, and particularly of the application of this philosophy to human beings and relationships. Oastler criticised '[t]he law-makers of the present age' for having 'imbibed the utilitarian notion that men are mere things, without rights or feelings...in this system of strange Philosophy, wealth, not man, is the object of regard' (*Fleet Papers*, 1843, pp. 9–10). Brotherton, similarly, denounced the state of society 'in which so many hundreds and thousands of human beings were regarded merely as machines or instruments of labour' (*Hansard*, 1836, vol. 33, col. 755).

The THM articulated a clear vision of the good home. But all the activities which it regarded as essential to a satisfactory family life required time. No advance in domestic life was possible without wresting time back from the workplace. But time could be gained only through collective action. Individuals had no power to alter their hours of work. Collective action was a necessary prerequisite for bringing into being the practices of home life that working-class activists desired. The Movement perceived a tension between the needs of families in the short-term, which led to practices damaging to its members, and their interests in the long-term. Its strategy offered a way of overcoming this tension and facilitating a transition to a different, and more humane set of family practices.

## Critique of working-class family practices

While the main objective of the THM was to persuade public opinion of the desirability of legislating for shorter hours, and to press Parliament to pass this legislation, its spokesmen were also engaged in a dialogue with factory workers themselves. The Movement's demands were not simply the expression at the political level of the aspirations of individual households. The desire for material improvement and security may have been felt by all working-class families, but the means for achieving this were not clear cut. Dialogue was thus necessary to convince workers of the accuracy of the Movement's analysis and the viability of its strategy, to win their commitment to the struggle, and to counter the employers' assertions that the ten hour day would reduce productivity and lead to a commensurate cut in wages. Against the latter, Ten Hour activists argued that productivity would be affected only marginally, if at all, and that reduced pressure on labour markets would maintain or even increase wages in the medium-to-longer term. Even if wages should fall in the short-term, the qualitative improvements in family life would more than offset the loss of income.

Furthermore, the campaign challenged the immediate household preferences of many. It condemned parents who were willing to disregard the welfare of their younger children for the sake of the small amount of extra income that their employment brought in and criticised, in particular, husbands who spent scanty wages drinking or gambling instead of meeting their families' basic needs for food and clothing. Expenditure should be devoted to the requirements of the family rather than the satisfaction of individual desires.

The operation of the family as a collective enterprise involves a constant interplay between individual, relational and collective needs and identities (Epp and Price, 2008). Different cultural moments balance these in different ways and give rise to different tensions. The discourse of the THM emphasised the collective and relational above the individual. This was partly a response to the pressures of survival but it also had an explicit ideological component. Confronting the tendency of market relations and individual wage-earning to encourage individualistic and often self-centred behaviour and expenditure, the THM emphasised the importance of obligations to other family members and to the family as a unit. It thus constitutes one particular moment in the long history within working-class culture of the salience of a relational experience of self that Gillies (2007) and others have drawn attention to and which contrasts so markedly with middle-class individuality.

But while THM activists were strongly critical of uncaring fathers and mothers, they generally defended working-class family practices against the aspersions of middle class observers, arguing, for instance, that most parents sent younger children to factory work only with the greatest reluctance, under the pressure of poverty and the dictates of the Poor Law. Oastler went even further, in his defence of the working class, arguing on many occasions that its members, as a whole, displayed a higher morality and greater devotion to family than did the upper and middle classes (Creighton, 1992b, p. 20). Moreover, unfeeling parents were themselves the product and victims of the system. 'It is the system of slavery in factories which destroys all parental feeling', declared Oastler (Alfred, 1857, p. 228).

The Movement constantly emphasised the powerlessness of factory workers, adults as well as children, and stressed that most parents were motivated less by selfishness, ignorance and greed than by structural constraints and the sheer need to survive. Once constraints were eased, behaviour would improve, at least amongst those who had not been completely dehumanised by the pressures upon them. At the same time, while the reformers were adamant that a change in household preferences could not happen without structural change, they were conscious that ideological struggle was also necessary to ensure that the maximum number of households would alter their behaviour and that concessions won from bitter struggle would not be wasted.

## Outcomes

The difficulty of evaluating the outcomes of social movements is well-recognised (Staggenborg, 2012, p. 46; Snow et al., 2004). If we confine ourselves to the legislative objectives of the THM, this stricture would not apply, for in this regard the Movement was remarkably successful. The Factory Act of 1847 conceded the Ten Hour day, and while legislative ambiguities allowed employers, initially, to avoid its full implementation, supplementary bills, culminating in the Employment of Children in Factories Act of 1855, closed the loopholes. With this, all protected workers and the men who laboured with them gained the reduction in hours that the Movement had striven for. But when we turn to domestic practices, the cautionary advice is well-taken. We have only limited information about domestic practices in northern towns in this period. Moreover, evaluating the precise extent of the contribution of shorter hours and the discourse of the THM to these changes would be a complex task. However, such evidence as we do have indicates that behaviour was indeed modified following the legislation, and generally in ways which conformed to the Ten Hour objectives. Ten Hour delegates, for instance, reported in 1849 that workers in various towns were attending schools, night classes and Mechanics' Institutes, and cultivating gardens and allotments. Local clergy commented on the religious and educational benefits and Shaftesbury considered that the Manchester operatives 'are morally and physically improved' (Ward, 1962, pp. 404–405). In the same year Leonard Horner, the chief factory inspector, carried out a survey of 1,153 operatives whose wages had (temporarily) been reduced following the Act. He found that even among this relatively disadvantaged group there was majority support for the reduction in hours, most particularly because 'it enabled them to attend evening schools' (P.P., 1849, XXII, p. 146).[7]

More detailed information about how operatives spent their additional non-employed time is provided by the investigation carried out by Angus Bethune Reach, also in 1849, for the Morning Chronicle. His respondents reported that their homes were cleaner and more comfortable, that they could spend more time at home and with their children, that their own health had improved, that their children were better educated and that they themselves were able to learn to read and write at night school (booksellers corroborated this claim, noting the 'very decided increase' in the number of copybooks sold). Among the specific domestic tasks that Reach recorded from his female respondents were the following: '[c]an do her own washing now, which she had always put out before', '[h]as learned crochet work, "a many patterns"', and '[m]akes her own dresses, "polkas and visites [sic] as smart as you like"' (Ginswick, 1983, pp. 117–119).

Similar reasons for welcoming the Act were put forward in the replies that the secretary of the Manchester Short-Time Committee received in the spring of 1849 from operatives in cotton towns in both Scotland and the North of England. Homes were better looked after and more comfortable, health had improved, operatives had time to read and time to attend night school, children were being better educated. In addition, many factory workers were devoting time to gardening (Ginswick, 1983, pp. 122–123).

A further issue, of considerable significance for the development of family practices, is how far, and in what ways, the THM influenced gender identities in the domestic sphere. It is indisputably the case that the movement was male dominated to an even greater extent than other radical social movements of the period, and much of its discourse related to the performance of domestic labour, which was seen as overwhelmingly the responsibility of women. The gendered rhetoric of the Movement has led several authors to suggest that it played a significant role in the development of the male breadwinner family (Walby, 1986; Valverde, 1988). At the ideological level, there is certainly much evidence to support this interpretation. Speeches frequently contained calls for men to be able to support their wives and for married women to be withdrawn from factory work so that they could devote themselves to the care of home and family. Policy, however, did not correspond to rhetoric. The actual demands of the movement were for shorter hours for all categories of workers, and since such reductions would significantly ameliorate the tensions between the demands of work and home, they can be seen as offering a different path to that of the male breadwinner family (see also Gray, 1987, p. 177). It is consistent with this interpretation that the textile areas, throughout the nineteenth century and well into the twentieth, were among the most resistant to the male breadwinner family as many of its communities registered some of the country's highest proportions of married women workers and shared domestic labour more equally than was generally the case amongst working class families in other parts of Britain (Gittins, 1982). Having said this, it is undoubtedly the case that the ideology of separate spheres was a deeply embedded component of the outlook of the time, and that changes in behaviour were negotiated within this constraint. It seems highly probable, therefore, that the campaign served to deepen the domestic division of labour and to reinforce women's identity as housewives and mothers. It is noticeable that women and men, following the factory acts, seem to have used their additional 'free' time in differing ways, even within the confines of the home. Thus women did more sewing and dressmaking, in addition to other aspects of domestic labour, while men did more gardening. There is need, however, to further research the precise impact of the THM and factory legislation upon domestic practices, the extent of variation between communities and occupational groups and the attitudes of women themselves towards these changes.

## Conclusion

More and more families in the second quarter of the nineteenth century were confronting the repercussions of the split between work and home, and the apparently relentless demands of the factory, over which they had less and less control. This split was a fundamental structural feature of industrial capitalism which required new responses if the claims of the workplace were to be curbed to give time for family life.

Family interaction and the socialisation of children could no longer be combined with production, as had been the case in domestic industry, but had to be squeezed into the few hours remaining after waged work had ceased. This situation required restrictions upon the length of the working day and week. Until this concession could be obtained, the options open to individual households were extremely limited.

For this reason, accounting for change in domestic practices requires attention to the level of collective struggle. A reduction in working time could not be achieved by households acting alone in their self-interest. Individuals had no power to negotiate shorter working hours. In theory, households could have acquired more time by withdrawing married women from the factory, as de Vries (2008, chap. 5) argues took place later in the nineteenth century. The desirability of this objective was voiced by some participants in the THM, but at this juncture the call was more of an aspiration than a concrete demand and could not in any case have been achieved while wages were so low. Moreover, as indicated above, this strategy would have been at odds with the Movement's stated aim of securing a reduction in working time for all members of the family, in order to improve domestic management, child-rearing and family closeness. The withdrawal of married women would not have provided the family time that men also desired nor, most crucially, would it have provided sufficient protection for children and time for their education and recreation

Collective action has a further function since, as argued earlier, demands are not simply an aggregation of the preferences of individuals or households. An agreed stance has to be forged out of varying and often conflicting opinions. They arise from processes of discussion and experimentation through which certain objectives are selected at the expense of others and appropriate mechanisms identified for achieving these objectives. The support for shorter working hours was not universal among members of the industries concerned. Individuals and households varied in their valuation of trade-offs between 'leisure' and income. Moreover, workers had to be reassured that legislation would not, as employers alleged, damage the household economy by putting children out of work and reducing wages.

Furthermore, campaigns involve confrontation with existing practices, practices which are rational in terms of the immediate needs of the household but which may not cater for the long-term interests of its members. In short, through a combination of legislative change and ideological struggle, the collective action of the THM gave families the opportunity of pursuing long-term goals in place of the short-term tactics that they had been forced to resort to, and was a prerequisite for allowing households to move from one set of domestic practices to another.

## Acknowledgements

I should like to express my appreciation of the helpful comments of the anonymous reviewer of this chapter.

## Notes

1. One notable exception is Smelser's (1959) study of the very period under investigation here. He argues that the THM was a regressive movement inspired by the desire to retain family work groups within the factory environment. For a critique of Smelser see Anderson (1976).
2. My usage of the term domestic practices follows closely David Morgan's concept of family practices (Morgan, 1996, 1999) except that it has a narrower focus, concentrating upon practices within the realm of the family-household.
3. The standard treatment of the movement is Ward (1962). Driver (1946) provides a stimulating life of Oastler.
4. Note especially the candidacies of Sadler at Leeds in 1832 and Huddersfield in 1834, and Oastler at Huddersfield in 1837 (Driver, 1946, pp. 194–202, 256–259, 344–350, 358–360; Ward, 1962, pp. 66–80, 116–117).
5. Northern workers did make one strenuous effort, in 1834, to cut hours by direct action, but this failed totally (Ward, 1962, pp. 114–115, 117–119; Kirby and Musson, 1975, pp. 272–301).
6. The role of Oastler in adapting evangelical ideals of domesticity to the realities and aspirations of working class existence has been examined in Creighton (1992b).
7. For a statistical breakdown of the respondents' attitudes to hours of work by income and marital status, see Smelser, 1959, pp. 308–312).

## References

*A Brief View of Medical Evidence and Opinion ... on the Factories Regulation Bill* (1832, n.p.).

*Address of the United Delegates from the Factory Districts ... assembled at Manchester to Their Operative Friends.* Manchester: 1834, though internal evidence suggests 1836.

Alfred (1857) *A History of the Factory Movement.* London: Simpkin, Marshall and Co.

Anderson, M. (1976) 'Sociological History and the Working-class Family: Smelser Revisited', *Social History*, 1(3), 317–334.

Bailey, J. (2010a) '"Think Wot a Mother Must Feel": Parenting in English Pauper Letters', *Family and Community History*, 13(1), 5–19.

Bailey, J. (2010b) '"A Very Sensible Man": Imagining Fatherhood in England c. 1750–1830', *History*, 95 (July), 267–292.

Basu, K. and Vann, P.H. (1998) 'The Economics of Child Labour', *American Economic Review*, 88, 412–427.

Berg, M. (1980) *The Machinery Question and the Making of Political Economy, 1815–1848*. Cambridge: CUP.

Brown, R. (1991) *Society and Economy in Modern Britain 1700–1850*. London & N.Y.: Routledge.

Bull, G. S. (1832) *A Respectful and Faithful Appeal … on Behalf of the Factory Children*. Bradford: n.p.

Bull, G. S. (1833a) *Factory Children: At a Public Meeting of the Borough of Bradford Held on … February 19, 1833* (n.p.).

Bull, G. S. (1833b) *Factory Children: speech in Bradford to a Meeting of Children … on Tuesday June 11, 1833*. London: n.p.

Creighton, C. (1992a) 'Richard Oastler, Factory Legislation and the Working-Class Family', *Journal of Historical Sociology*, 5(3), 292–321.

Creighton, C. (1992b) 'Richard Oastler, Evangelicalism and the Ideology of Domesticity', Occasional Paper No. 9, Department of Sociology and Social Anthropology, University of Hull.

Creighton, C. (2012) 'The Ten Hours Movement and the Rights of Childhood', *International Journal of Children's Rights*, 20(4), 457–485.

*The Crisis and National Co-operative Trades' Union Gazette* (1833).

Davidoff, L. and Hall, C. (1987) *Family Fortunes: Men and Women of the English Middle Class, 1780–1850*. London: Hutchinson.

Della Porta, D. and Diani, M. (2006) *Social Movements: An Introduction*. Malden, MA and Oxford: Blackwell.

De Vries, J. (2008) *The Industrious Revolution: Consumer Behaviour and the Household Economy, 1650 to the Present*. Cambridge: CUP.

Driver, C. H. (1946) *Tory Radical: The Life of Richard Oastler*. N.Y.: Oxford.

Edsall, N. C. (1971) *The Anti-Poor Law Movement 1834–44*. Manchester: MUP.

Epp, A. M. and Price, L. L. (2008) 'Family Identity: A Framework of Identity Interplay in Consumption Practices', *Journal of Consumer Research*, 35(1), 50–70.

*The Factory Bill: Lord Ashley's Ten-Hour Bill and the Scheme of the Factory Commissioners Compared* (1833, n.p.).

*Fleet Papers* (1841; 1843).

Gabb, J. (2008) *Researching Intimacy in Families*. Basingstoke: Palgrave Macmillan.

Giddens, A. (1992) *The Transformation of Intimacy: Sexuality, Love and Eroticism in Modern Societies*. Cambridge: Polity Press.

Gillies, V. (2003) *Family and Intimate Relationships: A Review of the Sociological Research* London: South Bank University.

Gillies, V. (2007) *Marginalized Mothers: Exploring Working-class Experiences of Parenting* . London & New York: Routledge.

Ginswick, J. (ed.) (1983) *Labour and the Poor in England and Wales 1849–1851*. London: Frank Cass.

Gittins, D. (1982) *Fair Sex: Family Size and Structure, 1900–39*. London: Hutchinson.

Gray, R. (1987) 'The Languages of Factory Reform in Britain, c. 1830–1860' in *The Historical Meanings of Work*, P. Joyce (ed.). Cambridge: CUP.

Gray, R (1996) *The Factory Question and Industrial England.* Cambridge: CUP.

Hall, S. (2011) 'Exploring the "Ethical Everyday": An Ethnography of the Ethics of Family Consumption', *Geoforum*, 42, 627–637.

*Hansard's Parliamentary Debates* (1832, vol. 11; 1836, vol. 37).

Hanson, J. (1831) *Humanity against Tyranny.* Leeds: n.p.

*Herald to the Trades' Advocate and Co-operative Journal* (1830–31).

Hilton, Boyd (2006) *A Mad, Bad and Dangerous People? England 1783–1846.* Oxford: Clarendon Press.

*The Home* (1851–1852).

Horrell, S and Humphries, J. (1999), 'Child Labour and British Industrialization' in *A Thing of the Past? Child Labour in Britain in the Nineteenth and Twentieth Centuries*, M. Lavalette (ed.). Liverpool: Liverpool UP.

Humphries, J. (2007) 'Standard of Living, Quality of Life' in *A Companion to Nineteenth-Century Britain*, C. Williams (ed.). Malden, MA: Blackwell Publishing.

Humphries, J. (2010) *Childhood and Child Labour in the Industrial Revolution.* Cambridge: CUP.

Jamieson, L. (1998) *Intimacy: Personal relationships in Modern Societies.* Cambridge: Polity Press.

Joyce, P. (1991) *Visions of the People: Industrial England and the Question of Class.* Cambridge: CUP.

Kirby, R.G. and A.E. Musson (1975) *The Voice of the People: John Doherty, 1798–1854. Trade Unionist, Radical and Factory Reformer.* Manchester: Manchester University Press.

Kirk, N. (1998) *Change, Continuity and Class: Labour in British Society, 1850–1920.* Manchester and New York.

Knott, J. (1986) *Popular Opposition to the 1834 New Poor Law.* London: Croom Helm.

*Lancashire and Yorkshire Co-operator* (1831–1832).

MacIntyre, A. (1981) *After Virtue.* London: Duckworth.

*McDouall's Chartist Journal and Trades' Advocate* (1841).

Money, A. (2007) 'Material Culture and the Living Room: The Appropriation and Use of Goods in Everyday Life', *Journal of Consumer Culture*, 7 (3), 355–377.

Morgan, D. H. J. (1996) *Family Connections: An Introduction to Family Studies.* Cambridge: Polity Press.

Morgan, D. H. J. (2011) *Rethinking Family Practices.* Basingstoke: Palgrave Macmillan.

Nardinelli, C. (1990) *Child Labor and the Industrial Revolution.* Bloomington: Indiana UP.

Oastler, R. (1832) *A Letter to Mr. Holland Hoole.* Manchester; n.p.

Oastler, R. (1833) *Infant Slavery. Report of a Speech Delivered in Favour of the Ten Hour's Bill by Richard Oastler, Esq..* Preston: J. Livesey and J. Walker.

Oastler, R. (1835) *Eight Letters to the Duke of Wellington.* London: J. Cochrane.

*Parliamentary Papers*, 1831–1832, XV.

Perkin, H. (1969) *The Origins of Modern English Society 1780–1880.* London: Routledge & Kegan Paul.

*The Pioneer* (1833–34).

*Poor Man's Advocate* (1832–33).

*Proceedings of a Public Meeting Held at Hebden Bridge ... 24 August, 1833*. Huddersfield: n.p.

Richardson, C. (1831) *The Factory System: or, Frank Hawthorn's Visit to his Cousin, Jemmy Cropper of Leeds*. Leeds: n.p.

Richardson, C. (1832) *Factory Children*. Derby: Wm. Bemrose.

*Rights of Industry. Catechism of the Society for Promoting National Regeneration* (1833). Manchester: n.p.

Sayer, A. (2003) '(De)commodification, Consumer Culture, and Moral Economy', *Environment and Planning D: Society and Space*, 21, 341–357.

Smelser, N. J. (1959) *Social Change in the Industrial Revolution: An Application of Theory to the Lancashire Cotton Industry 1770–1840*. London: Routledge and Kegan Paul.

Snow, D. A. and Benford, R. D. (1992) 'Master Frames and Cycles of Protests' in *Frontiers in Social Movement Theory*, A. D. Morris and C. M. Mueller (eds). New Haven: Yale UP.

Snow, D. A., S. A. Soule and H. Kriesi (eds) (2004) *The Blackwell Companion to Social Movements*. Malden, MA: Blackwell.

Staggenborg, S. (1998) *Gender, Family and Social Movements*. Thousand Oaks, Calif.: Pine Forge Press.

Staggenborg, S. (2012) *Social Movements*. Don Mills, Ont. & Oxford: OUP.

Stephens, J. R. (1839) *The Rev. J.R. Stephens in London: Three Sermons Preached by the Rev. J. R. Stephens in London on Sunday May 12, 1839* (n.p.).

*The Ten-Hour-Bill* (1831, Leeds: n.p.)

Thompson, W. (1834) *The Age of Harmony*. Glasgow: W. & W. Miller.

Tuttle, C. (1999) *Hard at Work in Factories and Mines: The Economics of Child Labor during the British Industrial Revolution*. Boulder, CO: Westview Press.

*The Union* (1842).

Valverde, M. (1988) '"Giving the Female a Domestic Turn": The Legal, Social and Moral Regulation of Women's Work in British Cotton Mills, 1820–1850', *Journal of Social History*, 21, 619–34.

Vickery, A. (2009) *Behind Closed Doors: At Home in Georgian England*. New Haven, Conn.: Yale UP.

Walby, S. (1986) *Patriarchy at Work*. Cambridge: Polity.

Ward, J. T. (1962) *The Factory Movement 1830–1855*. London: Macmillan & Co.

Ward, J. T. (1970a) 'The Factory Movement' in *Popular Movements c. 1830–1850*, J. T. Ward (ed.), London: Macmillan.

Ward, J. T. (1970b) *The Factory System. Volume 2: The Factory System and Society*. Newton Abbot: David & Charles.

# 2
# Buying the Ties That Bind: Consumption, Care and Intimate Investment among Transnational Households in Highland Ecuador

*Emma-Jayne Abbots*

## Introduction

Situated in a rural community of Jima in Highland Ecuador, this chapter reflects on the intimacies of consumption and the ways in which it is both embedded within and enacts affective relations. Specifically, it examines how the wives of migrated men invest in the long-term reproduction of their transnational household and maintain intimate relations with their geographically distant husbands – who are living in New York – through their everyday material engagements with commodities. The particular focus is on white goods, household appliances and clothing. Together with domestic architecture and food, which I have discussed elsewhere (Abbots, 2011; 2014a), these objects arguably bear the most emotional significance in this context and are drawn together through their intimate associations with migrated kin. As such, I explore the ways in which kinship, morality, commitment to family and transnationality are intrinsically interwoven through consumption and, in so doing, elucidate how the seemingly impersonal and alienated commodities of the market are made personal and intimate as they are brought into the domestic sphere. I thus draw attention to the ways in which public aspects of consumption, in terms of its capacity to construct and communicate social status and mobility, interplay with kinship and intimacy, as well as highlighting the gendered and class dimensions of these processes.

The women from Jima (Jimeñas[1]) with whom I conducted my research are members of previously peasant households whose main economic strategy, following the collapse of the rural economy in the late 1990s, is now premised on the transnational migration of, primarily male, kin and the subsequent receipt of remittances. As a consequence these households, like others in the region, have shifted from being units of production to ones of consumption (Abbots, 2012; Pribilsky, 2007), which channel remittances towards home extensions, household appliances, soft furnishings and items for children, particularly clothing, computers and motorbikes. In addition, migrated kin send gifts from New York to their Ecuadorian wives and children, which often take the form of white goods and clothing emblazoned with USA logos. These forms of consumption are commonly viewed as public expressions of status and framed as spectacular displays of new wealth that provoke dismay and alarm among local political elites and middle class professionals (hereafter governing classes). Throughout this chapter I question these depictions of consumption as being motivated by public display, social mobility and emulation, and argue that spending can also be understood as 'intimate investment' that reproduces the household and the relations contained within it. This perspective derives from my focus on the reproductive labour performed by Jimeña women, who transform the remittances and gifts received from their male kin into material objects and (re)produce domestic spaces in which their physically absent husbands are made symbolically present. I thereby demonstrate how ordinary household items help create and maintain bonds of affection between family members who are geographically separated, and look to illuminate the emotional attachments and social logics – of collectivity, intimacy and care – that inform Jimeña spending. As such, I highlight the moral frameworks and affective relations on which consumption is founded and critically reflect upon the definition and value(s) of consumption, as well as challenge the governing classes' notion that it can 'threaten' family life.

## Methodology

This chapter is based on a total of eighteen months fieldwork in the greater Cuenca region, in which the village of Jima is located. For twelve of those months, I lived and worked alongside a family who were, in many ways, typical of an emerging social group who originate from the lower rural, peasant classes but have recently acquired new wealth through the long-term transnational migration of their male kin. I refer to this social group as the migrant-peasantry throughout in order to reflect both their historical and current class position and the basis for much of their consumption, social life and household income. The husband, brothers and elder sons of Sonia, my hostess, had all been living in the United States for up to fifteen years, and I consequently shared Sonia's Jimeño home with herself, her two younger children and an array of casual and live-in domestic workers.[2] Being so enmeshed in the domestic life of a Jimeño household has both its advantages and disadvantages in terms of data collection. On one hand, I could easily observe the private practices of consumption and everyday engagements with objects within the home. This involvement also enabled me to access intimate data that my participants may not have been able to articulate in response to formal questionnaires; for example, the frequency of contact with migrants, the manner in which children and wives engage with their migrated kin, and the worries and pleasures which stem from male members of the household being physically absent. Much of Jimeño social life, and consequently my research, is centred on the house and, while the value of a methodological focus on the private home has been demonstrated in range of studies (see Bourdieu, 1973; Carsten and Hugh-Jones, 1995; Joyce and Gillespie, 2000; Lévi-Strauss, 1987) there is a distinction, as Carsten (1997) notes, between the domestic domain as an analytical concept and the subjective experience of living within it. The domestic environment, while providing valuable insights into everyday life and the intimacies of the household, can also become somewhat claustrophobic. I looked to offset those limitations by forging relationships, through snowball sampling and introductions, with other households. Consequently, in the following discussion I draw on the deep insights that can be gained from an intimacy with one household and contextualise these with the knowledge gained from working with a wider network of women and their households.

Migrant-peasant households comprise the majority of the Jimeño population, but they should not be regarded as a homogenous group, with households experiencing the consequences of sustained gendered migration in myriad ways. I have addressed a number of these distinctions and tensions elsewhere (Abbots, 2012; 2014b; 2014c), and in this chapter I specifically draw upon the voices and practices of those who come from the most established migrant-peasant households, as well as the views of some of my 'governing class' participants. I define this latter group as the rural and urban landed and professional social groups who differentiate themselves as much by their public criticisms of the migrant-peasantry as they do their cultural practices and labour relations. Although I hesitate to state that the migrant-peasant households

I discuss here are towards the end of the migratory cycle, as the times-cales for these processes remain unknown, their male kin are among the earliest and most successful migrants, and they number some of the wealthiest in the village.

Informal discussions and participant observation formed the core of my data collection methods, and it was through working alongside my participants in the kitchen and sharing leisure time that I collected most of my data. I paid attention to the embodied experience of living in the household and the ways in which my participants not only spoke about the objects in their homes, but also interacted with them. In addition, I attended to the quotidian casual utterances as well as the more 'formal' responses to my questions, and was involved in a number of group discussions that took place during communal gatherings and collective workgroups.[3]

### Consumption as disruption: the critique of the governing classes

I was sitting in Sonia's kitchen, observing two of her domestic workers, Carmela and Maria, prepare the food for Sonia's sons' First Holy Communion celebrations. Carmela was at the kitchen table, preparing the chicken that would later by roasted in the capacious oven that was installed in the corner. An array of saucepans bubbled on the rings of the two gas hobs, while the rice steamed in two electric rice cookers that stood on the counter alongside a food processor, a juicer and a micro-wave oven. Maria was sorting through one of the three freezers, trying to locate the ice cream that was to be served with the three-tier cake that had been brought from Cuenca city for the occasion. To her side was the door to the formal dining room, in which Zoila, another domestic helper, was arranging the ten wooden dining chairs around the polished table and dusting the dresser. As there were a number of guests, however, we would be eating in the lower salon, which could easily accommodate up to fifty diners. The stereo-system had been set up in this room, and the music emanating from its surround-sound speakers competed with the voices on the kitchen radio. Meanwhile, Sonia and her eldest son were in the upper salon, watching their favourite *telenovela* (soap opera) on the 55inch flat screen television, while her youngest played a game on the personal computer installed in the den.

As this brief description of Jimeño domestic life indicates, the migrant-peasantry are 'conspicuous consumers' (Veblen, 1994). Remittances are rarely saved, but are instead spent on an array of commodities, including house building and extension, kitchen appli-ances, electronic equipment and new technology, soft furnishings, and items and clothing for children. Such conspicuous consumption and seemingly ostentatious displays of wealth have come to characterise the socio-economic change resulting from migration – a change that is often cast in negative terms by the governing classes. As these critiques are premised on assumptions about the public role of consumption, as well as notions of the ideal family, I first wish to unpack such discourses and situate them within the broader concerns about migration that circulate across the region, as well as placing them in the context of a firmly embedded social hierarchy and the class consciousness that permeates every facet of social life in the Highlands (Miles, 2004, p. 27; Wibblesman, 2003, p. 279).

The greater Cuenca region is 'the locus of massive, predominantly male migration to the United States and Spain and the inflow of remit-tances that serve to transform the livelihood of the poor' (Whitten, 2003, p. 10). Migration from the Cuenca region to the United States was reported as early as the 1930s (US Department of Homeland Security, 2006) and continued slowly and persistently throughout the 1970s (Kyle, 2000; Jokisch and Pribilsky, 2002), although it was the two major economic crises of the 1980s and late 1990s that triggered the sustained widespread migration that has resulted in the transformation of the social lives of many Ecuadorians in the rural Highlands today (Jokisch, 2007; Jokisch and Pribilsky, 2002). Scholars in the area have commented on the profound social and cultural consequences of this economic strategy (Abbots, 2012; 2014b; Klaufus, 2006; Kyle, 2000; Miles, 2004; Pribilsky, 2007; Weismantel, 2003), not least in terms of demography, with some communities effectively becoming villages of women. Jima could also be defined in this way, with a large proportion of men between their late teens and early sixties no longer physically present and the majority of the village's core population comprising women of all ages, children between the ages of four and their mid-teens, and elderly men. A common argument, held both locally and in academic discussions, is that this inevitably leads to disruption in reproductive cycles and the breakdown of the family unit, with the female kin of migrants being deserted and suffering 'de facto' divorce (see, for eg. Kyle, 2000). However, none of my participants self-identified, or were classified by others, as 'deserted' women. Instead, they consistently asserted that they remained married and their household, intact. It was this assertion that led me to explore the mechanisms through which they maintain transnational kin rela-tions and reproduce their household, and to question the values and understandings of consumption and models of the family on which the 'family rupture' argument is premised.

This argument is particularly evident in the discourses of the governing classes. Their stance to the high levels of consumption practiced by the migrant-peasantry is generally one of condemnation, and they regard the gendered migration, the remittance wealth it creates, and the subsequent consumption as leading not only to the break up of the household, but also to the spoiling of children and a decline in moral and cultural values. As one governing class participant, Lucio, told me when directing my attention to a particular migrant-peasant house in the village:

> There are only children living there now, the parents have gone to the United States. But they send the money back and the eldest girl – well she must be about thirteen, fourteen, maybe – she looks after the rest. But they run wild, completely wild – what can you expect, with no parents and all that money? The parents, they think they are doing the right thing, but they're not.

This view is also presented in a Jimeño magazine, *Revista Huinara*, and is made especially clear in an article that focuses on the consequences of the prolonged absence of fathers on both young children and teenagers. The discussion directly associates gendered migration and consumption, and then goes on to draw correlations between these economic practices with rises in teenage alcoholism, poor educational achievement, and premature sexual activity (with its associated unwanted pregnancies, abortions and transmitted diseases). It concludes:

> (parents) without exception fall into a deep error because they send dollars and presents, wanting to fill the hole of their absence, without realising that the most important thing they are missing is the love of their parents, turning the teenagers into cold people, without aspirations, dependent on easy money. (*Revista Huinara*, 2005–2034)

This quote, which is less sympathetic perhaps than Lucio's, warrants some unpacking in the way it makes seemingly intuitive statements about consumption and intimacies. Here consumption is constructed as antithetical to kinship and affection, with parents misguidedly 'filling the hole of their absence' with commodities. Money and objects are thus associated with coldness and a lack of love. Yet it is also implied that the parental motivation for sending gifts is to support the continuation of a

relationship between parents and children, and for the parents to maintain a presence in their children's lives. This motivation is, however,
glossed over in favour of the seemingly inevitable consequences of
such practices. The message is clear: money, as materially manifested in
consumer goods, has a destructive capacity. Consequently, money and
commodities become diametrically opposed to affection and intimacy.
Such polarisations and fetishisations have, of course, been subject to
significant critique and demonstrated to be ideological constructs, and
the substantivist argument that economic transactions are embedded
within social relations and moral frameworks is well established (see
Parry and Bloch, 1989). Nevertheless, it appears to remain a particularly
salient notion in the Jimeño context and one that pervades much of
the criticism that is levelled at the consumption practices and economic
strategies of the migrant-peasantry.

Miles (2004), whose research is located in neighbouring Cumbe,
further notes that the Cuencano governing classes utilise a number of
mechanisms by which to circulate the view that migration, remittances
and the resulting consumption is resulting in the demise of morality and
family values. These mechanisms include the retelling of urban myths
and parables that focus on failed migrants and the dangers of sudden,
increased wealth, as well as the promulgation of narratives that mock
the consumption practices of the peasantry: for example Miles refers
to a published article, which echoes the sentiments of *Revista Huinara*,
that makes reference to stereo systems which no-one knows how to
use and typewriters covered in guinea pig droppings (p. 30). I was also
introduced to such narratives by my governing class participants, and
there are striking similarities between the tales they were keen to regale
to me and those that others have reported. Klaufus (2006, pp. 79–80),
for instance, refers to being told an anecdote about a house in which
the elevator is used for storing pigs, whereas I was asked by one of my
participants, amongst others, whether I knew that 'there is one house
that is so big – three storeys – that is has an elevator. And they keep
sheep in the elevator – all those sheep going up and down!' Moreover,
as another participant, Elena, showed me, these narratives are not just
casually circulated, but also make their way into more formal texts.

On first meeting Elena, who lives and works in Cuenca city as a
teacher, the conversation quickly turned, upon her hearing that I was
living and researching in the *campo* (countryside), to outward migration and the consumption practices of the migrant-peasantry. 'How
do you find it?' she asked me, 'the *campesinos* (peasants), they're don't
know what they are doing'. She continued, 'they have all this money

now – so much money – and they don't know what to do with it, so they just keep on buying things; it's a bit crazy, no?' The discussion continued in this vein, with Elena drawing upon examples, very much like those cited by Miles (2004) and Klaufus (2006), of houses with elevators, lifts containing sheep, and computers and new televisions strewn with animal droppings. On our next meeting she presented me with a book published by the local government, entitled *Migration Is a Right Not an Obligation* (2006), explaining that this would tell me much of what I needed to know about the consequences of migration and remittance incomes. The book contains a series of narratives and drawings collected from school children that elucidate the 'familial crisis' that has arisen as a result of being 'abandoned' (p. 67) and contains a series of warnings such as 'stay in your country: money is not happiness' (p. 47).

Miles' analysis of this governing class discourse concludes they regard the migrant-peasantry as 'ignorant peasants who have been blinded by the lure of earning dollars and do not really know what they are doing to themselves, their families, and, most distressingly, the cultural patrimony of Cuenca' (2004, p. 28). This 'ignorant peasant' discourse is perhaps compounded in Jima by the manner in which a number of commodities purchased by the migrant-peasantry are rarely used and ultimately end up being discarded to outhouses, as well as the scale of their consumption, whether it is building 'oversized' houses or having three freezers. As such, there is a seeming disparity between the extent of items consumed and their need and level of use. The theme of (perceived) waste and surplus and the need to put remittances to 'good use' thus starts to emerge – a narrative thread that points, perhaps, to the prevalence of the self-maximising, rational 'economic man' model embedded within this critique of consumption. This is further highlighted in the way the governing classes promote investment of economic resources to produce further capital, whether it is by encouraging the migrant-peasantry to invest remittances into farming and increasing agricultural yields, or to become petty entrepreneurs and set up small businesses, or to save money in higher interest bank accounts and saving schemes. As such, the seeming triumph of symbolic value of objects over their use-value together with the assumption that money and affection are ideologically irreconcilable is, I suggest, at the root of the governing classes criticisms of migrant-peasantry consumption. To the governing classes, the consumption of objects at a level seemingly above what a migrant-peasant household requires – or more accurately is understood to require – is a clear-cut example of peasant irrationality and the material manifestation of a less sophisticated mentality. The 'spend, spend, spend' philosophy of the migrant-peasantry appears to be without purpose, futile, and ultimately misguided. This theme has also been echoed in academic discourse (see, for example, Veblen's 1994 account of middle class consumption) yet, a closer look at the interplay between consumption and intimacies, from the perspective of the domestic rather than the public realm, presents a different picture: it is to this that I now turn.

## The public and private aspects of consumption: white goods and the entanglement of kinship, progress and economic security

Rosa's kitchen is one of the most intimate and social areas of the house, as well as being the space in which an extensive range of commodities are housed and displayed to her immediate kin and members of her closest social networks. It is fully fitted and equipped with hot and cold running water, a gas oven, two five-ring hobs, three fridges, a washing machine, and a number of smaller appliances such as electric rice cookers, juicers, a microwave, food processors and sandwich makers. Rosa's spending on household gadgets is not exceptional, and all of my participants made frequent purchases from one of Cuenca's many *electrodoméstico* (white and electrical goods) stores, which sell a range of washing machines, flat screen televisions, DVD players, cameras, and stereo equipment alongside smaller electrical household items. *Electrodomésticos* is one of the largest economic growth areas in the greater Cuenca region, and it seems that every other shop in the city now sells electrical goods, with new stores constantly opening. For example, the building next to the Jima bus company's office, which is located on the outskirts of Cuenca city, was, at the start of my fieldwork, a general food store but this was shut to make way for a new *electrodoméstico* store, much to the delight of many of my research participants who spent the time waiting for the bus browsing for their next purchase. It is not possible to quantify the amount of money spent, although, as an indicator, a number had invested in LCD and Plasma flat screen televisions which retail between US$ 2000 and US$ 4400. In addition, Miles (2004) and Klaufus (2006, p. 77) also comment on the success of the *electrodoméstico* industry in the region, with Klaufus stating the area is a 'paradise' for such enterprises.

This level of consumption appears, at first glance, to be motivated by social aspirations and it is tempting to interpret it through a lens of distinction (Bourdieu, 1984) and competition (Walmsley, 2001). My migrant-peasant participants tended not to see their consumption practices in this manner, although they did draw my attention to the ways in which the commodities they consume symbolise 'progress' and a shift towards economic security and modernity. Yet this does not suggest that it is only the public aspect of consumption that is of import here, as my participants often emphasised and entangled progress, continuity and stability of their own household and kinship relations within these broader social commentaries. Thus, the intimacies and domestic resonance of consumption is entwined with its capacity to broadcast claims to 'society'.

This is illustrated in Luisa's oral history. Having never been asked to reflexively consider their consumption before, many of my participants found it difficult to articulate the reasons behind their spending. However, wider conversations about the changes in the village and their domestic life, in which my participants were often keen to talk about their *'progreso'* (progress) and 'modern' lifestyles, gives some indication as to the ways in which the public and the private characteristics of commodities are drawn together. As Luisa elucidates:

In 1938, the radio arrived. But we only had electricity from 6pm to 6am. I remember seeing this large, wooden box [in a wealthier relative's house]. He paid 400 sucres for it[4]. Then there were only twelve, thirteen cars in Cuenca, and now they say there are 80,000 in Azuay. We have so many cars now, seventy years ago there weren't any, now there are hundreds. Only ten children in the whole area had bikes, and now, look, all the children here, these children [pointing to her great nephews] have bikes; some have two, three, four or five bikes.

Back then, a worker would earn one *sucre* a day and he would walk six kilometres to the hacienda and back – all the time barefoot – for his day's wage. Ninety percent of the people in the *campo* [countryside], the peasants, didn't have shoes in those days; now everybody has shoes. The first time I had shoes was my first communion. They were borrowed from my uncle so were too big. But I was very pleased and proud to have them.

Only rich people had shoes in those days; it was very bad. When I was young only three men had shoes, the priest, the teacher and one rich man. But the workers without shoes, they had children and sent them to school, and they had children who go to the United States and look [gesticulating around the dining room in her niece's house]! The grandchildren of the people who used to work for one sucre a day – they now have these big houses, and bikes and shoes and fridges. It's because we are more stable now, more economically stable. Things are much better now.

Unlike the governing classes, Luisa did not look to pass judgement on the consumption she observed but instead used it as material evidence of progress and security. Her narrative weaves personal memories and observations, which are embedded in her own kin relations, into a broader social history, and she situates these against a temporal framework in which the presence of specific commodities, particularly those which are commonly purchased with remittances, and the capacity to acquire these objects, are representative of the social and economic changes experienced in the village. Yet I also want to suggest that it is not just the evolution of Jima that is being narrated in Luisa's account, but also that of her household and family. The family has progressed (in her terms) to a 'much better' and 'more stable' situation and, while there has been change in terms of income and material possessions, there is also continuity of kinship. The household, then, has not only successfully reproduced itself, but has also economically improved its situation; a process which, it is hoped by its members, will also better its social status and the opportunities this affords to its younger members.

Luisa is not alone in emphasising the way that migration has engendered financial security and improved living conditions for the household, and I was frequently told that 'we are more secure now' and that 'life is much easier'. Considering the dire financial predicaments that many of my participants' families experienced before migration, it is perhaps not surprising that this factor comes to the fore. This interpretation is somewhat at odds, however, with that of the governing classes, who promulgate a discourse of 'easy money' while concomitantly highlighting the insecurity of remittances and the particularly precarious position of the children and female kin of those who remain in the village (see also Kyle, 2000). Hence a clear difference in the way the two social groups interpret consumption and the conspicuous presence of commodities emerges: for the governing classes, consumption is a sign of cultural and social breakdown whereas for the migrant-peasantry it marks progress – in time, in social status, and economically.

The ability to consume, for the migrant-peasantry, thus indicates economic and social 'success'. Yet, while there may be public elements of social status and emulation in the migrant-peasantry's notion of success, Luisa's account suggests that it also incorporates domestic elements, such as the 'betterment' of the household, its position in the village and its reproduction. Pribilsky (2007) draws similar conclusions from the perspective of migrated men. He shows that the consumption of commodities is motivated just as much by affective relations as instrumental status gains and argues that, through consumption, migrants can build relationships with their families while simultaneously establishing social distance between their household and those which cannot provide such objects (p. 270). He thereby draws attention to both the public and intimate aspects of consumption, while demonstrating how commodities facilitate the (re)production and reconfiguration of transnational familial relationships.

This entwining of the public and private comes further to the fore when we consider the ways in which the array of commodities held by a household comes to represent a migrant's journey and social reputation. White goods come into households via two mechanisms. They are either received as gifts directly from migrants or remittances are transformed by purchasing commodities from the market. Notwithstanding this distinction, once brought into the home, my participants firmly associated the objects purchased by remittances with the migrated male kin who had enabled their acquisition. This was seen in the way they would associate houses built in a migrant style with good husbands (see Abbots 2014a) and drew my attention to the source of key items, narrating to me how they had acquired it and who had provided the resources to do so. This process of imprinting objects so that they become known as originating from a specific individual is not uncommon in the Andes. As Colleredo-Mansfield (1999) argues, material items enable an individual's presence to be experienced, even if they are not physically present. Likewise, Pribilsky contends that gift-giving enables migrants to make 'status-claims' and maintain their position in their home community (2007, p. 243).

Gell's (1986) seminal critique of anthropological interpretations of competitive spending provides one of the most illuminating ways of thinking through this process. He contends that objects can be regarded as works of art that transcend their utilitarian capacity by objectifying the consumer's labour and personal sacrifice. Commodities thus 'totalise' the biography and career of their owner. It would seem a similar process is occurring in Jima as the migrant-peasantry invest the majority of the remittances earned by migrant labour into the permanent fabric of the household. The materiality of the items consumed is pivotal in this process: In concentrating much of their spending power in *electrodomesticos* and domestic architecture, the migrant-peasantry are selecting commodities that are hard-wearing, durable and materially robust. Hence there is a sense of solidity, as consumption transforms remittances into concrete commemorations of the migrant's journey. An appreciation of this practice thus provides us with a more nuanced view of the status commodities are capable of conferring, as it places the individual migrants and their 'successful' journey at the heart of public expression.

As such, commodities can be understood as a celebration of migrant kin and a material manifestation of their migratory success. This argument has been made in reference to migrant architecture, with commentators noting how houses materially demonstrate the success of migration (Klaufus, 2006; Thomas, 1998) and legitimise economic action (Colloredo-Mansfeld, 1994; Fletcher 1997). Following Pribilsky (2007), I wish to further extend this argument to the objects contained within the home, although this celebration and legitimisation differs in some aspects insomuch as that it is more intimate. Returning to Rosa's and Sonia's kitchens, we see that the core objects symbolising her kin's success – her domestic appliances – are contained in the private spaces of the home, rather than being on public display. Hence the relationship between consumer, migrant and object is one that is more private than public, an observation that further questions the notion that consumption is motivated by public expressions of status. Moreover, while not wishing to downplay the transformative practice of converting money into objects and the gendered labour relations that are potentially involved in this process, the recognition that bringing a commodity into the home and, in turn, displaying and interacting with that commodity, is the critical act in the materialising of migrated male kin raises a question as to 'what constitutes consumption' in the context. In crossing the boundary between public market and private home, the commodity appears to be transformed into a different type of object, one that is imbued with domesticity and personal meaning. I wish to suggest, then, that consumption can be a constructed as a transformative act in which an object moves from the public to the private sphere and its meaning is subsequently personalised.

The issue of who enacts these transformative processes consequently comes into view, and returning to Jima I wish to posit that, although objects are associated by my participants with their migrated male kin, two social actors are present: the one who has acquired the income through his own labour, and may have purchased the object directly – the migrated male kin – and the one who has physically brought the object into the domestic domain, by possibly purchasing it, by interacting with it and displaying it in their home – the wives of migrated men. This not only indicates that consumption is perhaps less concerned with the practice of transforming money into objects than in transforming objects and shifting them across boundaries, but also that it is not just the biographies of migrated male kin which are being materialised here, but also that of their female kin and the continuing relationship between them – an observation that extends Gell's (1986) concept of totalised biographies. I now therefore turn to explore how both men and women, and their the relationship between them, are embedded and totalised in another key objects consumed by the migrant-peasantry – clothing.

## Consolidating a migrant's presence: consumption and clothing

Scholarship on dress in the Andes has tended to focus on costume and its relation to ethnic identity rather than being considered through the lens of kinship, consumption and socio-economic transformation (see Meisch, 1987, Rowe, 1998, Salomon, 1981). An exception to this is Lentz's (1995) account of dress in the context of new wealth and migration, in which she highlights changes in 'traditional' dress and a shift towards 'modern' clothing, albeit still within a framework of ethnicity and relations between Indian and *mestizos*. In Jima, alongside domestic construction and household appliances, a shift in dress practices –particularly that of women – is one of the most conspicuous material changes emerging from male migration and the receipt of remittance incomes. All of my migrant-peasant participants were at various stages of rejecting the 'traditional' dress of the *pollera* and Panama hat that identify them as belonging to the rural lower classes in favour of clothes they define as 'modern', including jeans, tracksuits and sweatshirts.[5] As Carmela told me;

> I don't wear *polleras*; my mother used to too; but I wouldn't now. It's a tradition here, and the *polleras* are beautiful, but only the *indígenas* [indigenous women] and older women wear those clothes. My children, my girls, they wear blue jeans now. It's more modern.

Her view was echoed by the two remaining Panama hat makers in the village, who both explained that fewer and fewer women were purchasing and wearing their products, despite the rise in disposable incomes and increased wealth in the village. They attributed this decline to the migrant-peasantry, especially the younger generation, no longer being 'interested in the traditions' and 'want[ing] to wear other clothes – from the United States – now'. Dress then, like household appliances, is one of the mediums through which Jimeños chart and evaluate progress and socio-economic change, and the hat-makers' views resonate with those of the governing classes in the manner they point to cultural erosion and the role young people and increasing incomes seemingly play in this process. As such, the new styles of clothing worn by the migrant-peasantry can be framed as just another emulative commodity that expresses social status, distinction and modernity, and which is ultimately leading to, and indicative of, a decline in social values and established cultural practices. Yet, as with the other consumer objects discussed above, once brought into and embedded in the intimacies of the domestic sphere and the family, Jimeña dress can express and reproduce relationships with migrated male kin, while concomitantly constituting and communicating the social reputation of those kin and consolidating their presence in the village.

One evening as I sat and spoke to a group of women about the changes in their lives since their male kin had migrated, I noticed that none, with the exception of the elderly Doña Teresa, were wearing the uniform of *pollera*, shawl, Panama hat, and braided hair. This parallelled what I had observed in the village on a quotidian basis and during other group discussions and interviews, with women preferring, as part of their everyday or festive costumes, to wear trousers and sweatshirts. Hats and shawls were still visible, but had taken different, more individual, forms, and the women seated around the table with me wore a variety of baseball caps, knitted bonnets, straw boaters and leather caps, and a range of sweatshirts, tracksuit tops and bottoms, and jeans of various styles. Yet despite this seeming diversity, one symbol remained consistently prevalent – that of the flag of the United States. The stars and stripes was prolifically emblazoned across many items of clothing and often, during our group meetings, all my participants were wearing USA symbols in some shape or form. If the stars and stripes was not present, then other symbols and images of the United States, such as 'the Big Apple' or the New York Yankees logo, were displayed to a greater or lesser extent. Moreover, a closer look at Doña Teresa's seemingly traditional and unchanged dress revealed that she was also wearing knee-high socks embroidered with the USA flag underneath her wellington boots. My participants were not, therefore, dressed in a manner that looked to emulate the style of the governing classes, but had rather developed their own 'costume' that appropriated aspects of 'traditional' dress and blended them with clothes they regarded as 'modern', overlaid with images and symbols of the USA. As such, there is a distinctive style discernible in the clothes of the female kin and children of migrated men and they appear to have swapped one uniform – of the *pollera* – for another, derived from United States.

Upon being asked how they had acquired the clothes they and their children were wearing, I was told that a large proportion had been received as gifts from their male kin and had been sent directly to them from the USA. Moreover, in other more casual conversations, seemingly unrelated to clothing, many of my participants would draw my attention to the clothes they were wearing, telling me that their husbands and sons had purchased and sent the items from the United States. As Rosa informed me, she didn't need to buy clothes with USA logos from the shops in Cuenca 'like some of the other women' because her male kin had sent them 'directly from New York'. This gives some indication of the personal motivation informing their distinctive style adopted by the families of migrated men which is, I suggest, the desire to publicly demonstrate not only that their kin have made the journey to the USA, but also that they are sufficiently economically successful to purchase and send gifts. Moreover, and perhaps more importantly, it also demonstrates continuing relations with migrated kin; in wearing gifts that are clearly from the USA, a wife or child is showing that they are being remembered, not deserted, and that those who have migrated are continuing to care and provide for their Jimeño household. This, in turn, constitutes the reputation of the migrated men as both moral family men and economic success stories. The extent that Jimeñas chose to wear their gifts from migrated kin when they have other choices aside from 'traditional' dress, and the recognition that these other choices could also facilitate their self-presentation and constitution as 'modern', further indicates the robustness of the relationship between Jimeñas and migrants, and also draws attention to the ways in which gift exchange maintains this relationship across transnational space (see Abbots, 2011). Through this lens, the items of dress worn by my participants can, like household appliances, be seen as a material manifestation in Jima of a migrant's journey, his labour, his current geographical location, and his continuing commitment to his family.[6]

The ways in which the intimate consumption of objects can create and articulate an individual's reputation, even if they are not present, has been illuminated, albeit in very different social contexts, in anthropological accounts of kula exchange. Munn (1986), for example, tells us that the exchange of kula shells enables men to acquire a fame which transcends and extends their bodily being and concludes that 'fame is a mobile, circulating dimension of the person: the travels of a person's name apart from his physical presence' (1986, p. 105). She thus demonstrates the 'spatial extendibility' enabled through the exchange and display of material objects, a process expanded upon in

Gell's (1998) concept of distributive personhood, by which he argues that objects can embody social actors and thus become extensions of the self across space and time. Migrants' gifts of clothing are not exchanged in the same manner as kula shells, but there are striking similarities in the ways in which these material commodities appear to embody and carry a migrant's reputation beyond the physical confines of their body. Although Munn does not explicitly develop the theme of embodied practice in relation to kula shells, their unique characteristic, as with clothes, as items worn upon the body is significant. Entwistle (2000) notes that dress is a situated bodily practice, and Lurie (1981) and Wilson (2003) both highlight that clothes can be understood as an extension of those who wear them. As Tarlo confirms, clothes' 'peculiar proximity to our bodies gives them a special potential for symbolic elaboration' (1996, p. 16), and she emphasises how personal meanings can be imbued into dress in the construction of a self-image (see also Tranberg Hansen, 2000). As such, she points to the ways in which the meaning of dress can lie in the creative act of the wearer. Hence dress is located on the boundary between public and private (Wilson 2003 p. 2), in that it can express public statements while forging personal intimacies and relationships.

I wish to extend these conclusions by suggesting that, in Jima, the construction of the self through dress is, perhaps, of less import than the circulation of the reputation of migrated kin. This is not to deny that the processes of self-construction through engagements with clothing and other commodities is not taking place, as the reproduction and expression of an ongoing transnational relationship reflects on the women who remain at home in that they can demonstrate to society that they have not been deserted. Instead, I want to highlight that women's social reputations are, at least in part, embedded in that of their migrated kin. Thus, I want to raise the possibility that the wearing of USA emblemed clothes, as with the consumption of household appliances, is less concerned, in this context, with the construction of the self and more related to the construction of another member of the household, the relationship between the other and the self, and the self as the other half of that relationship. Thus consumption can be seen as a practice in which relationships are solidified and materialised, and in which both actors – the purchaser and the wearer – are drawn together in one item (of clothing). This raises questions, of course, as to gender relations and the labour that women perform in the construction, consolidation and circulation of male reputations and it is to this that I now turn.

## The labour of women: gender and the reproduction of the transnational household

It is Munn who further points to the gendered dimensions of intimate consumption by elucidating how women, through their bodily display of kula necklaces, perform their male kin's kula prowess and sustain male reputations. Women thus, she argues, become the 'fame of men' (1986, p. 112). Likewise, Pribilsky argues that women tacitly accept 'the burdens of representing men and their status in their home communities' (2007, p. 272). In this final section I thereby wish to explore the gender dynamics that are embedded in Jimeña consumption of household appliances and clothing and attend to the hidden labour of women in the reproduction of the transnational household. In so doing, I return to Jimeño class relations and indicate the role that migrant-peasant women potentially play in contesting and resisting the hegemonic discourses of the governing classes.

Scholarship on consumption and migration has tended, perhaps unsurprisingly, to focus on the practices and status of migrants, as opposed to those of whom they are intimately related. This, I suggest, significantly underplays the labour of women who, the evidence from Jima suggests, are critical to status-making and the (re)production of a dispersed household. For example, Thomas' (1998) discussion of migrant house-building in Madagascar addresses the labour involved in house construction to be that of migrants and pays little heed to the transformative practices of those – namely women – who remain in the exporting community. Pribilsky takes a more nuanced approach in highlighting the active role that women play as 'remittance managers' (2007, p. 266), but he also refers to women *sharing* the status claims of men, rather than attending to the possibility that women may be engaged in *making* this status. As such, consumption in this context is often represented, to a greater or lesser extent, as being driven by those (men) who have migrated. This perspective, however, obscures – and ignores – the labour of a key social actor – that of the individual who transacts the object and shifts it from the public market into the domestic domain. As I have demonstrated, it is the wives, mothers and sisters of migrated men who take the remittances they have received and transform them into the material objects that consolidate a migrant's presence in the home and village. Without this transformative practice, remittances would remain undisplayed numbers on a bank balance or stored as invisible dollar notes. Furthermore, while many objects are received as gifts – and migrated men have therefore performed their own transformative act by converting their wages into a commodity – it is through the labour of women that these objects are displayed and made present both within the home, in relation to domestic appliances, and on their own bodies, in terms of clothing. While men provide the economic wherewithal, it is their female kin who perform the act of consumption. And it is this seemingly insignificant and overlooked act, I argue, that is of crucial importance in this context; it takes that which is acquired in the public sphere and draws it into the personal realm of intimacy and kinship. In other words, the substances of production are transformed into the foundations of reproduction. An analytical focus on the intimate practices of consumption, then, can reveal previously unnoticed gendered performances of labour, as well as question taken-for-granted notions about which social actors consume and the social consequences of such consumption.

The role that Jimeña women play in the transformation of remittances into a form which maintains the moral integrity of the family unit and sustains kinship is reminiscent of Carsten's (1989) account of 'cooking money' in which she describes the process by which the wives of Malay fisherman take the profit received from trade and purify it by transforming it into food that is shared and, in turn, sustains the household. Carsten thus highlights the critical role that women play in investing a substance that is locally regarded as anti-social with the values with which they themselves are associated – cooperation, kinship and unity. She concludes: 'divided male money becomes united kin money through the interposition of women' (p. 136). From this vantage point, the consumption practices of Jimeña women can be regarded as a moral, reproductive practice. They are the moral agents who de-pollute remittances and seek to minimise the threat of disruption presented by the migratory journey by transforming new wealth into objects that embody and make manifest a migrant's relations to their Jimeño kin and ancestral home. Without women – and women's labour – constructing and filling houses with appliances and furnishings and wearing USA emblemed clothes, the continued presence of their migrated male kin would arguably be minimal. Moreover, as these objects embody and make manifest the intimate relationship between migrated men and their kin, they can be seen as providing one of the foundations for the reproduction and continuation of family life.

The reproductive labour performed by women thus comes into view, as does the ways in which their migrated kin continue to potentially regulate the bodies and domestic spaces of their female kin. Woodward suggests that dress is an indirect form of control as it 'allows other people's intentions to penetrate deeply into the intentions of the wearer' (2005, p. 22); an argument which is also found in work centring on religious dress codes as a medium of, frequently patriarchal, power (Arthur, 1999; Winter, 2001). Yet dress can also be a mechanism for agency and subversion, as Tarlo (1996) has demonstrated, and attending to the labour that women perform further indicates how their actions provide a counter-discourse to that of the governing classes. As I have suggested, attempts to regulate and publicly criticise the consumption practices of the migrant-peasantry, and particularly those of the women of this social group, are laden with class dynamics, and in rejecting the governing classes 'ideal' dress code for rural lower-class women – the *pollera* and Panama hat – and replacing it with USA emblemed clothes, Jimeña women can be seen to be potentially contesting, through their consumption practices, these hegemonic discourses. In other words, the manner in which migrant-peasant women continue to consume and display the commodities and gifts associated with remittance wealth and migration can, in the face of such consistent and blatant public criticism, be interpreted, at least in part, as resisting attempts by the governing classes to determine their actions and the way they live their everyday lives. I am not contending that a desire to challenge these discourses is the primary motivating factor for Jimeña consumption, and in contesting the cultural authority of the governing classes they may well be reinforcing the authority of their male kin, but I would like to raise the possibility that continued consumption in this context can be a mechanism for class empowerment, and that women can be the key actors in this process.

This emphasis on female agency and action extends scholarship on male migration, which has tended to emphasise the precarious position of the women who remain behind and/or obfuscate their action and agency. Kyle (2000), for example, argues that patriarchy facilitates and legitimates gendered migration, and portrays men as active agents in the public realm of production, with women being consigned to a somewhat stagnant domestic sphere. However, the model invoked assumes that kinship cannot be performed at a distance and little attention is paid to the ways in which seemingly domestic practices, such as shopping, not only involve the performance of labour, but also reproduce social relationships and intimacies (Miller, 1998). Consequently, women are either invisible or represented as without a social role, as they are left immobilised, helpless and without purpose. My interpretation of Jimeña women's consumption and labour presents a very different view and show that kinship relations and marriages are not as ruptured or as fragile as the governing classes depict. Migrant-peasant households may have shifted from being units of economic production to sites of consumption, but they remain the locus for reproduction.

## Conclusion

Throughout this chapter, I have intended to show that shift in analytical perspective that unpacks assumptions about consumption and kinship provides an additional dimension to discussions of dispersed transnational households by demonstrating the myriad ways migrated men remain embedded within their home-households. Thus, far from an immoral, irresponsible misguided economic activity that rupture family life and 'spoils' children, as the governing classes – and some academics – portray, consumption can be regarded as a reproductive practice that perpetuates and solidifies a household and the relations contained within it. The view from Jima suggests that both migrated men and their kin work hard to maintain their intimate relations and that consumption is crucial to this process. This conclusion provides a deeper understanding of the nature of intimate family life within this migratory context, and the role of consumption within it. It becomes evident that intimacies are reproduced across transnational boundaries through the transformation of remittances into material objects, and the shifting of those objects from the public space of the market to the private spaces of the home.

Consumption in this context, then, can be understood as a transformative process that shifts commodities from the public space of the market and draws them into the intimate domestic sphere of the home. Through this process, the meanings of objects are transformed as they become embedded within, and make manifest, familial relations. This is not to deny that they continue to broadcast claims to 'society' and are a mechanism through which social reputation and status are constituted and expressed. Rather, I have looked to demonstrate the ways in which the public and private characteristics of consumption are entangled, as claims to the progress and betterment of households are entwined with its reproduction, and the reputations of migrated men are built on both their prowess in the United States labour market and their demonstrable commitment to their Jimeño household. Women, I have argued, play a critical role in constructing and circulating this reputation and keeping their migrated male kin symbolically present in the village and in the home. Thus I hope to have drawn attention to oft-obscured labour that women perform and the ways in their consumption practices draw together and root their dispersed household.

# Notes

1. Throughout this chapter I refer to Jimeña(s) specifically when referring to women from Jima and female-specific practices and Jimeño(s) when referring to men and male practices. I also use Jimeño to refer to gender neutral practices and collectively to male and females individuals from Jima.
2. See Abbots (2012) for a discussion on changing domestic labour relations in this context.
3. The informal methods of collecting data and the domestic environment in which most of my data collection occurred raises a number of questions regarding research ethics, particularly concerning informed consent, as the informality and intimacy of the surroundings in which many of our discussions and my participant observation occurred made it difficult for my participants to remember my role as researcher. I attempted to minimise this issue by explaining the purpose of my stay in Jima to my friends and informants not only at the start of my fieldwork and during introductions, but also regularly throughout the duration of my stay. Consequently my research was discussed frequently and at length by my participants who further demonstrated their own awareness of my research by commonly asking questions about its progress. However, in recognition of the personal nature of some of the information I acquired during intimate conversations, I have made a judgement to withhold some data from academic analysis.
4. The sucre was Ecuador's unit of currency until it adopted the US dollar in March 2000. The exchange rate at the time of conversion was 25,000 sucres to 1USD.
5. I have discussed this process and its personal and social consequences in more depth elsewhere (Abbots, 2014b).
6. Pribilsky (2007, p. 237) further notes the importance of 'authenticity' in relation to objects received from migrated kin and the demand from children for '*cosas auténticas*' that indicates further distinctions between migrant households.

# References

Abbots, E-J. (2011) '"It Doesn't Taste as Good from the Pet Shop"; Guinea Pig Consumption and the Performance of Class and Kinship in Highland Ecuador and New York City', *Food, Culture and Society*, 14(2), 205–224.

Abbots, E-J. (2012) 'In the Absence of Men? Gender, Migration and Domestic Labour in the Southern Ecuadorean Andes', *Journal of Latin American Studies*, 44(1), 71–96.

Abbots, E-J. (2014a) 'Investing in the Family's Future: Labour, Gender and Consumption in Highland Ecuador', *Families, Relationships and Societies*, 3(1), 143–148.

Abbots, E-J. (2014b) 'Embodying Country-City Relations: The Figure of the *Chola Cuencana* in Highland Ecuador' in *Food Between the Country and the City: Ethnographies of a Changing Global Foodscape*, N. Domingos, J. Sobral and H.G. West (eds), pp. 41–57, London: Bloomsbury.

Abbots, E-J. (2014c) 'The Fast and the Fusion: Class, Creolization and the Remaking of *Comida Típica* in Highland Ecuador' in *Food Consumption in Global*

58    *Emma-Jayne Abbots*

*Perspective. Essays in the Anthropology of Food in Honour of Jack Goody,* J. A. Klein and A. Murcott (eds), pp. 87–107. Basingstoke: Palgrave Macmillan.

Arthur, Linda B. (ed.) (1999) *Religion, Dress and the Body.* Oxford: Berg.

Bourdieu, P. (1973) 'The Berber House' in *Rules and Meanings,* M. Douglas (ed.), pp. 98–110. Harmondsworth: Penguin Education.

Bourdieu, P. (1984) *Distinction: A Social Critique of the Judgement of Taste.* New York and London: Routledge.

Carsten, J. (1989) 'Cooking Money: Gender and the Symbolic Transformation of Means of Exchange in a Malay Fishing Community' in *Money and the Morality of Exchange.* J. Parry and M. Bloch (eds), pp. 117–141. Cambridge: Cambridge University Press.

Carsten, J. (1997) *The Heat of the Hearth: The Process of Kinship in a Malay Fishing Community.* Oxford: Clarendon Press.

Carsten, J. and S. Hugh-Jones (eds) (1995) *About the House: Lévi-Strauss and Beyond.* Cambridge: Cambridge University Press.

Colloredo-Mansfeld, R. (1994) 'Architectural Conspicuous Consumption and Economic Change in the Andes', *American Anthropologist,* 96(4), 845–865.

Entwistle, J. (2000) *The Fashioned Body: Fashion, Dress and Modern Social Theory.* Cambridge: Polity Press.

Fletcher, P. L. (1997) 'Building from Migration: Imported Design and Everyday Use of Migrant Houses in Mexico' in *The Allure of the Foreign: Imported Goods in Postcolonial Latin America* B. Orlove (ed.), pp. 185–201. Ann Arbor: University of Michigan Press.

Gell, A. (1986) 'Newcomers to the World of Goods: Consumption among the Muria Gonds' in *The Social Life of Things: Commodities in Cultural Perspective,* A. Appadurai (ed.), pp. 110–138. Cambridge: Cambridge University Press.

Gell, A. (1998) *Art and Agency: An Anthropological Theory.* Oxford: Clarendon Press.

Jokisch, B. (2007) 'Ecuador: Diversity in Migration' in *Migration Information Source* Migration Policy Institute (ed.) available at http://www.migrationinformation.org/USfocus/display.cfm? ID=575, [accessed on 5th April 2007].

Jokisch, B. and J. Pribilsky (2002) 'The Panic to Leave: Economic Crisis and the "New Emigration" from Ecuador', *International Migration,* 40(4), 75–101.

Joyce, R. A. and S. D. Gillespie (eds) (2000) *Beyond Kinship: Social and Material Production in House Societies.* Philadelphia: University of Pennsylvania Press.

Klaufus, C. (2006) 'Globalization in Residential Architecture in Cuenca, Ecuador: Social and Cultural Diversification of Architects and their Clients', *Environment and Planning D: Society and Space,* 24, 69–89.

Kyle, D. (2000) *Transnational Peasants: Migrations, Networks and Ethnicity in Andean Ecuador.* Baltimore: The John Hopkins University Press.

Lentz, C. (1995) 'Ethnic Conflict and Changing Dress Codes: A Case Study of an Indian Migrant Village in Highland Ecuador' in *Dress and Ethnicity: Change across Space and Time,* J.B. Eicher (ed.), pp. 269–293. Oxford: Berg.

Lévi-Strauss, C. (1987) *Anthropology and Myth: Lectures 1951–1982.* Oxford: Basil Blackwell.

Lurie, A. (1981) *The Language of Clothes.* London: Heinemann.

Meisch, L. (1987) *Weaving, Costume, and the Market.* Quito: Ediciones Libri Mundi.

Miles, A. (2004) *From Cuenca to Queens: An Anthropological Story of Transnational Migration*. Austin: University of Texas Press.

Miller, D. (1998) *A Theory of Shopping*. Cambridge: Polity Press.

Munn, N. (1986) *The Fame of Gawa: A Symbolic Study of Value Transformation in a Massim (Papau New Guinea) Society*. Cambridge: Cambridge University Press.

Parry, J. and M. Bloch (eds)\ (1989) *Money and the Morality of Exchange*. Cambridge: Cambridge University Press.

Pribilsky, J. (2007) *La Chulla Vida: Gender, Migration and the Family in Andean Ecuador & New York City*. Syracuse N.Y: Syracuse University Press.

Rowe, A. P. (ed.). (1998) *Costume and Identity in Highland Ecuador*. Seattle: University of Washington Press.

Salomon, F. (1981) 'Killing the Yumbo: A Ritual Drama of Northern Quito' in *Cultural Transformations and Ethnicity in Modern Ecuador*, N. E. Whitten (ed.), pp. 162–208. Urbana: University of Illinois Press.

Tarlo, E. (1996) *Clothing Matters: Dress and Identity in India*. London: Hurst and Company.

Thomas, P. (1998) 'Conspicuous Construction: Houses, Consumption and "Relocalization" in Manambondro, Southeast Madagascar', *The Journal of the Royal Anthropological Institute*, 4(3), 425–466.

Tranberg Hansen, K. (2000) *Saluala: The World of Second-hand Clothing and Zambia*. Chicago: Chicago University Press.

Veblen, T. (1994 [1899]) *The Theory of the Leisure Class*. New York: Dover Publications.

Walmsley, E. (2001) Transformando Los Pueblos: La Migración Internacional y el Impacto Social al Nivel Comuntario. *Ecuador Debate* 54. Available at http://www.dlh.lahora.com.ec/paginas/debate/ [accessed 17 April 2008].

Weismantel, M. J. (2003) 'Mothers of the *Patria*: La Chola Cuencana and La Mama Negra' in *Millennial Ecuador: Critical Essays on Cultural Transformations and Social Dynamics*, N. E. Whitten (ed.), pp. 325–354. Iowa City: University of Iowa Press.

Whitten, N. E. (2003) 'Introduction' in *Millennial Ecuador: Critical Essays on Cultural Transformations and Social Dynamics*, N. E. Whitten (ed.), pp. 1–45. Iowa City: University of Iowa Press.

Wibblesman, M. (2003) 'Appendix: General Information on Ecuador' in *Millennial Ecuador: Critical Essays on Cultural Transformations and Social Dynamics*, N. E. Whitten (ed.), pp. 375–388. Iowa City: University of Iowa Press.

Wilson, E. (2003 [1985]) *Adorned in Dreams: Fashion and Modernity* London: I.B. Tauris.

Winter, B. (2001) 'Fundamental Misunderstandings: Issues in Feminist Approaches to Islamism' in *Journal of Women's History* 13(1): 9–41.

Woodward, S. (2005) 'Looking Good: Feeling Right – Aesthetics of the Self' in *Clothing as Material Culture*, S. Küchler and D. Miller (eds), pp. 21–50. Oxford: Berg.

# 3
# Interconnectivities and Material Agencies: Consumption, Fashion, and Intimacy in Zhu Tianwen's 'Fin-de-Siècle Splendor'

*C. Laura Lovin*

The material girl who craves for world's splendour is Mia, the main character of 'Fin-de-Siècle Splendor,' one of the seven stories published by Zhu Tianwen in her 1990 collection *Fin-de-Siècle Splendour*. A volume of exquisite lyrical power, *Fin-de-Siècle Splendour* marked Zhu's break into mass popularity, particularly among urban readers of the Greater China region. Literary critics praised the volume for its modernist and postmodernist valences, more specifically for its capacity to present 'the unpresentable' and to enable its readership 'to see only by making it impossible to see' (Lyotard qtd. in Chiang, 2002, p. 53). At the core of *Fin-de-siecle Splendor* are the residents of 1992's Taipei – '"the new species" (*xin renlei*) of young men and women zipping about on their red Fiat scooters; the McDonald's waitresses, homosexual artists, fashion models and soap opera directors' (Chiang, 2002, p. 50). Among them is Mia, a fashion model and the main character of the title short story. 'Fin-de-Siècle Splendor' takes place in the future, two years after its publication, close to the turn of the century, in 1992 Taipei. The title of the story contains the French for 'end of century,' a phrase that references a generation of artists and thinkers who decried the cultural and social effects of modernisation as it unfolded across many European countries at the end of the nineteenth century. The fin-de siècle rejection of materialism, rationalism, and positivism went hand in hand with an endorsement of subjectivism and irrationalism (Mestrovic, 2010). Mia; her close girlfriends, Baby, Ann, and Joey; and her fashion-model male friends Kai, Yang Ge, and Ou live in a glamorous Taipei, a big city whose history and present are constructed through a language replete with popular-culture references from the US and Japan, designer brands of global prestige, and fragrances, textures, colours, tastes, forests, flowers, and herbs. Mia's incessant interest in fashion, fabrics, scent, and colour is read as a symptom of 'a culture that is saturated with commodities and in which the individual is subsumed in commercialism' (Wallace et al., 2013, p. 586). Her memories, pleasures, intimacies, and desires are woven into fragmented narrative lines that resist emplotment, rendering past episodes of immersion into the splendours of the world and thus creating histories of fashion, intimacy, love, and urban transformation.

I came across 'Fin-de-Siècle Splendor' in February 2010, at workshop with Michael Hardt[1] organised by several graduate students in the Comparative Literature Program at Rutgers University. The workshop was designed to complement Hardt's talk 'The Politics of the Common,' in which he discussed his conception of the common in relation to questions of urban space and included a discussion of several short stories portraying cities around the globe. I was thus introduced to the city of Taipei through Mavis Tseng's[2] selection of 'Fin-de-Siècle Splendor.' Since then, I have been haunted by the story's complicated relation to postmodernist, materialist, and new materialist urban writing. In this chapter I seek to foreground the new materialist valences of the title story of Zhu's *Fin-de-Siècle Splendor* by positing it as an exploration of interconnecting affects, sensations, and memories. The material interconnections between Mia's human body and her 'more-than-human worlds' (Alaimo, 2010, p. 2) require a different kind of critical attention than that afforded by the postmodern lenses of literary theory. I argue that while *Fin-de-Siècle Splendor* is generally claimed as part of postmodern literature, a new materialist feminist reading of the story foregrounds certain novel ways of writing about the materiality of consumption in relation to the interactions and interconnections between sensorial-affective, psychic, biological, social, architectural, informational, technological, and nonhuman natural elements. Such aspects further add to the coordinates of a postmodern approach by producing a reading that could potentially enrich the ethical and political criticism of consumption, urban-environmental injustice, and modern epistemologies.

The interactions and interconnections that Zhu's narrative constructs between Mia and her worlds will first be contextualised by considerations that explain the relevance of new materialist paradigms to contemporary feminist praxis and then by a brief discussion of Zhu's own literary and political orientations. I will then turn to an overview of the critical approaches to consumption and consumerism that were mostly developed prior to the emergence of new materialist thinking. Since fashion is one of Mia's passions and fashion modelling is her profession, my analysis also undertakes an examination of the fashion industry in relation to gender, pleasure, consumption, and global affective economies. I conclude this chapter by summarising the ways in which new materialist feminist accounts that foreground sensorial-affective interconnections may enrich our understanding of critical consumption by providing a fresh reconceptualisation of interconnections and agencies that shape human practices as well as the living and non-living material worlds.

## Tenets of new materialist feminisms and more-than-representational geographies

New materialism is a term that unites the theoretical interventions that developed in the interdisciplinary space of social theory, the humanities, and biological sciences to criticise the anthropocentrism inherent in social constructivism. By reconsidering the suppressed agencies of inhuman biological forces, non-living material entities, and more-than-human and nonhuman phenomena, new materialism discovers new terrains for ethics that address current crises of economic and environmental justice.

The shift to the analytical lens of new materialism developed in response to the linguistic turn in the humanities and the social constructionist turn in social sciences. The erasure of the agency of matter within postmodern analytical frameworks that foregrounded language, signification, and discourse constitutes the central tenet of new materialist theorisation. Postmodern and poststructuralist thinkers who reacted to the epistemologies of modernism claimed that objective access to the natural world, or by extension, to reality, was enabled by the categories of the natural and the real, which are in fact knowable only inasmuch as they are constituted by language. At the same time, for feminists, the foregrounding of discourse and language as the constitutive ground of reality enabled invaluable theoretical and political gestures that aimed to deconstruct concepts that defined women and femininity as subordinate categories. Furthermore, postmodern feminists contested, resisted, pluralised, and redeployed notions of femininity and masculinity in ways that demonstrated that gendered meanings form within complex systems and are co-constitutive with other binary and hierarchised notions such as class, race, sexuality, disability, geopolitical location, or citizenship status. They also argued that gendered dichotomies undergird all the other signifying binaries of Western thought: mind/ body, rational/emotional, subject/object, and culture/nature (Alaimo and Hekman, 2008). And whereas exposing the mechanisms of meaning that inform and normalise dichotomous thinking bore outstanding theoretical and political gains, the ambivalence that postmodern thinkers manifested in relation to the language/reality binary called for closer critical attention. I argue that as early as 1990, Zhu Tianwen's writing in fact expresses the tensions inherent in this ambivalence and that in *Fin-de-Siècle Splendor,* Zhu finds ways to narrate the materiality of the human body, the human-made world, and the natural world in ways that do not replicate the language/reality dualism.

In their quest for alternatives to the theoretical assumptions of social constructionism, feminist scholars thus became concerned with the conceptualisation of bodies and natures as the inactive material ground for rational thought. Many turned to instances that demonstrated that the human body is a wilful, active force and inquired what discursive possibilities might be available in order to render such moments and the lived experiences of pain, pleasure, disease, or joy intelligible in ways that account for biological substance (Alaimo and Hekman, 2008). In reference to the social constructionist idea that the material world cannot be accessed in and of itself, Karen Barad called for recognition of the fact that cultural intelligibility and the materiality of bodies and natures form a system of intra-actions (2007). Questions of knowledge, representation, epistemology, and ontology came to the fore in inquiries employing methodologies that sought to capture relations between the material and the discursive and to account for the part played by 'the physicality of the body in the constitution of our embodied subjectivity' (Jagger, 2014). In order to find an answer to these queries, Barad took up Niels Bohr's physics to refute the atomist view according to which the world is a collection of individually determinate 'things' and proposed an ontology of 'phenomena,' which would account for 'the inseparability of "observed object" and "agencies of observation"' (Barad, 2003, pp. 813–814). Thus, matter is always within such 'phenomena,' which are essentially material-discursive, with no primacy afforded to either side (Jagger, 2014). The relationality of intra-actions is dynamic and ongoing. It is thus continually stabilising and destabilising properties, meanings, boundaries, and patterns. Barad's intervention makes possible an understanding of the body as continuous with the world rather than as a bounded entity, separated from its environment by its epidermal barrier. It also opens new ways of understanding that the ongoing transformative potential of the world emerges in the context of intra-actions that intimately link discursive, corporeal, material, human, technolog-ical, and nonhuman phenomena (Alaimo and Hekman, 2008).

In keeping with the ontology of phenomena outlined above, Zhu Tianwen describes her own writing as a form of expression committed to the non-ordering representability of reality. The poetic register enables her 'to present reality in "reflection" ... instead of by way of contrast' (Zhu in Chiang 2002, p. 50). Her lyrical descriptions of fluid embodiments, of bodies that pulse alongside the energies of other matters, converge with the approaches of feminist scholars whose investment lies in fore-grounding material interconnectedness. In this sense, sensoriality and affective intensifications are invoked by new materialist thinking as a way of addressing the forces that, in Elizabeth Wissinger's terms, 'may only be observable in the interstices between bodies, between bodies and technologies, or between bodily forces and conscious knowledge' (Wissinger 2007, p. 232). Affects connect bodies, intensify their sensa-tions, focus their attention and orient them onto paths of knowledge. Ultimately, affects, sensations, and interpretations are inseparable. Affects are forces that throw signification off balance and move individ-uals into becoming other than what they are (Bruno, 2008). Accounting for affects, sensations, and interpretations is deemed to enable a better understanding of the world, but most importantly, they are simulta-neously seen to hold the potential for restructuring social meaning (Hemmings, 2005; Massumi, 2002; Sedgwick, 2003).

The emphasis on sensoriality and affects described above is also found in the field of critical geographies, where new materialism is combined with an analytical orientation towards nonrepresentational theory, which seeks to make better sense of 'our self-evidently more-than-human, more-than-textual, multisensual worlds' (Lorimer 2005, 83). For geographer Nigel Thrift, the nonrepresentational project, rather than orienting its inquiries toward representation and meaning, is concerned with rendering 'practices, mundane everyday practices that shape the conduct of human beings towards others and themselves in particular sites' (1997, p. 142). Nonrepresentational geographers also foreground the nonhuman, the 'more-than-human,' and the material world – all the elements within which the social is emplaced (Patchett, 2010; Valentine, 1999; Thrift, 1997).

Ordinarily, representation is bound to a specific form of repetition: the repetition of the same. Marcus A. Donel writes: 'Through representation, what has already been given will come to have been given again. Such is its fidelity to an original that is fated to return through a profusion of dutiful copies; an original whose identity is secured and re-secured through a perpetual return of the same and whose identity is threatened by the inherent capacity of the copy to be a deviant or degraded repetition, a repetition that may introduce an illicit differentiation in the place ostensibly reserved for an identification' (2010, p. 117). The feminist social constructionist critique of modern epistemologies was also concerned with claims for mimetic representability, realism, and truth, and thus many methodological innovations emphasised notions of power, agency, subjectivity, and reflexivity. The challenge that remains, however, is how to bring materiality back into social theory in ways that do not lose sight of the valuable concepts and methodological innovations enabled by social constructionist perspectives. In this sense, Zhu's construction of Mia is relevant to issues of materiality and social constructionism in that it is choreographed to open the human onto the nonhuman and to interconnect biological elements and cultural practices to form a story about the phenomenon that we call Taipei.

## Critical inquiries into consumption and consumer cultures

Since the 1970s, consumerism has become one of the driving forces of global capitalism, extending its scope from the United States and Europe to other regions of the globe and, in particular, to the ascending economies of East and South Asia. David Harvey links the contemporary operations of global capitalism with the radical reshaping of the urban environment (1985). He argues that the global recession of the 1970s launched a new regime of accumulation which was reliant on accelerated production and consumption turnover times, flows of capital resources and of people across national boundaries, as well as on the deindustrialisation of Western economies. Following Marx, consumer culture based on production is considered the ideological counterpart of these economic phenomena. Many critical arguments regarding global forms of commodified capitalist mass culture continue to be inspired by the contributions of the Frankfurt School thinkers who, as early as the mid-1940s, decried inauthenticity and the manipulative purpose and unsatisfying nature of mass culture and mass production (Barker, 2008, p. 49). Meanings, representations, and practices were thus mobilised in the articulation of consumption as a way of life and of consumer choice as an attribute of citizenship. The act of consumption changed from the 'mere acquisitions of commodities' to the 'basis for identity and selfhood' (Dunn, 2008, p. 8). While critical approaches to consumption have most often been developed in relation to concepts of class, lifestyle, subjectivity, and identity, as well as structural divisions among producers and consumers, the framework of cultural hegemony implied by such arguments was later challenged by cultural studies scholars, who discussed the creative meaning-producing activities that accompanied communal forms of consumption. John Fiske emphasised the significance of consumers' 'popular vitality and creativity' as potential forces that motivate and enable social change (Fiske, 1989, p. 8). In terms of postmodern consumption, the relation between consuming subjects and commodities sheds light on the fragmentations and contradictions caused by the arrival of post-Fordist globalised economies, under which accelerated turnover rates for goods and the rapid recoding of product differentiation affected consumers' identity formation. Furthermore, in the context of globalisation, consumer culture arguably converged with postmodernism in the decentring of the Western world and its epistemological categories, on the one hand, and in blurring the lines between art, culture, and commerce, on the other, through an aesthetic praxis of everyday life (Featherstone, 1991).

A writer of postmodernity, Zhu creates worlds in which trends and fashions change swiftly, producing a visual overabundance of competing colours, textures, and forms. In this sense, the theoretical treatments of consumerism as hedonism as well as the Marxist critiques of commodity fetishism are also relevant to Zhu's excursions in the sensorial-affective world. From the perspective of commodity aesthetics, commodities compensate for the sensual and social pleasure of rationalised and disenchanted modern societies (Dunn, 2008, p. 108). Zygmunt Bauman argues that the power of commodities rests not so much with their capacity to respond to needs for personal status, possession, and accumulation but in fact commences prior to the enjoyment of their functionality. Their power lies in their capacity to connect pleasurably with the human sensorium: 'The excitement of a new and unprecedented sensation – not the greed of acquiring and possessing nor wealth and its material tangible sense – is the name of the consumer game. Consumers are first and foremost gatherers of sensations, they are collectors of things only in secondary and derivative' (1999, p. 3). According to the interpretive framework of hedonistic consumption, desires and pleasures are derived from social meanings that are linked to the notions of gratification through personal growth, fulfilment, enjoyment, happiness, and pleasure. Commodity-oriented societies are thus also predicated on individualism, which invests the self with a heightened sense of agency in relation to the material world of commodities as well as to its own self-making and self-realisation (Dunn, 2008, p. 112). If consumerist pleasures are not primarily, or even exclusively, located within the mean-ing-making processes of consumer culture, the question then becomes: what possibilities for critical consumption could be imagined around the subjectivity and materiality of the sensing consumer? Whereas it is undeniable that we experience the world through our senses, affects, and emotions, contemporary sensory studies scholars signal that the human body has already been mapped and incorporated by the hyper-consumerist orientation of contemporary capitalism. Phillip Vannini, Dennis Waskul, and Simon Gottschalk note that the 'enhanced sensory pleasures that are embedded in the shapes, textures, and the designs of new commodities' downplay sense-making and augment the impact of the sensorial to the point that memory is also altered through the promise of enhancements to prior sensory experience (Vannini, Waskul and Gottschalk, 2012, pp. 156–157).

Feminist sociologists have recently introduced the notion of 'inti-macy' into their exploration of consumption in order to unearth the ways in which 'emotions intersect with cultural and economic forms of exchange' (Casey and Taylor, 2014, p. 131). The framework of inti-macy has thus allowed them to foreground the experiences of women and the scale of the household, but more importantly this approach has opened up an understanding of how socialities of help, caregiving, and support are mediated by consumption in the neoliberal contexts of welfare reform and austerity (Casey and Taylor, 2014, p. 132).

## Zhu Tianwen's cultural politics in the context of a rapidly changing Taiwan

Considered one of the best known women writers in Taiwan's contem-porary literature, Zhu Tianwen's writing bears the marks of her own cultural politics in the context of Taiwan's historical relations with mainland China, Japan, and the Western capitalist world. In tracing the genealogy of Zhu's cultural politics, Shu-Chen Chiang differenti-ates between her initial commitment and passionate support of China's mainland-oriented promotion of traditional high Chinese culture and the author's later critical approaches to notions of cultural authenticity. Zhu's subsequent adoption of more complex and multi-layered cultural politics is reflected in texts that portray Taiwan's multiplicity of differ-ence, intranational traditions, complicated identities, and social realities (Chiang, 2002).

Taiwan's realities are shaped by regional and global colonial and neo-colonial relations. It is currently a multiparty democracy under the

Republic of China government. Japan renounced its territorial rights to Taiwan in 1952, bringing to an end the colonial governance of Taiwan as one of the Japanese Home Islands and its attendant policies of assimilation (Katz, 2005). Following the end of the Second World War, Taiwan entered a four-decade-long single-party rule by Kuomintang (KMT). Under the KMT the notion of 'Taiwanese' became a regional identity, oftentimes deployed against mainland Chinese people living on the continent as well as against the mainland Chinese people who followed the KMT to Taiwan between 1945 and 1949. The political liberalisation of 1970s and 1980s reshaped the concept of 'Taiwanese' into a politicised ethnocentric category deployed by social movements against the authoritarian KMT regime (Corcuff, 2002). During the KMT government, Taiwan was defined in anti-communist terms and strategically constructed as the 'last outpost of traditional Chinese high culture' (Chiang, 2002, p. 47). Zhu's initial political views and cultural politics thus aligned with the mainland majority's devaluation of Taiwanese culture for being a mix of 'the Chinese outback and Japanese imperialism.' A second-generation mainlander born in Taipei, Zhu encountered a group of progressive young filmmakers (who later became known as 'the New Cinema'), many of whom had similar upbringing trajectories that intertwined 'mainland Chinese heritage, Taiwanese upbringing, and Western and Japanese influences' (Chiang, 2002, p. 47). The works of these young filmmakers challenged the grand narrative promoted by the KMT government in their commitment to relaying multiple voices and to presenting a plurality of narratives; they thus left an indelible mark on Zhu's cultural politics. Critics agree that after her encounter with the New Cinema group, the postmodern themes characteristic of globalisation moved to the core of Zhu's prose.

Compared to mainland China, Taiwan moved faster towards modernisation and industrialisation (Chia, Allred and Jerzak 1997, p. 138). From the first decade of KMT rule, women's work was summoned in support of the consolidation of the state. Policies encouraging more active roles for women outside of the family were adopted simultaneously with the implementation of programs of formal education aiming to develop motherhood skills and of welfare measures seeking to address the economic needs of mothers (Chen, 2009, p. 235). The economic development that was encouraged by U.S. economic aid in the 1950s relied significantly on an economic model of growth that placed cheap labour at the centre of its mechanisms for capital accumulation. From the mid-1960s to mid-1980s, women's cheap and flexible labour constituted the primary resource of Taiwan's labour-intensive export-oriented economy. The ripples of the 1967 Cultural Revolution in mainland China shored up traditional notions of gender and family, realigning women's work with the space of the family rather than with the economic needs of the state (Chen, 2009, p. 237). However, in the mid-1980s, pressures for change in the ways that the government was managing labour came from both social movements and the administrators of neoliberal global capitalism. Women's groups required 'a reasonable social and legal system of gender equality' (Chen 2009, 237), whereas capitalists pushed for further labour deregulation as a means to 'enhance their flexibility to utilize labor to cope with the changing economic environment' (Chen, 2009, p. 237). As neoliberal arguments for 'economic efficiency' won more and more ground, women became more politicised and demanded that their right to work not be dictated by the needs of the state or those of the free market. They exposed the patriarchal operations of both state and market and required the state and private employers to share the costs of social reproduction beyond the paradigm of child-care provision for the purpose of accumulation. With the globalisation of care work for children and the elderly, Taiwan became a receiving country. Nevertheless, the government strictly controlled the number of 'foreign maids' entering the country in order to prevent a too-sharp increase in the employment of local women – a trend that, according to neoliberal economists, runs parallel with the presence of immigrant care workers. Concurrently, starting in the 1980s, the mass media engaged in a twofold ideological project: on one hand, they targeted local audiences with messages that espoused 'native patriarchies and nationalist/nativist sentiments,' while on the other hand, at a regional level, they operated fully in the service of consumption, 'strategically suppressing native patriarchal and nationalist sentiments in order to maximize market expansion' (Shih, 1998, p. 288). Youths in particular became the main target of contradictory messages, some of which encouraged them to partake in the new consumer lifestyle of the booming urban environments, while others tried to curb consumption. The rationale behind the latter surpassed the motivational force of nationalist sentiments. The government of Taiwan also encouraged people to put a large portion of their income into savings as a way of avoiding becoming dependent on international borrowing. At the turn of the century Taiwan was among the nations with the highest capital reserves in the world (Chua, 2000). Moreover, its anti-welfarist orientation deprived its citizens of the consumption subsidies usually provided as public services in the so-called developed nations (e.g., child care and elderly care), which forced young middle-class families to hire domestic workers from the poorer neighbouring countries and ultimately reduced their income for discretionary expenditures (Chua, 2000, pp. 10–14).

The gender relations in Zhu's portrayals of global postmodernity are generally considered to be at odds with feminist ideas. Chiang writes: 'Unlike other Taiwanese women writers, she never enacts familiar feminist motifs such as selfhood, economic autonomy, sexual awakening, patriarchal domination, motherhood or sisterhood. These issues for her are no longer problems as they are already subsumed under the spectacular decadence termed as "postmodern" by the writer herself' (Chiang, 2002, p. 45). I argue that in fact, Zhu's writing illuminates significant feminist concerns about the cultural and economic transformations that were introduced, embraced, or challenged in the rapidly changing world of post-1970s Taiwan and is thus relevant to the feminist interventions that critique neoliberal globalisation. Besides, the feminist tropes identified by Chiang (selfhood, economic autonomy, sexual awakening, patriarchal domination, motherhood or sisterhood) are in fact tackled in 'Fin-de-Siècle Splendor,' but not in the recognizable vocabularies of liberal or difference feminisms. Such feminist tropes are subtly implied in Mia's sensual memories, in her observations of Taipei's rapidly transforming urban environment, as well as in her explanations of fashion trends. By profession, Mia is a fashion model. Her work in the global world of fashion places her at the intersection of significant transformations of production, work, and consumption practices. Fashion styles, products, affects, trends, pleasures, and ideas of beauty cross borders swiftly, and their impact is spatial, cultural, social, and aesthetic. Mia feels that her homeland is the 'city-confederacy of Taipei, Milan, Paris, London, Tokyo and New York. She lives here, steeped in its customs, well versed in its artistry, polished by its culture, ready to merge as one of its permanent representative' (Zhu, 2007, p. 401).

The feminist politics of the story are partly oriented toward epistemology, partly oriented toward imaging new worlds out of the current terms and practices of global capitalism: 'The world men have built with theories and systems will collapse, and [Mia] with her memory of smells and colors will survive and rebuild the world from here' (Zhu, 2007, p. 402). From childhood, Mia revolts against the patriarchal ordering of things. While her lovers are men, her circle of intimacies challenges heteronormative dictates. Her friendship with Baby constitutes one of the more ample narrative arcs of the story. In their younger years Mia and Baby were inseparable. With Baby embracing more conservative values, their friendship is challenged first by Mia's bold fashion choices, then by her materialism, and ultimately by her decision to pursue a relationship with wealthy yet married Duan. Baby's decision to get married could have been made in order to spite Mia. Years later, Mia finds Baby, who is now divorced and the mother of a three-year-old daughter. Mia runs a flower shop – also selling food – which becomes the space for her girlfriends' meetings. Mia recalls:

> The flower shop with its complex mixture of scents is like a Byzantine tapestry; the aroma of coffee wafts in the air, recalling the ancient age of handicrafts. Joe is responsible for the food served in the flower shop: homemade fruitcakes, cheese pie, oatmeal biscuits and flower-petal puddings. (Zhu, 2007, p. 397)

Baby's flower shop is the space where consumption, production, and commercial endeavours intersect with intimacy and thus form nonheteronormative affective and social relations. The threads of Mia's observations call for a consideration of the discursive and material investments that form and maintain the categorical impositions that establish 'the domestic' as economically irrelevant (Waring, 1989) and render heterosexual nuclear families as the norm for the organisation of sexuality, sociality, work, care, and solidarity in 'the private' sphere (Berlant 2000). The forces that orient and connect Mia and her intimate others exceed both the boundaries of human bodies and the restrictive meanings of sexuality. Many of these forces are nonhuman and of great sensorial-affective impact. Duan, girlfriends, best friends, and past boyfriends constitute Mia's social milieu, yet her recollections thread seamlessly encounters with gestures, colours, fragrances, feelings, textures, the island's climate, personal styles, fashion trends, friends, skylines, forests, and the rest of the world's splendours. The realisation of the world's inexhaustible beauties turns Mia to materialism: 'She did not have time enough to feast her eyes on the world's many splendours; she decided that she'd create a brilliant future for herself whatever it might take. Material girls – why not? She'd worship things and she'd worship money. Youth and beauty were on her side; she worshiped her own beautiful body' (Zhu, 2007, 402).

It is important to note that in gendering her characters and constructing their nonheteronormative sexual pleasures and intimacies, Zhu converges with the politics of women's groups who mobilised to challenge and change gender and sexuality norms by voicing their erotic thoughts, feelings, grievances, and desires, thus breaking with the culture of silence that used to envelope sexuality.

Furthermore, Mia's profession as a fashion model and her intimate relationship with Duan, an older married businessman, mirror key demographic and economic transformations undergone in Taiwan, as well as ideological processes engaged in the attendant redefinition of gender in relation to work, family, and the nation. As Shu-mei Shih points out, patriarchal representations of mainland women in popular media form at the intersection of multiple overdeterminations. She explains the emergence of the figure of the *dulamei*:

> the 'mainland women' as a category becomes overlaid with meanings beyond the biological and economic determinations ordinarily apparent. Although these are the bodies that serve as prostitutes and wives in Taiwan and Hong Kong, as mistresses and surrogate mothers for Taiwan and Hong Kong businessmen in coastal cities in China ... and accordingly their representation is heavily 'bodied', they also carry potent political and cultural meanings in their signification. ... When this power was threatened by the dalumei's clever maneuvers, the Taiwanese businessmen were reminded of their status as 'simpleton compatriots,' and the dalumei has increasingly come to embody threat. She is not merely a threat to Taiwanese businessmen's pocketbooks, but a generalized threat to Taiwan's capital and industrial advantage as Taiwan becomes more and more dependent on Chinese labor and the mainland market. She is even a threat to Taiwan's national security. (1998, pp. 293–294)

Shih also notes that Taiwanese feminists were slow to take on the representational violence directed at women immigrants from the mainland. While there is no textual evidence to link Mia and Duan to a specific ethnicity, their love story comes intriguingly close to expressing the region's 'new geopolitics of desire' discussed by Shih (1998, p. 294). However, the relationship between Mia and Duan does not conform to the representational conventions that newspapers and magazines use when portraying Taiwanese businessmen and people living on the mainland. By no means the classical *dalumei*, Mia is undeniably beautiful and materialistic yet as far as one can get from the standards of the media's flat character. In this sense, Zhu's nuanced treatment of local and regional, past and present patriarchies appears to fill in a critical gap left behind by Taiwanese feminists.

Regional and global geopolitics have thus shaped Taiwan culturally, economically, and politically. Global capitalism has left its marks – ubiquitous commodification and reification – on Taiwanese society, while

Taiwan's speedy economic take-off into the circuit of global capital and into the world market of the 1970s virtually compressed the two hundred years of industrial modernity in the West into just a few decades (Wang, 2007). As flows of images, commodities, and capital criss-cross the globalised terrain of Taipei, critics of global capitalism warn against the lost cultural integrity of nations, against the hegemonisation of the global vocabulary of consumerism, as well as against individualism. 'Fin-de-Siècle Splendor' could be read as a lyrical critique of the societal changes brought about by global capitalism at the end of the twentieth century. In his reading of Zhu, Ban Wang encounters a suffocating Taipei that deprives 'the residents of breathing room' (2007, p. 374). The city's youngsters are caught in circuits of imitative performance, modelling their behaviours after those 'of superstars and celebrities in the metro-politan centers of the West' (2007, p. 374). Similar forces shape Taipei residents' 'lifestyles...looks, and aesthetic tastes,' while an engulfing commodification 'erases the memory of how objects and life environments are made by humans, over long period of time' (2007, p. 374). From Zhu's story, Wang teases out the effects that modernisation and global capitalism inflict on subjectivities, social relations, and urban spaces. In his view, their emergence is accompanied by the dissolution of pre-modern communities. Thus, the operations of economic development, mass culture, and industrialised production account for the loss of the world of collective attachments, feelings of belonging, memories of the past, local knowledge, and non-alienating forms of work. Moreover, commodity manufacturing and consumption lead to the transformation of the organic world of the village and its networks of kinship, intimacy, work, and pleasure into the alienating, abstracting, and reifying socio-culturalmilieu of the metropolis (Wang, 2007, pp. 371–372). In a Marxist vein, these changes result in the reification of human life and labour. Furthermore, media and advertising colonise the human sensorium and cognition, transforming citizens into a mass of passive consumers. Ultimately, Wang sees in Zhu's writing a nostalgic gesturing towards the past, as her characters take refuge in the memory of 'things, feelings, relations, stories, myth – the green grass beyond the dreary and monotonous cityscape' (Wang, 2007, p. 376).

While the temporality of post-1970s material-discursive transformations of Taiwan are undoubtedly central themes that Zhu tackles in 'Fin-de-Siècle Splendor,' I argue that that the politics of the story are more ambivalent and could in fact be read as future-oriented. Moreover, in Mia's recounting of her childhood, Zhu articulates one of her most overtly feminist critiques of social and material practice. Fragrances, textures, clothing, work, family members, and concepts of gender come together in a recollection triggered by White Orchid powdered detergent:

> In those days, Mia has seen clothes hung out to dry on bamboo poles stuck between a willow tree and a wall....After a whole day in the sun, the clothes became hard and rough. When she put them on, the distinct difference between cloth and flesh reminded her of the existence of her clean body. Mother folded the family's clothes up for easy storage; women's clothes has to be put under men's, just as she insisted that men's clothes had to be hung in front of women's. Mia fought openly against this taboo; her young mind wanted to see whether this would bring a natural disaster. After the willow tree has been cut down and the land repossessed by the government for public housing, her elder sisters got married and her mother grew old. (Zhu, 2007, p. 390)

Wang's own nostalgic inclination reduces Zhu's complex worlds to an economically deterministic argument that romanticises Taiwan's Chinese rural past. While never direct or didactic, Mia's 'gentle memory' reminds us of the gendered forms of work and gender hierarchies of pre-modern Taiwan. What then are the elements, ideas and, forces that orient Zhu's story toward the future?

Mia's observations of the architectural environment relay the understanding of the built environment as always and already incorporable and entangled with climatic forces and geo-agencies of the island. In their turn, these nonhuman forces and agencies have long been incorporated in the unique life experiences, knowledge, and material production practices of the island's dwellers. In a conversation with Duan, Mia remarks: 'Our predecessors' accumulated life experiences has given us a building style that copes well with Taiwan's climate: light-weight. It is different from the West and again different from Japan: light in form, in space, and in visuality, it provides breathing space for the crowded sun-baked cities of Taiwan. According to I.M. Pei, style emerges from problem solving.' Duan, a constructor and architect himself, responds: 'If Pei had not had a group of technicians to help him solve the problems, the glass on his pyramid at the Louvre would not have had the glittering transparency' (Zhu, 2007, p. 389). Zhu deftly renders the interaction of culture, history, technology, biology, and geology, without privileging any of their agencies. While all the recounted thoughts, sensations, feelings, affects, emotions, memories, and judgments contained in 'Fin-de-Siècle

Splendor' are Mia's, they continually weave her existence into past and present worlds, where the distinctions between the intimate and the public are at times hard to set apart. Mia and Duan's moments of aesthetic intimacy on the terrace of her ninth-floor apartment, her trips to the mountains with her boyfriends from the fashion industry, and her visits at Baby's flower shop allow for the consideration of entanglements among intimacy, urban infrastructures, capitalist forces of development, homophobia, postcolonial conditions, and national security. A materialist reading of Mia's intimacies invalidates Wang's decrying of suffocating Taipei, at least inasmuch as her existence is concerned. But surely, Wang's observation is correct in many other life contexts. Critical geographers already pointed out that cities have never developed evenly and equitably. Urban decay, development, and creation follow the tracks of existing inequalities, adding new elements to the phenomenon of poverty (Wilson forthcoming 2015).

## The human and more-than-human agencies of fashion

One of the core engines of contemporary consumer societies is fashion. Its critics, consumers, and supporters would most likely agree that, as one of the most materialist industries, fashion is the epitome of contemporary consumerism. The meanings of the word 'fashion' connect the material world of clothes and garment industry to the abstract ideas of trend and style. Its constant creation of new products and desires goes hand in hand with the creation of new global geographies of natural labour and natural resources extraction. Fashion thus matters beyond the symbolic functions of its signs, meanings, embodied practices, and performative styles. The fashion industry is currently a system of global material relations with intimate ties to local ecologies.

Many cultural theorists and sociologists turn to fashion in order to critique the conformist pressures of advanced capitalist consumer cultures. Being 'in fashion' simultaneously evokes notions of conformity, markers of status and wealth, and a sense of belonging to certain groups, which renders fashion a component of complex articulations of social and cultural identity. In 1949, Simone de Beauvoir denounced fashion for its power to enslave women, negate their independent individuality and potential for transcendence, and ultimately subsume them under male agency and desire (Beauvoir, 1953). Three decades later, U.S. author activist-author Susan Browmiller identified feminine fashion as one of the social-aesthetic practices that maintains gender difference and fuels female oppression. She was a strong advocate of women wearing trousers, arguing that by obscuring sartorial differences between women and men, sexism might diminish (Henry, 2012, pp. 17–18). Whereas versions of these arguments still inform the sartorial codes of professional and corporate cultures, the rejection of feminine fashion and the endorsement of masculine dress codes as a feminist statement or a gender-free alternative came, however, under critique as soon as the 1980s. Georg Simmel pointed out that despite its firm grounding in imitation, fashion allows individuals to act upon their desires for 'union and segregation' (1971, p. 297). Judith Butler, on the other hand, explained that 'style is never fully self-styled, for living styles have a history, and that history conditions and limits possibilities' (Butler, 1988, p. 521).

Zhu constructs Mia's relation to the world of fashion in ways that capture the forces of subjectivity formation, their moments of creative repletion, resistance to old meanings, and resignification. Mia's career in fashion modelling takes off with an outstanding performance of imitation: she impersonates the ultimate material girl, Madonna, in a look-alike competition. She is a fine aesthete, and as with fashion, her preference for certain styles changes with the passing of time. On her life trajectory, army-style outfits follow the 'beggary trend' of perforated clothing that she used to love at the age of fifteen. Pierre Cardin's fashion and the rose-red cashmere V-neck pullovers entered Mia's life along with her crush on the Japanese actor and model Abe Hiroshi. Then follows the trend of androgyny. She observed how '[t]he fear of AIDS led to a new fashion trend: feminine clothes for women and gentleman's look for men; unisex clothes all disappeared,' and she too 'said good-bye to her hermaphroditic dress code, which has passed through phases of David Bowie, Boy George and Price' (p. 395). Mia is also an astute observer of her friends' relations to fashion. When her friend Gee decides to part with her three-piece suits with heavy shoulder pads, Mia explains: 'The career women's stiff outfit is like a housewife's apron; wearing it constantly equals giving up your rights as a woman.... She fully intends to take advantage of the fact that she is a woman, and the more feminine a woman is the more she can get out of men. Gee has learned to camouflage her vicious designs with a low profile and since then success has come with much less effort on her part' (390–391). Thus, Gee's disavowal of business attire and her reorientation towards femininity mirror the changes in feminist critiques of fashion, where the rejection of the feminine aesthetic and the gendered normativity of beauty coexists with reformist arguments that advocate diversifying notions of beauty, femininity, and masculinity (Henry, 2012, p. 24) and exposing the artifice and performative character of clothing, gender, and sexual normativity.

In Mia's world, 'doing' gender through fashion creates spaces of intimacy and manifestations of desire that transgress the limits of heteronormativity. Fashion, pleasure, intimacy, material cultures, and work connect Mia and her friends, Ann, Joey, Wanyu, Baby, Christine, Gee, Kai, and Ou in a network of sociability that includes material agencies. Mia's reflections indicate clearly that the mutability of fashion trends is accompanied by societal and personal shifts in notions of femininity and masculinity, the emergence of new health and disease ecologies, geographical and climate forces, transformations in the human-built environment, and subsequent reorientations and reemplacements of pleasures and intimacies. Mia and her best friend Baby wear 'a pair of moon and star earrings: one was on Baby's right ear, the other on Mia's left ear.... Together they mapped out their dream-plan of opening a shop someday.' (2007, 395). Comradeship is the term that Mia uses to describe her relation to Kai, her male partner for magazine fashion features, yet she is also in love with him. Kai is a very handsome man, who 'loved only himself, and he treated Mia as his beloved brother, Narcissus' (2007, p. 393). Ann, a beautician who 'exudes a cold smell of scrub creams' and prefers her vibrator to having sex with men or women, dislocates sexuality from the realm of essentialism and binary notions, through her desirous orientation to sexual gratifications outside the realm of interpersonal encounters. In their youth Mia and her friends, Yang Ge, Ah Xun and his wife Ou, 'Ant,' Kai, and the Yuan brothers, would drive to the mountains, where they smoked a marijuana joint and passed around a bottle of Chinese liquor. Such nights gave Mia the feeling that '[they] were making love with Nature' (2007, p. 392). Mia is also in love with Yang Ge and the attraction between them formed somewhere between the vegetal world of 'dead bamboo trees and sharp bamboo shoots' where 'his warm, fleshy hand [let] her know his intentions' in the 'air of nonchalance created by his old blue jeans and faded khaki' (2007, p. 393).

All her recollections take Mia from a sensorial-affective present into a recollected past or critically appraised present. A magazine photo shoot that recreated the image of the Duanhuang cave painting has Mia and Wanyu model a collection of cutwork rayon. The encounter with rayon triggers Mia's scrutiny of this semisynthetic fibre, its emergence and existence at the intersection of material, technological, economic, creative, and destructive forces: 'Rayon is made from wood paste; it has the feel of cotton but it is more absorbent and hangs better. Besides, rayon chiffon is just a third the price of silk chiffon.... In damp, sizzling weather rayon turns moldy easily' (2007, p. 391). Mia's reflections on the degradation of rayon prompt her to worry about 'the jars and bunches of dried flowers and dried reeds in her house,' which constitute the objects in both an epistemological quest and a business project, as she plans that soon after retiring from fashion modelling, she 'will be able to support herself with her handicrafts' (2007, p. 402). Among 'dried flowers and herbs...Chinese orchids, African violets, potted pineapples, Peacock coconuts, and all sorts of nameless ferns,' Duan often gets the sense that he is with a medieval monk. Oftentimes, Mia and Duan get lost in the contemplation of the city skyline:

> Prawn-red, salmon-red, linen-yellow, reed-yellow; the sky turns from peach to emerald.... They indulge themselves aesthetically so much that either their energy is exhausted in the process or their spirit shattered by the overwhelming spectacle, and very often they do not even do what lovers are supposed to do. (2007, p. 389)

The colour and shapes of the natural world are synaesthetically connected to the taste of peppermint herb tea and to the colours and shapes of the 1990 summer show and the previous 1989 autumn/winter trend:

> Those were not the colorful prints of the Caribbean but of the North Pole shores. Several icebergs from Greenland floating in the misty North poles seas, every breath was ice-cold. All was snow-white, with hints of green or traces of emerald. The details were a continuation of the 1989 autumn/winter trend – lace was given new life with mesh patterns or braided with motifs of fish fins and shells. (2007, p. 389)

However, the appropriation of nature by fashion operates not only in relation to aesthetic ideas but also in relation to material life. Zhu traces lines of continuity between the animal fur featured in the 1989 collections by Christian Lacroix, Moschino, and Ferre and the old British Empire's visual vocabulary of exploration and its attendant commodities: 'the stuffed animals...imported from their colonies' (2007, p. 397). Ecological protection, observes Mia, led to the subsequent trend of fake fur in the winter of 1990. While she disagrees with the concept of fake fur that 'could pass for the real thing,' the trend of the following year converges with her views on fashion and environmentalism. Mia reflects:

> But what's the point of imitating the real thing? It's just foolish. Much better for the fake items to be self-mocking, which is in line with the

modern spirit, somewhat witty and quite cute…. Mia's '91 anti-fur show, with its variations of fake furs dyed red and green was cute and trendy. (2007, p. 397)

Elizabeth Wissinger situates the development of affective economies within the larger context of the consolidation of the service sector and the consumer economy of global post-industrial capitalism, where 'capital shifts its domain of accumulation to bodily pre-individual forces such that value is produced through enlivening, capacitating, and modulating affect' (2007, p. 234). Affective labour and the production of care and emotions sits thus at the core of the industries subsumed into the affective economy. In certain industries, these outputs require unmediated forms of presence and proximity, however in other industries such as fashion modelling, the production of affect can be achieved through mediated contact. Clearly, fashion models must produce and maintain bodies that measure up to the aesthetic standards of the industry. However their bodies and work reach past the manufacturing of mere appearance. Fashion models also 'manipulate affect or feeling by acting, engaging, and connecting with themselves and others, with the goal of stimulating and projecting a feeling of vitality and aliveness' (2007, p. 235). While representational critiques of fashion and modelling focus on the production and hegemonisation of particular ideas of femininity, masculinity, beauty, attractiveness, health, and happiness, the new materialist approach supplements the narrative of subjectivity formation with an effort to account for moments of intensified sensation, focused attention, and augmented feeling which ultimately fuel our orientations and connections with the world. Wissinger's fieldwork in the world of fashion shows unequivocally that the goal of modelling work is in fact 'the stimulation of affective energy' (2007, p. 241). The production of affect reaches past the contagious communication of facial and corporeal expression, as many fashion models emphasise that they strive to enable unplanned and unexpected moments that translate into images and energies that are 'beyond the borders of conventional interpretation' and thus 'not immediately assimilable to consciousness' (Wissinger, 2007, p. 243).

In writing Mia and in writing about Mia's worlds of works, loves, friendships, affects, feelings, and sensations, Zhu Tianwen interlaces social, symbolic, aesthetic, economic, and material agencies. Her relation to the material culture of the fashion industry is at once aesthetic, social, sensual, and economic. While creative expressions that foreground individuality and enable nonheteronormative intimacies materialise every so often, the speed of commodification prompts Mia to adopt a state of continued critical alertness. From an affective perspective, the temporality of fashion is simultaneously orientated toward the past and the future. Deconstructed looks, bold and punchy aesthetics, militaristic prints, power suits, cashmere sweaters, and flowing silks in vibrant hues feature in looks and trends that will elicit affective notes of familiarity and nostalgia along with enthusiasm for novelty and innovation (Henry, 2012, p. 25). Beyond these, textures and colours take hold of the body's sensorium and grant fashion material forces of attraction that supplement those operating within the realm of the symbolic. Tracing the emergence of fashion icons and iconoclasts in relation to the current phenomena of 'globalization, cultural imperatives of self-expression, dilemmas of sexualization that trade on racial and gender politics, co-optation and cultural appropriation, and casual rhetoric of social change' (Tarrant and Jolles, 2012, p. 9) is key to the development of critical accounts to contemporary consumption. Yet the attention given to embedded and situated actions should reach past the limit of the human and its socio-culturaldimensions. By opening the scope of such inquiries toward the realm of the more-than-human and the agency of bodies and natures, a better understanding of the current global order and its potential alternatives can emerge.

## Conclusion

The interconnections between the human, more-than-human, and nonhuman material agencies captured by Zhu Tianwen in 'Fin-de-Siècle Splendor' open up new analytical, ethical, and political perspectives. Mia's work in the fashion industry further destabilises the distinctions between the psyche and the market, the local and the global. As a fashion model, her existence is interwoven with phenomena, bodies, and technologies that are constitutive of the global affective economies. Mia's work entails more than producing meanings, representations, and images. She is never engaged in acts of conspicuous consumption or in the construction of consumerist subject identities that would already be meaningful, interpretable, and identifiable. Her own sensual descriptions that link the human sensorium to the elements of urban infrastructure and the natural world are nevertheless interconnected with the other technologies of contemporary capitalism (e.g., biotechnology, surveillance, information and entertainment technologies), which are primarily invested in intensifying the flow of energy between bodies. Under particular material circumstances, some of these flows morph into desires, and some desires further materialise in acts of consumption. Thus, for the critic of consumerism, the identification of the material-discursive conditions that slow down such flows could aid in imagining a new ethics and a new politics of consumption. Finally, the very possibility of the stagnation of flows or of a stoppage in consumption calls for the imagination of *an outside* to capitalism. The latter can be better understood in relation to the concept of affective labour, which has been theorised by Michael Hardt and Antonio Negri (2000, 2004). The emergence of affective labour under conditions of global capitalism makes it impossible to distinguish between production and reproduction, which renders human subjects simultaneously products and producers of the unitary machine of capitalism, leaving no signs, subjects, values, or practices that are outside of it (Hardt and Negri 2000). I would argue that the materialist portrait of Taipei's turn-of-the-century global capitalism proposed by Zhu maintains the hope that even in the absence of an absolute outside to capitalism, alternative economic practices, socialities of care, and an ethics of justice could emerge within the multitude of material and discursive conditions of which we are part.

## Notes

1. Michael Hardt teaches at Duke University and is best known for his trilogy of books – *Empire* (2000), *Multitude* (2004), and *Commonwealth* (2009)– which he wrote with Antonio Negri.
2. Mavis Tseng was at the time a PhD candidate in Comparative Literature at Rutgers and was one of the organisers of this event.

## References

Alaimo, Stacy (2010) *Bodily Natures: Science, Environment, and the Material Self.* Bloomington: Indiana University Press.

Alaimo, Stacy and Susan Hekman (2008) 'Introduction: Emerging Models of Materiality in Feminist Theory' in *Material Feminisms*, Stacy Alaimo and Susan Hekman (eds). Bloomington: Indiana University Press.

Barad, Karen (2003) 'Posthumanist Performativity: Toward an Understanding of How Matter Comes to Matter', *Signs* 28(3), 801–831.

Barad, Karen (2007) *Meeting the Universe Halfway: Quantum Physics and the Entanglement of Matter and Meaning.* Durham: Duke University Press.

Barker, Chris (2008) *Cultural Studies: Theory and Practice.* London: Sage.

Bauman, Zygmunt (1999) *Culture as Praxis.* London: Sage.

Beauvoir, Simone de (1953) *The Second Sex.* New York: Knopf.

Berlant, Lauren (2000) *Intimacy.* University of Chicago Press.

Bruno, Juliana (2008) 'Cultural Cartography, Materiality and the Fashioning of Emotion' in *Visual Culture Studies*, Marquard Smith (ed.). Los Angeles: Sage.

Butler, Judith (1988) 'Performative Acts and Gender Constitution: An Essay in Phenomenology and Feminist Theory', *Theatre Journal*, 40(4), 519–531.

Casey, Emma, and Yvette Taylor (2014) 'Introduction: Intimacies, Families and Practices of Consumption', *Families, Relationships and Societies*, 3(1) (March 1), 131–133. doi:10.1332/204674313X13808737332960.

Chen, Ya-chen (2009) *Women in Taiwan: Socio-cultural Perspectives*. University Press.

Chiang, Shu-chen (2002) 'Rejection of Postmodern Abandon: Zhu Tianwen's Fin-de-Siecle Splendor' in *Feminism/Femininity in Chinese Literature*, Chen Peng-hsiang and Whitney Crothers Dilley (ed.). Amsterdam: Rodopi.

Chia, Rosina C., Linda J. Allred and Page A. Jerzak (1997) 'Attitudes toward Women in Taiwan and China Current Status, Problems, and Suggestions for Future Research', *Psychology of Women Quarterly*, 21(1) (March 1), 137–150.

Chua, Beng-Huat (2000) *Consumption in Asia: Lifestyle and Identities*. New York: Routledge.

Corcuff, Stéphane (2002) *Memories of the Future: National Identity Issues and the Search for a New Taiwan*. Armonk, NY: M. E. Sharpe.

Donel, Marcus A. (2010) 'Representation and Difference' in *Taking-place: Non-representational Theories and Geography*, Ben Anderson and Paul Harrison (eds). Ashgate.

Dunn, Robert G. (2008) *Identifying Consumption Subjects and Objects in Consumer Society*. Philadelphia: Temple University Press.

Featherstone, Mike (1991) *Consumer Culture and Postmodernism*. London: Sage.

Fiske, John (1989) *Understanding Popular Culture*. Boston: Unwin Hyman.

Hardt, Michael and Antonio Negri (2000) *Empire*. Cambridge, MA.: Harvard University Press.

Hardt, Michael and Antonio Negri (2004) *Multitude: War and Democracy in the Age of Empire*. New York: Penguin.

Hardt, Michael and Antonio Negri (2009) *Commonwealth*. Cambridge, MA: Harvard University Press.

Harvey, David (1985) *The Urbanization of Capital: Studies in the History and Theory of Capitalist Urbanization*. Baltimore, MD: Johns Hopkins University Press.

Hemmings, Clare (2005) 'Invoking Affect', *Cultural Studies* 19(5), 548–567.

Henry, Astrid (2012) 'Fashioning a Feminist Style, or, How I Learned to Dress from Reading Feminist Theory' in *Fashion Talks: Undressing the Power of Style*, Shira Tarrant and Marjorie Jolles (eds). Albany: State University of New York Press.

Jagger, Gill (2014) 'The New Materialism and Sexual Difference', *Signs* 40(2) (January 1), 321–342.

Katz, Paul R. (2005) *When Valleys Turned Blood Red: The Ta-pa-ni Incident in Colonial Taiwan*. Honolulu: University of Hawai'i Press.

Lorimer, H. (2008) 'Cultural Geography: Non-Representational Conditions and Concerns', *Progress in Human Geography,* 32(4) (February 8), 551–559.

Massumi, Brian (2002) *Parables for the Virtual: Movement, Affect, Sensation*. Durham, NC: Duke University Press.

Mestrovic, Stjepan (2010) *The Coming Fin-de-Siècle: An Application of Durkheim's Sociology to Modernity and Postmodernism*. London: Taylor & Francis.

Patchett, Merle (2010) *Putting Animals on Display: Geographies of Taxidermy Practice*. Ph.D thesis, University of Glasgow.

Sedgwick, Eve Kosofsky (2003) *Touching Feeling: Affect, Pedagogy, Performativity*. Durham, NC: Duke University Press.

Shih, Shu-mei (1998) 'Gender and a New Geopolitics of Desire: The Seduction of Mainland Women in Taiwan and Hong Kong Media', *Signs*, 23(2).

Simmel, Georg (1971) *On Individuality and Social Forms; Selected Writings*. Chicago: University of Chicago Press.

Tarrant, Shira and Marjorie Jolles (2012) 'Feminism Confronts Fashion' in *Fashion Talks: Undressing the Power of Style*. State University of New York Press.

Thrift, Nigel (1997) 'The Still Point' in *Geographies of Resistance*, Steve Pile and Michael Keith (eds). London: Routledge.

Valentine, Gill (1999) 'A Corporeal Geography of Consumption', *Environment and Planning D: Society and Space*, 17(3), 329–351.

Vannini, Phillip, Dennis Waskul and Simon Gottschalk (2012) *The Senses in Self, Society, and Culture: A Sociology of the Senses*. New York: Routledge.

Wallace, B. Alan, Kirk A. Denton and Ju-Chan Fulton (2013) *The Columbia Companion to Modern East Asian Literature*. New York: Columbia University Press.

Wang, Ban. (2007) 'Re-enchanting the Image in Global Culture: Reification and Nostalgia in Zhu Tianwen's Fiction' in *Writing Taiwan: A New Literary History*, David Der-wei Wang and Carlos Rojas (eds). Duke University Press.

Waring, Marilyn (1989) *If Women Counted: A New Feminist Economics*. Macmilan London.

Wilson, Ara (2015 forthcoming) 'The Infrastructure of Intimacy', *Signs: The Journal for Women in Culture and Society*, 41(3).

Wissinger, Elizabeth (2007) 'Always on Display: Affective Production in the Modeling Industry' in *The Affective Turn: Theorizing the Social*, Patricia Ticineto Clough with Jean Halley (eds). Dike University Press.

Zhu, Tianwen (2007) 'Fin-de-Siècle Splendor' [Trans. by Eva Hung] in *The Columbia Anthology of Modern Chinese Literature*, Joseph S.M. Lau and Howard Goldblatt (eds). New York: Columbia University Press.

# Part II

# 'Sticky' and Shifting Sites of Intimate Consumption

# 4
## 'My Bedroom Is Me': Young People, Private Space, Consumption and the Family Home

*Siân Lincoln*

### Introduction

A bedroom in the family home is often regarded by young people as one of the first spaces over which they are able to exert a level of control, ownership and regulation and in which they can achieve some level of privacy away from the challenges of everyday life. It is a space that young people can call their own, can decorate according to their current tastes and can regulate in terms of who and who cannot enter that space. While bedrooms are in many ways functional spaces for young people, e.g. they provide a space to sleep or do homework, they are also meaningful spaces that can tell us much about teenage life, youth culture and consumption. Bedrooms are worked upon, albeit at varying levels, and even when the space seems to change very little visually, the mere presence of a young person consuming within it, living out their social and cultural lives, means that it is a space that is never static. Moreover, for many young people, these are 'worked upon' spaces of identity and biographical display and representation, capturing both through cultural practices and the materiality of the space itself those often turbulent transitional years of growing up (Griffin, 1993; Roberts, 2008). Young people's bedrooms are also quite complex spaces to understand, often spaces of contradiction. For example, as sites of consumption they can have a dual role as both spaces within which to stabilise and authenticate one's identity, as well as to play and experiment with it (Larson, 1995; Baker, 2004; Lincoln, 2012). They are spaces that can offer refuge at difficult times, but also spaces within which those difficult times can be experienced. They can be spaces to escape to, from the control and regulation of parents, but also spaces subjected to this type of regulation too (Heath, 1999, 2004). Bedrooms are spaces whose use is influenced by geographic location, familial formations, gender, social class and age, all of which are intertwined in often quite complex ways (James, 2001; Abbott-Chapman and Robertson, 2009; Lincoln, 2012). In addition to this, the meaning of a bedroom to a young person is changing in the context of the current UK economic climate. Government reforms such as the 'Housing Benefit size criteria' ('Bedroom Tax') for example, are prescribing how such private spaces can be used by a family, often leading to multiple occupancy of a bedroom. Further, the parental home is increasingly being occupied by young people well into their twenties and way beyond the traditional youth period of one's teenage years. Biggart and Walther (2005) use the concept of 'yo-yo' transitions to understand young people's moves back into the parental home due to factors such as increased university fees, unemployment, cutbacks in welfare provisions and rising house prices that are rupturing traditional youth to adult transitions, even reversing them. In these instances the bedroom is more than just a transitional space but is site of permanence and stability amid a life trajectory that is anything but stable.

This chapter aims to get inside the often complex contexts of young people's uses of their bedrooms as spaces in the family home and as intimate sites of consumption, particularly in relation to their identities. 'Private' spaces like bedrooms take on a particular significance for the teenager that is different from other ages because they are experiencing their 'formative years' in which they are making key decisions about themselves and their future and defining who they would like to be (Larson, 1995). They are also times in which a young person feels in a perennial state of 'in-betweenness', in a state where they are precariously suspended in-between different boundaries at home, school and at work as well as well as in leisure related contexts such as bars and clubs where their age might just be keeping them out but their peers are pressuring them to go in. In the midst of those times, private spaces such as bedrooms can play a pivotal role in young people's lives because they provide a space for privacy, for intimacy, for respite, for the 'exploration of the self' a place to 'take stock' of their emerging adult lives and to think through these negotiations and dilemmas. However, the use of bedrooms by young people is subject to various 'layers' of regulation both inside and outside of the home, questioning the extent to which this is a truly private domain for the young occupant where they can 'be themselves': in which they can construct and consume their emerging identities. Similarly, the notion of 'private' space has become somewhat complicated for young people today as they find themselves entrenched in social media cultures whereby the boundaries of public and private become extremely blurred as Livingstone (2005), boyd (2014) and others have argued, or even 'collapsed' (boyd, 2007; Marwick and boyd, 2010; Vitak, 2012). In this chapter, I draw on ethnographic research data gathered for a project entitled *'youth culture and private space'* (Lincoln, 2012) to understand how young people make private space meaningful to them. I explore how as spaces of consumption bedrooms represent the ways in which young people work through and between multiple boundaries inside and outside the home and how this shapes their emerging identities and young adult lives. In the following section I outline some of the key work on teenage 'bedroom culture' (for example, McRobbie and Garber, 1976; Larson, 1995; James, 2000; Lincoln, 2012) to establish the significance of private space in the family home and the meaning of spaces like bedrooms to young people in this context.

## Seeking self, seeking space: teenagers and their bedrooms

The significance of bedrooms to young people as part of their everyday youth cultural lives is not a recent phenomenon. In their canonical paper *Girls and Subcultures*, Angela McRobbie and Jenny Garber (1974) questioned why teenage girls did not seem to be (at least according to accounts produced by the Centre for Contemporary Cultural Studies) participating in street-based youth subcultures. They argued that this didn't necessarily equate to their invisibility in street-based cultures but rather they argued that girls' cultures were located and lived out in a different sphere: that of the domestic. In her later work (1991) McRobbie noted that girls' lives in the 1970s were:

> ... more highly structured than their male peers and their actions are closely monitored by the school, by youth leaders and by parents. The girls are firmly rooted in the home and local environment, and lack the social knowledge and expertise which derives from being able to visit and explore different parts of the city by themselves in the ways that boys can. (p. 37)

In this respect, McRobbie argued, girls compensated for this lack of interaction in public spaces by 'creating culture based on each other, rather than on *doing things* together' (p. 37, original emphasis) and this culture existed in their bedrooms. Girls additionally had to live their lives under the shadow of the 'double standard' (p. 5): girls' reputations were everything and while they were seeking their male counterpart on the one hand, their interaction with boys in the public domain had to be carefully monitored. As McRobbie noted:

> Girls had to be careful not to get into trouble and excess loitering on street corners might be taken as a sexual invitation to the boys.... Girls who spent too much time on the street were assumed to be promiscuous. (p. 5)

Girls were considered to be more at risk in public spaces 'from attack, assault or even abduction' and thus greater restrictions were placed on daughters than sons by parents (p. 12). In addition, McRobbie noted that young girls also sought alternative ways of experiencing the leisure spaces they already inhabit (a theme that is evident in more recent accounts of girls using their bedrooms, see James (2000) discussed below).

More recent studies of youth culture and the private domain, particularly from the mid-1990s onwards consider the significance of private spaces not just to young women but to young men too. This is because young people in contemporary times are growing up in environments that are readily defined as 'risky', globalised, neo-liberal and driven by practices of relentless consumption (Rose, 1999). Valentine and McKendrick (1995), Livingstone (2002) and others have argued that since the 1990s there has been a marked shift of young people's leisure activities back into the domestic sphere as public spaces like streets and parks become increasingly defined as unsafe for young people and as entertainment media become more diverse and competitively priced. In this respect, parents have been 'buying up' technology in an attempt to create leisure space in the home where they could keep an eye on their children.

Even more recently, studies of 'the private' in contemporary youth culture (that often draws on spatial metaphors such as the bedroom (see Lincoln and Hodkinson, 2008; Pearson, 2009; Robards, 2010; boyd, 2014) have become of interest to academics. Social media have become ever-more ubiquitous in the lives of young people who are increasingly growing up in 'boundary-less' environments or environments of 'context collapse' (Marwick and boyd, 2010) which means that the dichotomies of public and private are no longer so clear cut and privacy takes on new meanings (boyd, 2014). As I have argued elsewhere (Lincoln, 2012), young people's bedrooms are not 'closed off' spaces confined to the domestic realm, but have become 'portals' from which young people can access a variety of different spaces and environments as they live out their everyday lives.

One of the consequences of this is young people's exposure to culture that doesn't just rely on what you 'go out and find' as described by McRobbie (1991); digital spaces don't require a physical presence in the public sphere (this is more a question of access to the technology). In this respect, it can be argued that private domestic environments like teenagers' bedrooms have become more complex because they can be infiltrated in a number of different ways. In this way, teenage bedrooms provide a microcosmic example of the layers of intervention and negotiation from public, private and virtual realms that take place in the domestic environment of the home and subsequently influence how that space is used and managed.

More recent studies of young people's bedrooms have focused on their meaning in the context of young people's emerging adult identities (for example, Larson, 1995; James, 2001; Lincoln, 2004; 2005; 2012). This is because as a child moves towards adolescence and their teenage years, he or she can experience a sense of 'in-betweenness' that pervades many aspects of their life that can make identities complicated or uncertain. For example, young people find themselves 'suspended' between adulthood and childhood, between dependence and independence, between public and private spaces (for example being too young to go to the pub while other peers start using similar environments), are starting to question the authority of parents and teachers but not necessarily being confident about the alternatives and so on. In this respect, spaces such as bedrooms offer a young person a place within which to work some of these uncertainties out, as well as giving them a space to work through the emotional, physical and psychological changes that come with adolescence too. This 'working out' is done in a number of different ways for example, through the materiality of the space (Lincoln, 2012; 2013), consumption of it and within it and through cultural and social practices. The bedroom can provide a 'canvas' to represent the interests, thoughts and feelings of the young occupant using the material resources available to them (Lincoln, 2012; Lincoln, 2014); can act as a 'portal' from which to communicate with others and engage in different (sub) cultural environments; and can be a social space in which to hang out with friends or a private space to escape from parents and siblings (Lincoln, 2012).

Kandy James (2001) pays attention to teenage bedrooms as 'alternative recreational spaces' for teenage girls in which they are able to resist social expectations or are a 'line of *least* enquiry' (p. 72, original emphasis) in comparison to other public spaces such as swimming pools or other public recreational spaces. Drawing on interviews with girls aged 15 and 16 years old, James engages with what she defines in her earlier work (James, 2000) as 'situational body image' (p. 71) a concept that helps to explore the ways in which the girls in her study modified their bodies in particular social situations and what level of ridicule was associated to specific audiences and recreational spaces. James' study found that boys are much more likely to engage in sport-related recreational activities than girls. In these public contexts girls felt pressure to look or perform in a particular way that they were not necessarily comfortable with and, like the girls in McRobbie and Garber's (1976) study were vulnerable in public environments where potentially they could be ridiculed. For James' girls, the bedroom provided a space of their own that they could control (p. 71). The girls' choice to use their bedrooms as sites of recreation were often the result of 'forced' choice; that is, private spaces such as bedrooms were deemed safe, a sanctuary, secure and a haven (pp. 78–79) in comparison to public spaces where they could potentially be judged, particularly in terms of appearance. James, like Larson (1995) below, notes that girls' use of private spaces such as bedrooms is particularly pertinent during the teenage years; as James puts it: 'adolescents are particularly vulnerable to embarrassment and are likely to avoid social situations or places where they perceive a potential for ridicule' (p. 73). For James' participants, the bedroom was considered a 'site of emotions' for them (p. 78). As participant Laura put it 'if I have to cry about anything it's in my room', or Beth: 'if I'm really depressed I cry in there, that's where I have to go if I have to cry for anything... security.' (p. 78). In addition, the bedroom was also a site of control for James' participants 'at a time when many aspects of a girl's life were beyond their control, the bedroom seemed to be the one place where they could exert authority' (p. 79). The bedroom was a place from which they could *escape* authority too. For example, the girls spoke of retreating to their bedrooms when avoiding their parents, particularly mothers who would ask the girls to do household chores; control of bedroom space was interrupted by the chores that they (but not their brothers) were expected to do. If you could successfully hide away in your bedroom then somebody else would be asked to do them.

The media also plays an important role in understanding the uncertainties of teenage life, providing a host of resources (film, television, literature, music) that can be drawn upon adding additional layers of meaning to bedroom spaces. Importantly, the consumption of that media is shaped by the spaces that young people use them in. In his work on adolescents' private use of media Reed Larson (1995) argues that bedrooms provide a crucial site for young people, especially those experiencing their teenage years. In this private domain teenagers can shut themselves away from family, friends and peers and can retreat from the stresses and strains of the outside world. Larson argues that spaces such as bedrooms take on new meanings and significance for young people experiencing these years. He argues that as they move into their adolescent years, young people are finding new ways of engaging with their cultural surroundings using cultural resources, for example those provided by the media as 'tools' with which to understand their emerging identities. He goes on to argue that as young people's engagement with media (for example, music) becomes more purposeful and their connection to particular songs becomes more pertinent because the lyrics or melody capture their teenage experiences, the role of private space also takes on a new significance. In this respect, media such as music is consumed in very specific ways in the private realm as a 'meaning-making' resource. Larson argues that 'it is in their solitary bedroom lives where media has some of its most significant functions...' (p. 536). When a young person begins to experience the physical, emotional and sociological changes associated with adolescence, a medium such as music becomes a resource with which that young person can work through different aspects of their maturing selves: it can become a type of 'self-help' tool. For example, the lyrics of a song become significant because they can be related to a personal experience: a young person associating a song with 'coming out' or breaking up with a 'first love'. In turn, the affection for a particular song may manifest further in private space, for example through a poster of the band or artist who has recorded the song adoring the bedroom walls.

In my work elsewhere (Lincoln, 2004; 2005; 2012; 2013; 2014) I have argued that young people's uses of media in their bedrooms can be understood through the concept of 'zoning' for eg. see (Lincoln, 2004, p. 94). 'Zoning' refers to the ways in which young people navigate and organise their own private domains, making their space meaningful as *their* space in the family home. Zones in bedrooms are both physical and virtual arrangements of bedroom space. 'Zoning' refers to the ways in which a young person utilises the physical space of their bedroom as well as the materials, items and objects that fill it as expressions and performances of identity and how a young person expands the physical space by opening and closing other realms in public and virtual spheres, primarily using media technologies such as a sound system, television, DVD player, games console, laptop, iPad, Smartphone and so on. The use of this technology, that fills many young people's bedrooms as their parents attempt to keep them off the risky streets, are particularly useful 'identity marking' resources. Take for example, the music blasting out of a teenager's bedroom that vibrates throughout the house in the form of a dull (or not so dull) thudding created by the cranked up bass. Playing music loud not only takes 'bedroom culture' outside the private realm of this space, spilling into other parts of the household, irritating parents and siblings alike, but it also signifies a statement of who the young occupant is and what their current tastes are. Playing music loud can be a form of rebellion if it is interrupting an otherwise quiet household. This can take on a further dimension if the bedroom window is open and the street is also subjected to the loud noise; that young person's musical choices become publically heard. Conversely, music can be 'zoned in' to be a highly private experience. Again, media technology facilitates this, for example through the use of an iPod or other mobile listening device or headphones plugged into a phone. In this respect, music is used to completely internalise the listening experience. Lying on the bed, listening to music through headphones is an intense, intimate experience. This intimacy can be experienced with another should headphones be shared, but the point is, this is a very individual and personal experience dictated by the feelings and emotions of the listener at that time. 'Zoning' then, is one way of conceptualising how young people manage a personal and private space that is subject to a range of invasions and interruptions as a room in the family home. Being in their bedrooms affords teenagers greater privacy than perhaps other parts of the house, although as I will explore in the next section of this chapter, this 'privacy' and the production and consumption of identity within it exists within the context of often quite complicated family politics as well as within the wider contexts of young people's youth cultures. What these studies collectively reinforce is the significance- and shifting meaning- of private spaces to young people transiting through their teenage years as critical sites within which the exploration of emerging identities can be explored through consumption, and how the production of a 'bedroom culture' by teenagers (primarily, but also by siblings and parents as will be discussed below) facilitates and regulates these identity-seeking practices.

### (Bedroom) space invaders

Young people's consumption practices in bedrooms are not straight forward primarily because they are spaces in the parental home that are shared with other family members and thus those practices can be distorted in a number of ways and regulated by others' positions and roles in the home. Bedrooms are not just entered into by their 'owners'; they can be 'invaded' by parents, siblings, friends or peers. This means that young people's bedrooms can take on different meanings, depending on who is and who is not occupying them and the extent to which the 'privacy' of that space is contained within the bricks and mortar of the home. According to my research, parents and siblings regularly invade a bedroom (Lincoln, 2012). Siblings, for example, may go 'snooping' into their brothers' or sisters' bedrooms when they are not in; rifling through their 'stuff', retrieving things that belong to them, borrowing clothes or music, going in to get the shared games console or other piece of kit that has otherwise been monopolised (McNamee, 1998). Going into an older siblings' space when they are not there serves as a rite of passage for the younger sibling. Crossing the boundaries of a space from which they might ordinarily be excluded or restricted, as well as transcending the affordances of their age to reclaim items that are supposed to be shared, such as a games console or to borrow items such as clothes without permission gives the consumption of these goods a new significance. This consumption represents a challenge to age-related hierarchies in the sense that the younger sibling does not have to negotiate with their older sibling in order to access these things and their enjoyment of them is enhanced through the crossing of age and space boundaries. Further, taking these items into their bedrooms represents a claim to ownership even if this is only temporary and until they are discovered by the older sibling only to be taken back into their space.

Parents go into their children's bedrooms too. The frequency of entry and the reasons for it can vary but often it is mothers who would go in and clean the room, pick up laundry or retrieve crockery as well as have input on how the room is decorated and fathers who tended to have more of a say in how the space is regulated, for example in terms of who was and who was not granted access, especially for teenage girls (Lincoln, 2012). Bedrooms can also be 'invaded' by parents for reasons other than practical ones, for example, if they are curious about what their illusive son or daughter is up to. A number of my participants were aware of that sort of 'snooping' happened when they were not at home and thus they would hide things like bottles of alcohol, cigarettes, condoms or porno-graphic magazines and films inside cupboards, in the back of the ward-robe, in drawers, in among box files for college and so on, in the hope that they wouldn't be easily found (Lincoln, 2012). As with the example of siblings above, the fact that these items are hidden away from parents makes the consumption of them in bedrooms even more significant. Their consumption represents a challenge to (domestic) authority; doing things your parents have told you not to-under their roof. It represents a negotiation of time and space (inasmuch as young people find ways of consuming such items so that they remain undiscovered although this is somewhat complicated by the consequences of their consumption- for example smell of smoke or alcohol). This consumption also serves as a stamp of a young person's identity on their bedroom space as well statement of their ownership and control of it. However, as I will discuss below hiding things in bedrooms might not always be so straightforward, particularly if parents regulate content. Bedrooms can be 'invaded' for other, more serious reasons too. For example if parents have serious concerns about their child's welfare (they suspect he or she is drinking alcohol excessively, is smoking or taking illegal drugs, has an eating disorder, might be pregnant or is being bullied) they might resort to entering their children's bedrooms to find clues.

Bedrooms can be opened up by their young occupants to friends and used as social spaces; an invasion that is more controlled and regulated (Hodkinson and Lincoln, 2008). Bedrooms can provide a space in which friends hang out before a night on the town, enjoying a few drinks and listening to music in preparation for the night ahead. They can also provide a space to return to after a night out to dissect the night's events, wind down, perhaps enjoy a few more drinks and listen to music (Lincoln, 2004), continuing the consumption practices of their night out. The now ubiquitous use of social media, and particularly social network sites (SNS) mean that the bedroom can be opened up or 'zoned' out (Lincoln, 2012) even further to include those 'friends' who exist on sites such as Facebook or Twitter who can also participate in these post-night out consumption practices even if they are not physically in the same space. Uploading images of the night or 'tweeting' about the events of the evening take the social activities of friends in a bedroom out into virtual domains and thus their night out becomes an experience mediated by other peoples' experiences represented through images and text-based comments from the same night out. The bedroom is further mediated through music used to set the tone for the night ahead as well as to create the right ambience for coming down and chilling out from the night out (Lincoln, 2004).

A young person's bedroom, then, is subject to various different invasions – some examples of which have been outlined here and many of which impact on the ways in which young people consume 'bedroom culture'. Sometimes the 'invasion' is controlled by the young people themselves, other times it is not. For the duration of this chapter, I wish to consider in more detail how consumption in 'private' space is managed by young people and how the intersections that these invasions create are worked though by a young person to create their own space. Referring specifically to three of my female participants Lisa aged 18, Sarah aged 12 and Lisa aged 14, I will explore how amidst all of this, the bedroom is a place where they can state 'this is me'.

## 'Mum hates A Clockwork Orange': bedrooms, identity and parental control

For Lisa, aged 18 and a first-year student living in university halls of residence, her bedroom had always been an important space. When talking about this with Lisa, it emerged that its significance was related to a range of complex family issues that she has experienced while growing up. These experiences were primarily marked by the divorce of her parents when she was 6, her mother meeting a new partner, then moving abroad when she was 14 years old, and her father also meeting a new partner. Lisa's mother had returned to the UK but was living in a different city to Lisa's father. Lisa's mother had remarried and was living with her son (Lisa's younger brother) and stepson. Lisa's father had also remarried and was living with his wife and stepdaughter. There were periods of her life where Lisa had lived in both households, but the very nature of the situation positioned her as 'in-between' those two family formations; part of both but partial also. Lisa had a bedroom in both her mother and her father's house, but the concept of 'her bedroom' was quite different in each:

> Well, I've got my own room at my mum's house in Carlisle but it's more of a guest room, but at my dad's, he still makes jokes that it looks like I never moved out, and there is just as much stuff [as there is in her room in halls] everywhere there...

While Lisa did have a room in her mother's house, she described it as 'more of a guest room'. This suggested a certain amount of disconnection from the room, acknowledging that while she did have a space of her own it didn't really *feel* like it belonged to her, but rather it was a space that anyone who *visited* the house can sleep in. On the other hand, the room that she has in her father's house was very much *her* space and was a space that was left alone by her father, even when Lisa was away at university- it was still full of her things and she could literally walk into it at any time and engage in the activities she'd always done in there. This was significant in a number of ways not least because it constituted the difference between Lisa having her 'own room' in her father's *home* or sleeping in the 'guest room' when she goes to her mother's *house* as well as reinforcing the importance to Lisa of having a space of her own.

From an early age Lisa's mother had exerted control over what Lisa could and could not have in her bedroom and according to Lisa that has caused many battles between them over the years. Often these battles were over content and were media-related (for example, about types of music or particular films) as when Lisa's mother 'banned Marilyn Manson from her house and [she] hates a *Clockwork Orange*,' according to Lisa. While Lisa had interests in both (influenced by her mother's dislike of them) in her early teenage years, she had not been allowed to have any paraphernalia related to either in her room. Lisa had put up a A *Clockwork Orange* poster on her bedroom wall, but her mother had regarded it as offensive and something that 'shouldn't be in her house', even if it was something that Lisa had an interest in, and demanded she took it down. Lisa explained that her reaction was also partly because she had a younger brother and her mother did not want him to see what she considered to be offensive imagery. Lisa's attempt to make her bedroom her own in this instance was intercepted by her mother and the offense she took to particular music and films. Lisa duly took down the poster knowing that she would be able to display it in her 'other' bedroom.

According to Lisa, her father took a much more liberal approach than her mother to what Lisa could have in her room. Lisa said he:

> didn't care – he's just painted my room and I decided to paint squares on one wall and stick things in the middle of the squares and he didn't care, he was just like 'if that's how you want it, that's how you can have it' kind of thing, he just let's me have it my way.

Lisa considered her room at her father's house to be 'her bedroom' because it was a space that she was allowed to do what she wanted with and a space that she knew her father also acknowledged as 'her space' through allowing her to decorate the room the way she liked. In her mother's house where she was often restricted in terms of what she could have 'on display' in the her room, Lisa did not feel a connection to the space regarding it as – and as her mother saw it – the guest room that she slept in when she visited.

Throughout my discussions with Lisa, it was clear to see that her life had been profoundly affected by the divorce of her parents, which had brought with it a sense of uncertainty into her family life and a 'diversity' in her family formation that she did not always find easy to deal with. For Lisa, then, the need to have her own space was very important because this represented consistency and stability, both of which Lisa desired. Being able to mark out her bedroom as 'her space' was paramount. It was a place in which she could deal with the emotions of growing up, like the girls in James' (2001) study discussed above, as well as the uncertainties that came with her sometimes unstable home life. This desire for consistency and stability was articulated primarily through the contents of her bedroom evident in both the room at her father's house and in her halls of residence where she later lived. Her bedroom at her father's house was, according to Lisa filled full of 'stuff'. A self confessed 'hoarder', Lisa explained how she held on to the 'clutter' because she saw anything from a receipt to a cushion as part of the fabric of who she was and the experiences she was encountering as she grew up. This 'hoarding' strategy meant that Lisa had a space that was literally full of things about her life. The fuller it got, the more permanent it became because the amount of things it in would be very difficult to move. Her bedroom in this respect literally became 'anchored' as her space in the home through her 'hoarding' of material possessions and a space in which her identity was 'brimming over': anyone who walked into that room know that it was Lisa's. This strategy was also employed when Lisa moved into hall of residence in her first year at university.

While hall spaces tend to be very generic in terms of layout and furniture, Lisa selected items from her bedroom at her father's house with which she was able to 'recreate' her bedroom in halls. This involved the use of very mundane generic items such as a washing basket that Lisa had put in her university room in exactly the same place that she would find it in her bedroom at her father's. Photographs were also significant in this 'translation', particularly photographs of her family when her parents were still together, a period of 'stability' in Lisa's life that she held onto through collages of photos in her room. For Lisa, the meaning of her bedroom at university (a space outside both parental homes) was constantly informed by the reference point of 'when my parents were together'. This, she claimed, was one of the reasons she considered herself a hoarder: she liked to hang on to things and not let go of the past. At every point in Lisa's room there was a story to be told about a particular object or item, from the Elvis cushions that her mother had made for her to the homemade 'Sponge-Bob Square Pants' made by her brother. More often than not, these stories would be told within the context of the time when her parents were together which was a particularly important reference point for her when things were not going so well:

> Ummm … there is pretty much everything, from when my parents were still together, there's stuff from school and then uni ones obviously, there is just pretty much everything from every part of my

life like my first day at School ... I think it's because the people in the pictures, if I needed them they would be there for me and it brings back memories looking at old photos so if I am feeling lonely I can look at them and think well it wasn't always like this so it won't always be like it kind of thing it makes you feel a bit better about it.

The private space of Lisa's bedroom operates as a container that is filled with material possessions that may appear meaningless to others (a supermarket receipt pinned on her wall, for example) but are meaningful to Lisa, particularly in the context of a stable family life (the receipt represented the first groceries she bought at university – a mundane, yet usually family-related, activity). Items like photographs help Lisa to maintain a sense of stability in her otherwise turbulent life and her bedroom is the place that accommodates those items. They also help her to navigate new experiences and provide her with a point of focus should she need it. Importantly, these items are transportable so Lisa was able to take old photographs with her to university, but equally she is able to take photographs back home from university as she becomes more comfortable with these new experiences and feels a part of them. Lisa said she would take back photographs of her boyfriend or of nights out with friends as constant reminders of the good times she was having at university. She said that this was particularly important when staying at her mother's house because 'when I go home [to my mum's house] I like to have my uni things just to remind me that I'm not going to be under my mum's watchful eye there!'

## 'She thinks she's our mam': bedrooms, identity and sibling control

Sara and Natasha aged 12 and 14 years old, were sisters who shared a bedroom. They were two of five siblings living with their mother in a single parent household. Sara and Natasha got on well because they were relatively close in age with only couple of years separating them. However, in discussions with them, they talked about their more difficult relationships, particularly with their eldest sister and, to a lesser extent, with their young sister who was 8 years old. This discussion demonstrates the ways in which the girls used 'age' as a strategy to articulate their place in the home, particularly their bedrooms, to regulate content and to make sense of frictions within the broader household. As mentioned above, Sara and Natasha shared a bedroom but at the time of the research the eldest sister, who was 18 years old, was also using their bedroom – as hers was being redecorated. As the girls spoke about how they all got along with each other it emerged that while an 'age'

hierarchy was evident in their relationship with each other, the responsibilities that the eldest sibling took charge of within the home were
a point of contention for Sara and Natasha, particularly as they were
temporarily sharing a room with her.

>**Sara:** The oldest one does our heads in, but the next one down [aged
>17], she's all right.
>**SL:** Do you argue a lot?
>**Sara:** We both argue with the other one, the eldest one
>**SL:** Why's that?
>**Sara:** Because she thinks she's our mam [mum].

Being the eldest of five siblings in a single parent family it seems
reasonable that Sara and Natasha's sister would take on significant
responsibilities in the family home, for example, she would do many
of the domestic chores, cook for her siblings and look after them while
her mother was at work. However, Natasha and Sara were not particularly sensitive to her plight and rather than supporting their sister
in this role, saw her as an 'intruder' who they felt was pretending to
be their mother. Natasha and Sara did not see her as worthy of her
assumed adult status; instead, they preferred to see her as their sister,
still within teen age and thus with little authority to tell them what to
do. This 'rejection' was particularly emphasised when the girls talked
about their eldest sister's use of their bedroom while her room was
being re-decorated.

The girls' bedroom, already 'invaded' by their 8-year-old sister who
liked to play in it and who had slowly introduced what Sara and Natasha
called 'girly' pink toys into their space. Now it was being 'invaded' again
by their eldest sister. Sara and Natasha's room had just been redecorated
and they had chosen a blue and silver colour scheme with accessories and furniture matching this scheme (hence the pink toys were not
welcome). They endeavoured to keep it tidy (perhaps a novelty given
its newness) and had storage space in which to keep all of their bits
and pieces. Their eldest sister however would 'just throw all her college
work all over the bed...she has her homework and everything all over
the bed...and shoes...' and, Sara added, 'I think that bed makes our
bedroom look a mess'. So in addition to the girls being 'mothered' by
their eldest sister, their space was also being 'invaded' and according
to them, disrespected by her through her frivolous throwing of items
into the room, causing further tension and animosity between them.
This was further exacerbated by the role of 'the boyfriend', Lee, the

relationship with whom, Sara and Natasha felt, added to their sister's adopted 'mothering' role.

> **Sara:** She's got a boyfriend called Lee and she's like 'oh, I can't go, I'm going out with Lee'
> **Natasha:** We call her Mrs Lee, us!
> **SL:** Does she bring him up to your room?
> **Natasha:** No, not in our room…oh, this is another thing. Say that we're downstairs watching telly or something before we're going to bed, if Lee comes in we've got to go upstairs.

On the one hand, the role of 'the boyfriend' is viewed by Sara and Natasha as just another way for their sister to establish her 'adult' mothering status, but she also uses Lee as a way to 'control' them and their use of the house. Like children, they were often 'banished' to their room so that their sister can be alone with her boyfriend which was especially important for her given that she didn't have her own room, albeit temporarily, to have any privacy. But in scenarios such as this, the girls' bedroom moved from being 'their space' that they have spent time redecorating and making their own, to a space that they have been sent to like children: its meaning is different in this context because they have not chosen to use the space but have been forced to use it by their sister who they struggled to take seriously an as authority figure in their home. The girls' bedroom in this household then is a site of union, conflict and contradiction and its use is suspended within rather complex family dynamics and tensions among siblings. The room is shared in the first instance, but Sara and Natasha get on well. Their bedroom had already been redecorated and they had spent time thinking about decoration and colour schemes and had taken this as an opportunity to make a room that represented them as they both moved into their teenage years (for example they had painted the white furniture they already had silver). But at the same time as they were 'working on' their space and making it their own, it got invaded by their other siblings, for example their 8 year old sister who brings her 'childish' toys into the room and leave them there and their 17 year old sister who just 'dumps' things because it is not her room, just a place she is using for storage while hers in re-decorated. Finally, the room, despite being 'owned' by Natasha and Sara is used by their eldest sister as a way of exerting power over them, particularly when her boyfriend is visiting the house. Natasha and Sara then, are constantly trying to reclaim their own space.

## Conclusion

So what does this tell us about young people, private space and consumption in the family home? First, the discussions above confirm that while a young person's bedroom is a space for basic functions such as sleeping and getting dressed, it is a space that plays an important symbolic role in the articulation of a teenage identity and of a sense of place in the home and beyond. As I noted in the introduction, young people's use of private space is particularly significant because they are experiencing a period of growing up when not-quite-fitting-in is synonymous with the period of transition that the teenage years brings. In this respect, a young person's bedroom, which is often one of the first spaces that young people feel any sense of ownership over, takes on an important role as a site of meaning-making and identity marking. However, young people's bedrooms exist within often quite complicated webs weaved through young people's interactions both inside and outside the home. In this respect, young people's uses of their bedrooms are caught up in a series of 'intersections' (Livingstone, 2005) whereby, on the one hand, they are using the space to work their way through different boundaries, regulations and restrictions across different spheres but, on the other, their use of private space is restricted, challenging the extent to which the young occupant can claim 'this space is me'.

Using the example of multiple and shared bedrooms, I have argued that young people experiencing their teenage years need private space in which to be themselves and to explore, construct and consume their own emerging adult identities. This need for space is influenced by a variety of factors that can be unique to different households. The dynamics of a family undoubtedly influences a teenager's use of their bedroom as well as the significance of it as a private space. Finding a space to call their own often involves negotiations with other family members; some members (mothers, fathers, older siblings) can even control its content, thus limiting, in the eyes of a teenager, the resources available to a young person to express their identity. Others have to 'find' space in a room that is shared or constantly invaded by other siblings and in such scenarios content and decoration become important symbols of ownership and identity.

Once in the bedroom, consumption within it occurs against a set of predefined criteria that in the scenarios above is determined by amongst other things: age, space and family relations. For example, items such as alcohol may be hidden in bedrooms and the fact that they are in a young person's bedroom does not by default mean that they will not be seen as parents and siblings can enter when the occupant is not around (therefore further privacy measures to hide such items are implemented to ensure they are not discovered). For this reason, taking those items 'out of hiding' to be consumed is in itself an act that reinforces the claim that 'my bedroom is me', is an act of rebellion and a signifier of growing up. While items may be hidden in bedrooms, so too can they be made more visible and taken out of one context to be consumed in another. The act of younger siblings invading bedrooms to borrow their older siblings' clothes demonstrates the new significance these items take when worn by the younger sibling in the context of their own room or even outside in the public realm. An example I elaborate on above is of siblings Natasha and Sara who were forced to share a room with their older sister while her bedroom was re-decorated. Fractures in their relationship occurred because of the older sibling's lack of consideration for Natasha and Sara's space. The 'just chucking things in' approach that she took to moving her stuff in temporarily represented a disrespect of their (newly decorated) room, messing up it up and disturbing the aesthetics that they had carefully considered. The temporariness of this move for the older sibling determined how she treated the space. In addition, their younger sister, desperate to share the space too, further dilutes the room's meaning when placing girly pink toys in the space.

Lisa's consumption practices were subject to multiple family formations and had to be adapted accordingly and in relation to different family contexts be it her mother's house, her father's or her room in halls of residence. Amidst these varying criteria that each context and formation presented, and in the quest to find stability in an often unstable life are Lisa's consumption practices that could be perceived as rather excessive to the extent to which she has so much stuff, it becomes difficult to move it – she is literally anchoring her identity through mass consumption. In working within the restrictions implemented by her father, mother or university, Lisa carefully manages her personal space exploiting the freedom she has in her father's house – the space which she considers to be the most authentic of her multiple bedrooms. These examples represent how consumption practices in private spaces such as bedrooms can be complex, negotiated, often pre-defined, constantly challenged, invaded and compromised for young people. However, while young people are working through the intersections of public, private and virtual life, the bedroom is a site where they can consume their identities and ultimately state 'my bedroom is me,' albeit with restrictions.

# References

Abbott-Chapman, J. and Robertson, M. (2009) 'Adolescents' Favourite Places: Redefining the Boundaries between Public and Private Space', *Space and Culture*, 12(4), 419–434.

Baker, S.L. (2004) 'Pop in(to) the Bedroom: Popular Music in Pre-Teen Girls' Bedroom Culture,' *European Journal of Cultural Studies*, 7(1), 75–93.

boyd, d. (2014) *It's Complicated: The Social Lives of Networked Teens*. New Haven: Yale University Press.

boyd, d. (2007) 'Why Youth (heart) Social Networking Sites: The Role of Networked Publics in Teenage Social Life' in *Youth, Identity, and Digital Media*, D. Buckingham (ed.), pp. 119–142. Cambridge, MA: MIT Press.

Griffin, C. (1993) *Representations of Youth*. Cambridge: Polity Press.

Heath, S. (1999) 'Young Adults and Household Formation in the 1990s', *British Journal of Sociology of Education*, 20(4), 545–561.

Heath, S. (2004) 'Peer-Shared Households, Quasi-Communes and Neo-Tribes', *Current Sociology*, 52(2), 161–179.

Hodkinson, P. and Lincoln, S. (2008) 'Online Journals as Virtual Bedrooms: Young People, Identity and Personal Space', *Young: The Nordic Journal of Youth Research*, 16(1), 27–46.

James, K.A. (2001) '"I just gotta have my own space!": The Bedroom as a Leisure Site for Adolescent Girls', *Journal of Leisure Research*, 33(1), 71–90.

James, K.A. (2000) '"You Can *Feel* Them Looking at You": The Experiences of Adolescent Girls in Swimming Pools', *Journal of Leisure Research*, 32(2), 262–280.

Larson, R. (1995) 'Secrets in the Bedroom: Adolescents' Private Use of Media', *Journal of Youth and Adolescence*, 24 (5), 535–550.

Lincoln, S. (2014) 'Mediated Private Space' in *Mediated Youth Cultures: The Internet, Belonging and New Cultural Configurations*, A. Bennett and B. Robards (eds), pp. 42–58. Basingstoke: Palgrave Macmillan.

Lincoln, S. (2013) 'Media and Bedroom Culture' in *The Routledge International Handbook of Children, Adolescents and Media*, D. Lemish (ed.). New York: Routledge.

Lincoln, S. (2012) *Youth Culture and Private Space*. Basingstoke: Palgrave Macmillan.

Lincoln, S. (2005) 'Feeling the Noise: Teenagers, Bedrooms and Music', *Leisure Studies*, 24(4), 399–414.

Lincoln, S. (2004) 'Teenage Girls' Bedroom Culture: Codes versus Zones' in *After Subculture: Critical Studies in Contemporary Youth Culture*, A. Bennett and K. Kahn-Harris (eds), pp. 94–106. Basingstoke: Palgrave Macmillan.

Livingstone, S. (2005) 'In Defence of Privacy: Mediating the Public/Private Boundary at Home', London. LSE Research Online, http://eprints.lse.ac.uk/archive/00000505 [date accessed May 5, 2014].

Livingstone, S. (2002) *Young People and New Media: Childhood and the Changing Media Environment*. London: Sage.

Marwick, A. E. and boyd, d. (2011) 'I Tweet Honestly, I Tweet Passionately: Twitter Users, Context Collapse, and the Imagined Audience', *New Media & Society*, 13(1), 114–133.

McNamee, S. (1998) 'The Home: Youth, Gender and Video Games: Power and Control in the Home' in *Cool Places: Geographies of Youth Cultures*, T. Skelton and G. Valentine (eds), pp. 195–206. London: Routledge.

McRobbie, A. (1991) *Feminism and Youth Culture: From Jackie to Just Seventeen*. Basingstoke: Macmillan.

McRobbie, A. and Garber, J. (1976) 'Girls and Subcultures' in *Resistance Through Rituals: Youth Subcultures in Post-War Britain*, S. Hall and T. Jefferson (eds), pp. 209–223. London: Hutchinson and Co.

Pearson, E. (2009) 'All the World Wide Web's a Stage : The Performance of Identity in Online Social Networks', *First Monday*, 14(3), http://firstmonday.org/htbin/cgiwrap/bin/ojs/index.php/fm/article/view/2162/2127 [date accessed January 30, 2012].

Robards, B. (2010) 'Randoms in My Bedroom: Negotiating Privacy and Unsolicited Contact on Social Networking Sites', *Prism*, 7(3), http://www.prismjournal.org/fileadmin/Social_media/Robards.pdf [date accessed January 30, 2012].

Roberts, K. (2008) *Youth in Transition: Eastern Europe and the West*. Basingstoke: Palgrave Macmillan.

Rose, N. (1999) *Governing the Soul: The Shaping of the Private Self*. London: Free Associations Books.

Valentine, G. and McKendrick, J. (1997) 'Children's Outdoor Play: Exploring Parental Concerns About Children's Safety and the Changing Nature of Childhood', *Geoforum*, 28(2), 219–235.

Vitak, J. (2012) 'The Impact of Context Collapse and Privacy on Social Network Site Disclosures', *Journal of Broadcasting & Electronic Media*, 56(4), 451–470.

# 5
# The Transgressive Potential of Families in Commercial Homes

*Julie Seymour*

## Introduction

The starting point for this chapter is a type of building: one that contains a hospitality establishment. The focus is on a particular form of such establishments – the family-run hotel, boarding house, or public house. Its distinctiveness comes not only from the commercial use to which the building is put, but the fact that it also serves as the home for the families who run the business. As such, these places have been labelled 'Commercial Homes' by (Lynch, 2005) and this phrase will be used throughout this chapter to discuss these dual-purpose locations.

The aim of the chapter is to focus not on those families 'consuming' leisure and holidays in these Commercial Homes – this has been done elsewhere (Haldrup and Larsen, 2003; Schanzel et al., 2012). Instead I will foreground those families who provide the hospitality for others to consume and for whom, the Commercial Home is the everyday, mundane setting in which their family lives unfold. This fits into the aim of this edited volume of looking at the diversity of domestic and intimate spaces of consumption by showing that these can also include spaces of public and commercial consumption. As such, it emphasises the multiple activities which can occur in domestic spaces and thus enhances the conceptual treatment of these locations (Seymour, 2007; McIntosh et al., 2011). In addition, it confirms that the management of the work-life balance does not always involve spatially discrete locations. By focusing on the lives of families in Commercial Homes this chapter serves as a reminder that considerations of family leisure need to also bear in mind the providers of hospitality and the impact of others' leisure consumption and production on their everyday family lives.

In order to examine this approach, I will draw on a body of work I have carried out on family-run hotels, pubs and boarding house which interrogated the sociological impact on family life of residing in such business establishments (Seymour, 2005; 2007; 2011a; 2011b). The data used comes from a range of sources. A small-scale empirical study was carried out in which fieldwork was split between two East Coast seaside resorts: one in the South and one in the North of England. 19 in-depth interviews were carried out with families (both parents and children) currently living in hotels, pubs or boarding houses. A further six interviews were undertaken with individuals and couples who raised their families in such establishments or grew up in them in the 1960s and 70s. Finally, secondary data analysis was carried out on fifty oral history interviews relating to participation in the tourist industry in one northern seaside town during the early and middle parts of the twentieth century.[1]

Typically in tourism and hospitality research, hotels are discussed as transgressive, liminal and carnivalesque sites (Pritchard and Morgan, 2006) for those who are consuming/producing (Lofgren, 1999) leisure but they are quotidian or commonplace to those who live in them. For the latter (as with other service personnel) their everyday work is to service others' holidays and this labour within a pub, boarding house or hotel then becomes mundane, that is repetitive and routinised (Edensor, 2007; Crang, 1997). This work happens alongside family life – sometimes in parallel and sometimes in a deeply interwoven manner (Adkins, 1995; Seymour, 2001b). As a result this, for most families in such establishments, impacts on the nature and practices of their family life. This chapter will show how this is particularly so with regard to spatial and temporal family practices.

An additional element of this impact on the host family is related to the nature of these hospitality establishments – the very fact that they are family-run hotels, pubs and boarding houses – means that a particular presentation of hospitality is required; one which emphasises the 'familyness' of the establishment. But this presentation of 'familyness' is carried out by the Commercial Home Family; that is a family that presents a model of 'normality' that can be recognised but one that operates in a business environment where, as commercial providers, there must be no privileging of the family over the guests.

The Commercial Home then presents a spatial area of considerable complexity. Guests are consuming and producing their own leisure (Lofgren, 1999), additional workers may be carrying out paid employment and the resident family are enacting their everyday family practices while (for most) also presenting themselves to guests as the Commercial Home Family. This latter activity is not continuous but is required at specific moments. Such moments constitute examples of what (Finch, 2007) has called 'family display' and this chapter will examine the applicability of this recent concept to a domestic setting which is also the location of business practices. In addition, the family practices of the host family are impacted on by the spatial and temporal requirements of the business such as holiday seasons, mealtimes and the use of public and guest bedroom spaces within the Commercial Home. As a result, the host family can find that their own family practices become a mirror image or inversion of those of the guest families as will be outlined below. The argument of this chapter is that by being resident in a hospitality business and, on certain instances, displaying the Commercial Home Family, the host family will actually develop family practices which are significantly different from those perceived as defining a 'normal' family. This then results in a paradoxical situation where the very presentation of a family-run hospitality establishment and the displays of the Commercial Home *Family* so distort the reality of the hosts' family practices that they performatively disrupt the discourse of the family life they are portraying and lead to a transgressive constitution of the family ideology they are trying to reproduce.

I will illustrate this process by using examples from three areas of my research on Commercial Homes: spatial and temporal disruptions to 'normal' family practices, the emotional labour that host children carry out as part of the hospitality business and the 'display' of Commercial Home Families within their familial hotel, pub or boarding house. I will then go on to discuss the relationship between the performance of everyday family practices by the host family and their 'display' of the Commercial Home Family and show how this leads to a potentially transgressive performativity which contests the ideological family. Through developing the recent concept of family displays, this chapter extends the work of (Gregson and Rose, 2000) on performance, performativity and spatialities of consumption. It also reminds us that family practices and displays are made up of both activities and discourses (Morgan, 1996; 2011; Seymour, 2011b).

The chapter's focus then on Commercial Homes helps to develop and nuance our consideration of domestic consumption by a concentration on the multi-purpose domestic location. Such family-run hotels, pubs and boarding houses truly exemplify sites where emotions, relations and domestic intimacies intersect with cultural and economic forms of exchanges. Their very 'homeliness' becomes a product subject to commercial exchange through the economic production and consumption of hospitality (Lynch et al., 2009). The outcome of these business activities has a considerable impact on the host family in relation to their family practices but, as this chapter will show, a detailed study of this impact can contribute to the growing heterogeneity of discourses relating to the constitution of contemporary family life.

## Family practices in commercial homes

Commercial homes are businesses *and* family homes and hence the site of economic *and* family practices. For most of the families in my study, the economic imperative and the requirements of running a hospitality establishment considerably influenced the spatial and temporal family practices of the host family.

For example, in relation to space, the home had both public (reception areas, guests' lounge, dining rooms, gardens), semi-private (guest bedrooms) and private areas (kitchens, host family rooms). These spaces were however fluid depending on the needs of the business and the seasonality of the Commercial Home; that is whether it was closed during the quieter times in the UK of Nov-April. Hence, when open to guests, family bedrooms could be used by paying visitors with the family squeezed together in a shared room, sleeping in another building or camping in the garden (Seymour, 2007). One boarding house owner remembers hiring out her teenaged daughter's bedroom to guests and sharing the marital bedroom with her:

> ... the first nine months we were here she didn't sleep in it [her bed].
> She was sleeping with us a lot of the time. (Interview 15, female)

The contemporary presentation of the home as a place where children have their own rooms for considerable lengths of time or at least as Sibley (1995, p. 129) puts it 'the child attempts to carve out its own spaces and set its own times' is, in the Commercial Home, problematised by the additional, and often privileged, requirements of paying guests. Conversely, if the establishment was closed during the off-season, then the family might occupy bedrooms previously used for guests, or hold family parties in the guests' lounges and dining rooms. However, not all interviewees' spatial family practices showed such flexibility. One boarding house owner had firm boundaries between the home and the business areas of the location. As a result, four children shared one bedroom throughout their childhood despite there being vacant bedrooms elsewhere in the building during the out of season months (Interview 2, female).

Interviewees often spoke of trying to define a 'family space', a material or symbolic space where only family members were allowed.

Nobody comes through the fire door in the hall [demarcating their family area] unless they're invited. (Interview 15, female boarding house owner)

In reality, such spaces were often breached by guests, staff, and telephone calls throughout the day and night.

With regard to temporal family practices, the requirement of a hospitality establishment that there is someone available, in the current idiom, 24/7 meant that there was little *guaranteed* private time. Dedicated family time – whether meals, helping with homework, or children's bedtime routines – was always potentially liable to be interrupted. This brought home to the Commercial Home families, their atypical family practices since they saw 'Normal' or 'proper' family life as drawing on a discourse of time and activities spent together with, *and only with*, family members (Seymour, 2011b). To achieve this familial exclusivity, paradoxically and, in an inversion of the common discourse, 'protected' family time may have to take place away from the home. This was exemplified by one of my respondents who commented that uninterrupted family time could only be achieved by having meals away from their own hotel (Interview 17, female hotel owner) hence highlighting the spatial consequences of temporal family practices in Commercial Homes.

In addition, family practices in Commercial Homes do not have the same temporal rhythms as those consuming the hospitality service. Due to the seasonality of much Commercial Home activity in the UK, family holidays cannot be taken between Easter and September or at Christmas. (Gillis, 1996) traces the emphasis on Christmas and summer holidays to the growth of family-centred time. As a result, for the businesses under consideration, their work timetables have grown to accommodate other people's family time. Hence Commercial Home families have temporal practices which are an inversion of the expected or typical rhythms of 'normal' family-centred time such as mealtimes and non-work periods and ideologically prescribed daily, weekly and holiday activities such as leisure time and school holidays. As one female hotel owner said:

We don't have the weekends to spend as a family like we used to do [prior to running the hotel]. (Interview 17)

In my study, family meals were taken before or after those of the guests. Family holidays were taken in the off-season months and public holidays could be delayed:

> 'so New Year was always our Christmas' (Interview 12, female B & B owner).

Again some families chose to reduce the impact of the business on family Christmas practices by not opening during this time but clearly this had a significant economic cost (Seymour, 2007).

These examples show that while the host family in a Commercial Home use the presentation of their everyday 'familyness' as a commercial selling point, their physical location in a business environment means that the actual performance of their own spatial and temporal family practices are starkly atypical. This then has implications for the performativity of spatial and temporal family practices which will be discussed later in the chapter.

## Children's emotional labour in commercial homes

This second topic contributes to the debates surrounding the emotional and material labour involved in producing and reproducing domestic and intimate spaces (Martens and Casey, 2007) but again adds the dimension of a location which also has commercial activities taking place in the home. Focusing on emotional labour and using the data from the study of Commercial Homes, I wish to highlight the contribution of children to the emotional labour involved in their family business. This widens the previous research on emotional labour in general by acknowledging the role of children in its production and that on children's emotional labour in particular by showing it can take place in a commercial environment.

Emotion work has been defined by (Hochschild, 1983) as 'explicit management of the emotions', both of oneself and of others and has been acknowledged as taking place in the home (Gabb, 2008). The emotion work performed by children has been recognised as an element of the contributions children make to the production of the domestic sphere in everyday interactions (Gabb, 2008), as carers (Becker et al., 1998) or in times of disaster recovery (Whittle et al., 2012). Under the name emotional labour, it has long been recognised as an element of paid employment (Hochschild, 1983; Toerien and Kitzinger, 2007a) However, the research on emotional labour as an economic activity has concentrated on adults and has not identified the role children play in the emotional labour of businesses. One reason for this is that emotion work and emotional labour have been presented as occurring in spatially discrete locations due to the tendency to see paid employment as located away from the private sphere. The study of Commercial Homes allows the consideration of where these two areas coalesce.

For hospitality workers, emotional labour involves relational work with consumers to enhance the latter's sense of well-being or the minimisation of one's own negative feelings. To be performed well it should not be visible and it is often carried out jointly with physical tasks (Toerien and Kitzinger, 2007b). Data from my interviews showed that for individuals running or living in a hotel, pub or boarding house such self-management took place as part of the labour process. This would either involve falsely putting on a friendly face in front of guests or conversely toning down 'bad' emotions so as not to be overhead by customers.

> If there was ever like a family argument or anything like that it was always 'Shush, we've got guests in'. (Interview 15, daughter of B & B owner)

Emotional labour is often associated with practical activities such as the serving of food and drink but can be carried out on its own as when a staff member asks a guest about their day (Seymour, 2005).

> They have to sit and tell you every detail and even if it's the most boring story you have ever heard, you have got to sit there and smile and say 'Oh was it nice?' You've got to make conversation even though you really don't want to. (Interview 16, daughter of hotel owner)

This interview excerpt shows how emotional labour differs from the emotional capital, which (Silva, 2007) discusses in her consideration of consumption and family life. Emotional labour can be bought and sold and requires a convincing performance by the worker. Emotional capital is seen as a more personal capacity to connect which then becomes a resource for consumption (Silva, 2007). While increased emotional capital in individual Commercial Home Owners – and their children – can be seen as a marketable asset (Silva, 2007, p. 144) as it will enhance the performance of their emotional labour and presumably make it more pleasant to carry out, the latter can be carried out without the former.

In this study of Commercial Homes, the emotional labour performed by *children* in these families as part of the economic imperative of the business became clear: an element that has not been emphasised previously in research either on family practices or consumption research. The interview data produced numerous examples of children growing up in hospitality establishments carrying out examples of emotional labour such as explicitly engaging guests in a conversation about their day, chatting to them while serving food and drink or reducing the volume of a family argument so that guests do not hear. These acts of emotional labour were recognised by parents and considered good for business. Parents discussed how their children carried out front management with guests, masking their 'real selves':

> Barry likes older people, even when he was little he got on well with older men and older women. He's a bit of an old man in hisself. He's very polite which goes down well. I mean it's not a true reflection of him, he's an untidy so-and-so but *he's got the image bang right, which is good from our point of view.* (Interview 17, female hotel owner, my emphasis)

Interestingly, although emotion work – and by extension emotional labour – is considered to be gendered (Duncombe and Marsden, 1993), there did not seem to be any differentiation in the requirement to perform emotional labour between male and female children. While the performance of emotional labour seemed to be a requirement of (many) children growing up in Commercial Homes:

> He's got to learn those social skills. (Interview 6, female B & B owner)

It was not done without some advantage accruing to the children. Following (Bolton and Boyd's, 2003) consideration of the way in which the worker calculates their own returns from the performance of emotional labour in a commercial setting, children showed agency by the manner in which they engaged with the emotional labour demands of the family business. They could show resistance by doing the minimum required, or benefit either economically by making money for themselves through tips or philanthropically by seeing their emotional labour as a 'gift' to either the business or themselves. As such, the performance of emotional labour by children for their family business appeared less of a situation of the former's passive exploitation and more one of mutual advantage (or at least mutual exploitation) for parents, children and guests alike (Seymour, 2005). With regard to the consideration of intimate consumptions, the emotional labour of children in Commercial Homes provides an atypical but stark domestically-located example of the intersection of emotions and economic forms of exchange.

## Displaying the family in commercial homes

Reflecting the fluidity of contemporary intimate relationships, the focus in family studies and hospitality/tourism research investigating family holidays has for the past two decades been less on family forms and more on family activities. Global North family studies have shown a widespread adoption of Morgan's concept of family practices – the 'doing' of family (1996, p. 186). Through these practices, families are able to represent the family-like quality of their relationships regardless of their biological or social constitution. Families in Commercial Homes carry out family practices by performing the everyday activities of family life which are embedded in the discourse of intimacy that identify the actions as 'doing' family. It is the atypical location in which these practices are enacted which results in them being inverted as outlined above.

Developing Morgan's work on family practices, (Finch, 2007) stated that due to the range of family forms which can exist, these activities not only need to be done but, on occasion, need to be *seen* to be done. That is they need to have a quality of 'display' to an audience in order to emphasise and sustain the familial nature of the relationships. Hence she introduced the concept of Family Display: 'the process by which individuals, and groups of individuals, convey to each other and to relevant audiences that certain of their actions do constitute "doing family things" and thereby confirm that these relationships are "family relationships"' (Finch, 2007, p. 67). The audience for such displays consist of both family members and others and the location of display can be in private or public spaces. In the intervening years since it was first proposed the concept of family display has been enthusiastically adopted and interrogated within family studies with more than 200 citations of the article to date and an edited collection dedicated to its review and development (Dermott and Seymour, 2011).

How then might family display be applied to the Commercial Home, a location where there are multiple audiences and multiple activities? I have suggested (Seymour, 2011a) that in Commercial Homes, as with families in purely domestic settings, there are instances of family practices between family members although they are constructed around the spatial and temporal requirements of the business as outlined earlier in this chapter. There will also be family displays which (due to the building's dual purpose as a home/workplace) take place in a business setting with audiences which may consist of family members and/or guests and other workers in the establishment. For example, family pictures and mementos may be displayed in guest lounges. These will no doubt be carefully chosen aesthetically-pleasing images, conveying an idealised view of the family in appropriately classed activities (Rose, 2010). Conversely, out of season family occasions may be hosted in the hotel or boarding house due to the number of bedrooms/function rooms available.

In addition though, and precisely due to the spatial nature of the location as a *family-run* hotel, pub or boarding house, the host family must present a display as the Commercial Home Family. Hence the mundane activities of family production and reproduction, such as eating meals, take place but in a manner which is appropriate to the Commercial Home Family as I shall illustrate below. As Morgan (1996) says, interactive activities can have more than one intent. Here displaying the Commercial Home Family addresses both the family and the business agendas. Alongside the display of 'this is my family and it works' as outlined by (Finch, 2007), the host family are also showing 'this is my family business and it works'. As such, this process exemplifies the combination of family and consumption practices which is at the core of this volume albeit from a consideration of those who service the leisure consumption of others.

In spatial terms, the family in the Commercial Home are occupying both their own homescape and the hospitality establishment's servicescape, that is the shared physical setting of a business (Bitner, 1992; Hall, 2009). Thus the family meal in the hotel dining room is a family practice of feeding, a family display of shared mealtimes and hence togetherness, but also a site of Commercial Home Family display often, as (Hall, 2009) suggests, demonstrating to guests how to behave 'properly' (for the hospitality establishment's aspirational market segment) during meals.

I have also proposed that there are specific aspects about the display of the Commercial Home Family which make it distinct from other family displays (Seymour, 2011a). The host family is displayed as part of the economic process of operating a family-run hotel, pub or boarding house. As one hotel owner put it:

> Rather than us being these figures kind of behind the business, I think it makes us more real to them, you know, *we are a family.* (Interview 17, female hotel owner, my emphasis)

It can be argued that, compared to a purely domestic setting, the need for family display in the Commercial Home is increased since the presence of a family is one of the establishment's marketing strategies (Seymour and Green, 2009). The forms of display in a family-run business are not necessarily different from those in a private home, but they become *essential* rather than optional due to the commercial nature of the context. In addition, they must be made absolutely explicit to ensure that they are 'effective'; that is, that the audience appropriately constitute (read) the meanings they are intended to convey (Finch, 2007, p. 66). These meanings are that a family live here in this homely location but that the guests come first. It must be made clear to the audience of 'relevant others' (Finch, 2007), which here consist of guests, staff and other family members, that, while they may be present, family members are in no way privileged over paying customers. Hence the Commercial Home Family will need to be hyper-visible but also make a clear show of 'displayed reticence' where they are, for example, in the dining room but seated at the worst tables and served last at mealtimes, or they are clean but not seen to be using the bathrooms at times of high demand (Interview 5, male ex-hotel owner).

Depending on the age of the members of the family, this 'displayed reticence' at mealtimes could be through a conscious adoption of the mechanism of 'Family Hold Back' where the Commercial Home Family waits until all the guests are served (Seymour, 2011a). Children of hoteliers were aware of these Commercial Home Family display demands (and that they differed from the displays of 'normal' families) but recognised them as an essential component of growing up in a family hotel.

> I suppose sometimes I felt that the best things whatever they were, the best cuts of meat for example, would go to the guests and, talking to other children, their parents would always try and get the best for the family. It's such a small quantity in terms of the whole, we managed without. (Interview 4, adult son of ex-hotel owner)

Where the children of the hosts were very young, they may not consciously display themselves but the display of a Commercial Home Family could be managed:

> They used to get plonked on table while we were serving meals and, I [was] just saying to somebody this morning, in hindsight we should have fed them first and then we wouldn't have had them saying 'I'm hungry, Mummy, I want something to eat' and my Dad'd be saying

'Oh for goodness sake, shut up till we're finished serving the visitors'. (Interview 12, female hotel owner)

However, the danger with hypervisibility, especially with children, is that displaying family can reveal a family that *doesn't* work or that feedback by the audience on the family display is negative. For the Commercial Home Family, this could be due to an assessment by the guests of perceived misbehaviour, damage to their goods or insufficient 'displayed reticence' by the host family. While this could result in economic conse-quences for the family in Commercial Homes, such financial outcomes may be less severe or violent than the responses to other displays which do not achieve legitimacy by reference to heteronormative discourses as has been shown in research on families in the areas of sexuality and migration (Heaphy, 2011; Seymour and Walsh, 2013). Further research is required on situations where family display does not result in positive outcomes.

The 'displayed reticence' of the Commercial Home Family is different from the decisions *not* to display discussed by Almack in her interviews with lesbian mothers (2007). Her work provides examples where choices were made as to whether or not family displays would be enacted in public. In contrast, 'displayed reticence' is a deliberate display of a family 'holding back'. Clearly as the above quotation from a hotel owner shows, the need to display the Commercial Home Family can conflict with the family practice of feeding and paying attention to children and may explain why a small number of proprietors and publicans chose to keep their homelife and work activities spatially discrete despite them occurring in the same location. As a result, their children were invisible rather than involved in 'displayed reticence' but this choice could have had economic implications arising from the guest's interpretations of the reasons why children were absent from the commercial premises:

Even when we lived in the pub, there were people who saw us being odd, and snobbish because we wouldn't let our kids socialise in the pub. [The customers asked] 'What's wrong with our kids then?'. (Interview 9, male ex-publican)

The need to display the Commercial Home Family has temporal vari-ations. Clearly when the hotel or boarding house was out of season or during public house closing times, the requirement to display to an audience of guests or staff ceased although the family may still display to other family members. Similarly, there would be particular times in the days when the hospitality establishment was open when display was either mandatory, such as during shared meal times, or part of good business practice, for example, family members being present when guests were first arriving or departing from the business.

These temporal demands of the business correspond with Finch's 'degrees of intensity' (2007, p. 72) when the requirement for family display is heightened. Finch suggested this can be when family circumstances change but it can also be when ideological discourses of the family and intimate lives are contested. This can take place in a number of contexts such as in Doucet's research on fathers as the main child carer (2011), Almack's study of lesbian mothers (2007, 2011) or, as in my study, when a family are living in a workplace. All exemplify that intensity is not necessarily about changing events in the lives of individual families, but can be about being perceived by others as going against heteronormative ideals. In my research, such counter discursive identities would constitute not living out family life in a purely domestic setting. In addition, families in Commercial Homes have cyclical changing identities rather than necessarily longitudinal ones. These are daily, weekly, and seasonal and may include the transition from a long-term family member to a hospitality worker. For each transition, change must be actively demonstrated and renegotiated as Finch (p. 72) suggests but in an iterative rather than linear manner.

However, a further issue arises. These periods of intensity in hospitality establishments require a family display because they are revealing a family living in an atypical spatial location, that of a business. Yet if the family carried out a normative family display in the hotel (i.e. not holding back) this would be detrimental to the business. The display of family they are required to do as part of their business practices appears to portray the normative family for marketing purposes. However, the family displays actually required by the business are those of the Commercial Home Family with its mandatory nature and its mix of hypervisibility and 'displayed reticence'. This then is itself transgressive of the ideological family it seeks to portray.

The very marketing device that family-run hotels, pubs and boarding houses sell themselves on, their normative 'familyness', is not found in their (inverted) family practices, their family displays (which take place in a business setting) or paradoxically in the business practice of displaying the Commercial Home Family. Indeed the act of running a Commercial Home means that the practices and displays of the host family contest the ideological image of the family they seek to market and hence are potentially subversive. It has long been recognised that the reality of the situation in which people 'do' family (the family they live with) often differs from the ideal to which they aspire, that is the 'imagined family we live by' (Gillis, 1996, p. xv). The issue here for the Commercial Home Family is that the presentation of homeliness and imagined family for which they accept money, can only be achieved by activities which make the attainment of these ideals impossible. Instead, the practices and displays which constitute the Commercial Family, result in a further reconstitution of the existing discourses of family life. To explain fully, requires a consideration of the processes included in family practices, the relationship between the concepts of family practices and family display and discussion of how these processes are enacted in the spatialities of consumption (Gregson and Rose, 2000).

## Family practices and family displays: engaging with activities and discourses

Family Practices include a consideration both of the activities of everyday family life and the discourses of the family. As Morgan puts it 'practices and discourses, the families we live with and the families we live by, are mutually implicated in each other' (Morgan, 2011, p. 68). Families reproduce themselves literally and ideologically. Thus Morgan (2011, p. 69) states that when engaging with 'the everyday and possibly routine family practices' one is also looking 'towards more public discursive constructions' of families. The family in the Commercial Home then will be engaging with ideological discourses of the family when performing their family practices. However as has been shown, the needs of the business results in these practices being significantly different from those of a 'normal' or 'proper' family resulting in a contestation of the dominant discourse.

Following this argument through to family displays, Finch's concept has taken 'the approach of family practices as its start point' (Morgan 2011, p. 61). It follows then that, conceptually, family displays consist of both the activities of the specific displays and the familial discourses within which they are situated – and against which they are judged successful or otherwise. The fact that this dual constitution of displays is not explicitly articulated in Finch's seminal article (2007) may explain why the concept has been critiqued as being overly agentic (James and Curtis, 2010). In relation to the topic of this chapter, the family displays which those in hotels, pubs and boarding houses carry out among family members to show that they are still 'a family which works' despite the business setting, are disruptive of the normative familial ideology. This is spatially because they occur in an atypical dual work/home location, temporally due to their inversion of 'proper' family-centred time (Gillis, 1996) and in terms of the atypical performance of gendered emotional labour as illustrated above. In addition, the business practice of displaying the Commercial Home Family (which has been shown to have unusual elements not found in 'normal' family displays) again transgresses the normative discourse of privileging family members over strangers as shown by the quotes below:

> Family meals, *after the guests always*. (Interview 5, male ex-hotel owner, my emphasis)
>
> Whenever I came home the guests were always more important than me. (Interview 13, adult son of ex-hotel owners and hotel owner)
>
> He's had to learn, you know, that the work has to come first. (Interview 6, female hotel owner)

Through the activities of family practices and displays, while drawing on a discourse of 'familyness' and normality, the families in Commercial Homes subvert this normative discourse through their 'unconventionality' (Finch, 2007). Heaphy (2011) focuses on gendered, classed, age and 'raced' dimensions of families which are viewed as unconventional against a white middle-class heterosexual norm. In this chapter, I have shown that we also need to consider spatial dimensions of family diversity rather than assuming the home is only a domestic location of consumption and production. For families in Commercial Homes the lived experience of 'familyness' is of inverted timetables, public spaces in the home and an enforced reticence on the part of family members. As such, their activities reinscribe rather than reproduce the ideological discourse from which they draw, making their actions transgressive at the discursive as well as at the practical level. As Heaphy (2011, p. 21) says display can be linked to reproducing the family as an institution but can also involve 'critical, resistive and creative operations of power'. The dual spatial nature of the Commercial Home calls forth particular family practices and displays from the host family but in doing so creates spaces where inverted family practices, fluid boundaries and hypervisibility become commonly performed. Such spaces then both draw on and make their own contribution to citational practices (Gregson and Rose, 2000) of family and consumption resulting in 'critical possibilities in different directions' (p. 447). An interrogation of family practices and displays has thus shown the transgressive potential of the Commercial

Home Family since they are 'constitutive of family and relational experience and not merely reflective of it' (Heaphy, 2011, p. 32).

## Conclusion

This chapter has outlined the importance of considering family leisure from the viewpoint of those who service rather than consume the carnivalesque. By doing so, it has shown that the processes of family practices and the tools of family display are used by families in Commercial Homes as in other homes, but that the specific outcomes of these processes look very different from those normatively ascribed to the domestic sphere.

Morgan (2011) has suggested that one way that the research employing the concept of family displays can be developed is to look at instances where display is being used to convey a particular type of family rather than just a family that works. That is to consider not just displaying family but displaying Family. Here the research would focus on 'the deployment of family members in displaying the idea of and the core values attached to family' (p. 63) and he presents as an example the Christian Family. The discussion in this chapter has addressed this proposed development in conceptual understanding by looking at the display of the Commercial Home Family. Unlike Morgan's example of the Christian Family, where the activity of display reinforces the discourse of a particular set of family values, the display of the Commercial Home Family serves to disrupt the discourse from which it appears to draw. This may be because it is in reality a business practice rather than a family practice with only a presentation of 'familyness', which is commercially expedient.

The tension for families living in hotels, pubs and boarding houses is that they are living in sites of multiple activities and attempting to manage the demands of both family and business practices. As such, they bring into stark relief the realities of the work/life balance and widen the conception of the domestic sphere as a place of consumption. Indeed they provide an empirical example of Gregson and Rose's (2000) call to investigate the 'multiple subject positions in spaces of consumption' (p. 447). Commercial Homes then have proved a particularly rich topic of investigation for considering the combination of family and consumption research. Analysis in this area has served to broaden the definition of spaces of domestic consumption and show how the everyday experiences of those who service the leisure activities of others can contribute to the developing discourse of family lives.

# Note

1. The interviews were funded by the Millennium Commission and conducted as part of the 'Looking Back, Looking Forward' project carried out by the North Yorkshire Museums Department. I am grateful to the project's organiser, Karen Snowden, the interviewers and particularly the interviewees, who allowed their thoughts and words to be passed on to other researchers.

# References

Adkins, L. (1995) *Gendered Work, Sexuality, Family and the Labour Market*. Bristol: Open University Press.

Almack, K. (2007) 'Out and About: Negotiating the Process of Disclosure of Lesbian Parenthood', *Sociological Research Online*, 12(1). http://www.socresonline.org.uk/12/1/lmack.html

Almack, K. (2011) 'Display Work: Lesbian Parent Couples and their Families of Origin Negotiating New Kin Relationships' in *Displaying Families*, E. Dermott and J. Seymour (eds), pp. 102–118. Basingstoke: Palgrave Macmillan.

Becker, S., Aldridge, J. and Dearden, C. (1998) *Young Carers and their Families*. Oxford: Blackwell.

Bitner, M.J. (1992) 'Servicescapes: The Impact of Physical Surroundings on Customers and Employees', *The Journal of Marketing*, 56, 57–71.

Bolton, S. and Boyd, C. (2003) 'Trolley Dolly or Skilled Emotion Manager? Moving on from Hochschild's Managed Heart', *Work, Employment and Society*, 17(2), 289–308.

Crang, P. (1997) 'Performing the Tourist Product' in *Touring Cultures: Transformations of Travel and Theory*, C. Rojek and J. Urry (eds), pp. 137–154. London: Routledge.

Dermott, E. and Seymour, J. (2011) (eds) *Displaying Families*. Basingstoke: Palgrave Macmillan.

Doucet, A. (2011) '"It's Just Not Good for a Man to Be Interested in Other People's Children": Fathers, Public Displays of Care, and "Relevant Others"' in *Displaying Families*, E. Dermott and J. Seymour (eds), pp. 81–101. Basingstoke: Palgrave Macmillan.

Duncombe, J. and Marsden, D. (1993) 'Love and Intimacy: The Gender Division of Emotion and "Emotion Work"', *Sociology*, 27(2), 221–241.

Edensor, T. (2007) 'Mundane Mobilities, Performances and Spaces of Tourism', *Social and Cultural Geography*, 8(2), 199–215.

Finch, J. (2007) 'Displaying Families', *Sociology*, 41(1), 65–81.

Gabb, J. (2008) *Researching Intimacy in Families*. Basingstoke: Palgrave Macmillan.

Gillis, J.R. (1996) *A World of Their Own Making: Myth, Ritual and the Quest for Family Values*. Cambridge, Massachusetts: Harvard University Press.

Gregson, N. and Rose, G. (2000) 'Taking Butler Elsewhere: Performativities, Spatialities and Subjectivities', *Environment and Planning D: Society and Space*, 18, 433–452.

Haldrup, M. and Larsen, J. (2003) 'The Family Gaze', *Tourist Studies*, 3(1), 23–46.

Hall, C. M. (2009) 'Sharing Space with Visitors: The Servicescape of the Commercial Exurban Home' in *Commercial Homes in Tourism. An International Perspective*, P. A. Lynch, A. McIntosh and H. Tucker (eds), pp. 60–72. London: Routledge.

Heaphy, B. (2011) 'Critical Relational Displays' in *Displaying Families*, E. Dermott and J. Seymour (eds), pp. 19–37. Basingstoke: Palgrave Macmillan.

Hochschild, A. (1983) *The Managed Heart: Commercialization of Human Feeling*. Berkeley: University of California Press.

James, A. and Curtis, P. (2010) 'Family Displays and Personal Lives', *Sociology*, 44(6), 1163–1180.

Lofgren, O. (1999) *On Holiday. A History of Vacationing*. London: University of California Press.

Lynch, P. A. (2005) 'The Commercial Home Enterprise and Host: a United Kingdom Perspective', *International Journal of Hospitality Management*, 24(4), 533–553.

Lynch, P. A., McIntosh, A. and Tucker, H. (eds) (2009) *Commercial Homes in Tourism. An International Perspective*. London: Routledge.

Martens, L. and Casey, E. (eds) (2007) *Gender and Consumption: Domestic Cultures and the Commercialisation of Everyday Life*. Abingdon, Oxon: Ashgate.

McIntosh, I., Dorrer, N., Punch, S. and Emond, R. (2011) '"I Know We Can't Be a Family, but as Close as You Can Get": Displaying Families within An Institutional Context' in *Displaying Families*, E. Dermott and J. Seymour, pp. 175–196. Basingstoke: Palgrave Macmillan.

Morgan, D. H. J. (1996) *Family Connections: An Introduction to Family Studies*. Cambridge: Polity Press.

Morgan, D. H. J. (2011) *Rethinking Family Practices*. Basingstoke: Palgrave Macmillan.

Pritchard, A. and Morgan, N. (2006) 'Hotel Babylon? Exploring Hotels as Liminal Sites of Transition and Transgression', *Tourism Management*, 27(5), 762–772.

Rose, G. (2010) *Doing Family Photography: The Domestic, the Public and the Politics of Sentiment*. Farnham: Ashgate.

Schanzel, H., Yeoman, I. and Backer, E. (eds) (2012) *Family Tourism. Multiple Perspectives*. Bristol: Channel View Publishers.

Seymour, J. (2005) 'Entertaining Guests or Entertaining the Guests: Children's Emotional Labour in Hotels, Pubs and Boarding Houses' in *The Politics of Childhood. International Perspectives, Contemporary Developments*, J. Goddard, S. McNamee, A. James and A. James (eds), pp. 90–106. London: Palgrave Macmillan.

Seymour, J. (2007) 'Treating the Hotel like a Home: The Contribution of Studying the Single Location Home/Workplace', *Sociology*, 41(6), 1097–1114.

Seymour, J. (2011a) '"Family Hold Back": Displaying Families in the Single Location Home/Workplace'in *Displaying Families*, E. Dermott and J. Seymour (eds), pp. 160–174. Basingstoke: Palgrave Macmillan.

Seymour, J. (2011b) 'On Not Going Home at the End of the Day: Spatialized Discourses of Family Life in Single Location Home /Workplaces' in *Geographies of Children, Youth and Families: An International Perspective*, L. Holt (ed.), pp. 108–120. London: Routledge.

Seymour, J. and Green, T. (2009) 'Selling the Family?: Family Imagery in Holiday Advertising', Turning Personal Conference, Morgan Centre for the Study of Relationships and Personal Life, University of Manchester, 16–17, September.

Seymour, J. and Walsh, J. (2013) 'Displaying Families, Migrant Families and Community Connectedness: The Application of an Emerging Concept in Family Life', *Journal of Comparative Family Studies*, Special Issue on 'Family and Migration', 44 (6),. 689–698.

Sibley, D. (1995) 'Families and Domestic Routines: Constructing the Boundaries of Childhood' in *Mapping the Subject: Geographies of Cultural Transformation*, S. Pile and N. Thrift (eds), pp. 123–137. London: Routledge.

Silva, EB. (2007) 'Gender, Class, Emotional Capital and Consumption in Family Life' in *Gender and Consumption: Domestic Cultures and the Commercialisation of Everyday Life*, L. Martens and E. Casey (eds), pp. 141–159. Abingdon, Oxon: Ashgate.

Toerien, M. and Kitzinger, C. (2007a) 'Emotional Labour in the Beauty Salon. Turn Design of Task-directed Talk', *Feminism and Psychology*, 17(2), 162–172.

Toerien, M. and Kitzinger, C. (2007b) 'Emotional Labour in Action. Navigating Multiple Involvements in the Beauty Salon', *Sociology*, 41(4), 645–667.

Whittle, R., Walker, M., Medd, W. and Mort, M. (2012) 'Flood of Emotions: Emotional Work and Long-term Disaster Recovery', *Emotion, Space and Society*, 5(1), 60–69.

# 6
# Belonging in Difficult Family Circumstances: Emotions, Intimacies and Consumption

*Sarah Wilson*

Much work on young people's material and consumer cultures has focused on the relatively affluent, and on those living with their parents. This chapter is concerned with the often more problematic material and affective circumstances of young people whose family difficulties have led them to be 'looked after' by the state. In particular, it focuses on the significance of material objects in helping to construct (or not) a sense of belonging, however ambivalent, in often successive places of residence. Further, while there has been much policy and research discussion of young people's use of consumer items affording access to the internet and other electronic means of communication (Livingstone and Haddon, 2008; Livingstone et al., 2012; Osvaldsson, 2011), this chapter focuses on the importance of items of lesser monetary but often great affective or 'sentimental' value. As such, it draws on and develops recent literature on the role of consumption and material culture (Miller, 2008; 2010) in producing the self as a person who 'belongs' (May, 2013), and who can 'display' a family (Finch, 2007).

In addition, this chapter discusses the research interview itself, in particular where, as in the project discussed, visual (and audial) methods are employed, as a place in which families and relationships may be 'displayed', through photographs of material objects and places or drawings of 'ideal homes'. The chapter also explores the consumption of the artefacts produced in such research. On the one hand, these artefacts are analysed as possible means of drawing sympathetic attention to the material and relational absences and fragility associated with difficult family circumstances. It is argued that these items, if carefully used, have the potential to evoke the type of 'haunting' in a wider audience discussed

by Gordon (2008) as a potential prompt for changes in the public imagination of groups whose difficult circumstances tend currently to be
understood in individual terms. At the same time, the potentially more
negative effects of research council requirements to evidence research
'impact' and to archive all data produced are addressed. In particular,
the potential for archived photographic data to fix and reinforce stig-
matised representations of difficult circumstances, and by extension of
those associated with them, is discussed.

The next section will introduce the study on which this chapter is
based, and the sensory methods (Pink, 2009; Rose, 2007) it employed,
before discussing participants' material cultures in terms of ideas of
'haptic belonging' (May, 2013), practices of family 'display' (Finch,
2007) and 'haunting' (Gordon, 2008).

## Methodological background

The ESRC-funded project on which this chapter primarily draws was
a qualitative study of the sensory and spatial construction of (not)
belonging, whether positive, negative or ambivalent, with currently
or formerly 'looked after' children in Scotland. From 2011–2012, the
researchers worked with 22 young people (13 men, 9 women aged 10–23
but primarily 10–18) from urban, rural and island communities across
Scotland, recruited through voluntary sector organisations or statu-
tory social work services. As such, the sample reflected consumption in
different geographical contexts, including less researched remote islands.
In addition, the sample reflected a variety of official living arrangements. Four participants were living independently having left care, but
all had experienced a range of different, and often successive, official
placements, including foster, kinship, secure and residential care. All
the young people participated in the first interview and 14 completed
a second interview. In these interviews, photos, sound recordings, and
drawings produced by the respondents were discussed. Subsequently, six
young people also participated in producing films and music to dissemi-
nate project themes.[1]

The interviews and the visual and audial methods employed in this
project built upon the researchers' previous work (including Milne
et al., 2012; Wilson et al., 2012a, b; Wilson, 2014) and guidance from a
project advisory group that included a young woman with experience of
multiple, diverse living arrangements in adolescence and subsequently
of being a kinship carer.[2] Ethical advice and approval was received from
a University ethics committee, and from several of the organisations

through which respondents were recruited. The first interviews were preceded by an introductory meeting in which potential participants were talked through the researchers' broad directions for taking photos and recording sounds (what Rose (2007) calls the interview 'running script'), as well as the ethical implications of taking pictures that might identify or incriminate themselves or others. In these interactive sessions, potential participants were also given the chance to play with the equipment, to ask questions, and to consent (or not) to differing potential uses of the data produced.

In preparation for the first interviews, participants were asked to record sounds (and one musical track) that were important to them and to take photographs of their favourite and least favourite spaces (where they felt most and least 'at home'). Reflecting the literature on different types of physical and less tangible spaces, the script did not limit the participants to where they lived, nor to conventional domestic spaces. Such 'photo-elicitation' – as well as drawing exercises – has often been used with children and young people in research into the meanings they give to particular places (Morrow, 2001; Rasmussen, 2004). However, unlike in this project, such exercises have often reproduced conventional distinctions between the 'home' and public spaces with explorations of the former limited to domestic spaces (Wilson, 2014). If participants did not want to, or could not, take a photograph of a particular place, they were asked to download an Internet image to represent it, or this was done during the interview itself. Particularly relevant to this chapter on consumption, they were also asked to take photographs of three highly personally significant objects or 'things'. The resulting visual and audial data or artefacts formed the basis for the first interview discussion. In the second interviews, participants' first interview data and responses were revisited. They were also invited to discuss music tracks, which contained messages they wanted others to hear, and to complete drawings of their ideal and current living places. The use of these methods was 'multi-sensorial' in the sense that it was not expected that the data produced from more visual methods would primarily reflect visual experience, or, indeed, that sensory experience can be so divided. As Rose (2007, pp. 238–239) argues, photos 'carry flesh and blood', encouraging talk that would not have been possible in their absence. Audial methods have been employed much less frequently. (Allett, 2010). The author drew on DeNora's (2000) and Bull's (2007) research into the uses of music in everyday life, and her sense of the importance of music and sound in general to lived experience, to develop the innovative audial methods employed in this project.

The respondents' photographs, sounds, drawings and music tracks were discussed in very loosely-structured, largely participant-led and often long (1–4 hours) interviews. Pink (2009, p. 9) advocates the use of participatory 'practices' that 'seek to understand and engage with other people's worlds through sharing activities, practices and inviting new forms of expression'. While we did not 'do' the activities identified alongside the participants in quite the manner Pink advocates, the process of downloading and looking at the data they produced seemed to lend a sense of non-threatening proximity and collective, creative endeavour to the interviews, providing insights into their attempts to create a feeling of belonging across a broad range of spaces. In addition to producing rich data, the use of such participatory methods, in which direct questioning employing emotive terms such as 'belonging' itself was avoided, seemed less intrusive than some of the author's previous experiences of conventional face-to-face interviewing (Wilson, 2014). At the same time however, later discussions with one older participant and the subsequent process of writing about the project suggested the potential for some of the images taken, and discussions of these, to 'stay with' or haunt (Gordon, 2008) the involved parties long beyond the project's practical 'end' in both positive and potentially more negative ways. This experience lead to further reflections related to the 'impact' of research projects.

This chapter will draw particularly on discussions of the photographs respondents took of favourite objects as well as material relating to photographs of spaces and drawings of 'ideal homes'. In the following sections, the project findings in relation to the artefacts produced will be discussed in relation to ideas of 'haptic' (or sensory) belonging (May, 2013), 'display' (Finch, 2007) and 'haunting' (Gordon, 2008) respectively.

## Haptic belonging, display and haunting

### Creating a sense of haptic or sensory belonging

The respondents photographed and discussed a wide variety of objects. These included many electronic items including computers and mobile phones, the significance of which in terms of communication, engaging with music and as techniques of self-care is discussed elsewhere (Wilson, 2015 forthcoming). In some instances, articles associated with substance or alcohol use were highlighted. Many objects had no such practical significance in everyday life, however, and often little monetary value.

These items included teddies and other soft toys, even among older respondents, as well as photos (of birth family members, former foster carers, siblings), a guitar, a family tartan, a set of samurai swords, wallpaper and several (sometimes broken) clocks. The significance of some of these items was further underlined over the course of the project as the circumstances of the participants changed.

The importance of 'transitional objects' has long been recognised in social work practices such as creating 'memory boxes' for the deposit of significant objects and 'life story work' to create records of little-remembered periods (Brodzinsky et al., 1998; Baynes, 2008). The importance of such work is often explained in terms of the difficulty that bereaved children, or those removed from their family, may have to remember or find out about significant people and important events, as well as their need to work through difficult past circumstances. The latter is also associated in psychological terms with developing 'emotional literacy' or the ability to express and discuss emotions.

In the context of this project, sociological work on belonging, relationships and material culture also proved helpful in thinking through the data. According to May, '[b]elonging can be characterised as feeling at ease with one's self and one's social, cultural, relational and material contexts' (2013, p. 14). Many of the items or keepsakes discussed seemed to be associated with a sense of 'haptic' (or sensory) belonging (May, 2013) or 'home' through their visibility, texture and smells. Drawing on Miller (2008), May argues for example that '[o]bjects can store and possess emotions, and can, for example, represent deceased people and allow the bereaved to continue a relationship with them even after death' (2013, p. 144). In this project, teddies and other soft toys provided something physical to hug and even to talk to. Furthermore, some respondents claimed that these toys also carried the familiar smells of important people including relatives, former social workers and others. Often it seemed unlikely that such an item could have retained a smell over so many years, but the 'reality' seemed less important than their imagination of this continued, tangible presence.

Similarly, in her first interview, Channel[3] (18, foster care) presented several photos of her aunt's living room, commenting at length on the 'feel' of the décor and colour scheme there, particularly the wallpaper. She spoke about the calming effects of this wallpaper during the day when she liked to spend time there alone, and at night when the silvery flowers on the darker background shone and the room was filled with people, many of whom were her relatives:

SW: Is that one of your favourite places...(A-ha). It is? What do you like about it?

CH: The room...the colours, the theme...

SW: The theme and the colours.

CH: I just like it. It's my favourite colours.

SW: Kind of brown?

CH: It's like silver and blue.

SW: A-ha. And is it soothing?

CH: It's calm and relaxing...

SW: OK. So when you go round there, is it usually full of your friends?

CH: No, just at night. But I'm in it myself during the day. To calm down....Aye, can you see the colours now?...(Yes) that's the colours that get lights that I like.

Through our discussion it emerged that she associated this place and the colour scheme –which she had also tried to reproduce in her re-decoration of the friend's flat where she spent most of her time- with her recently deceased and much-loved grandfather. This connection, and the fact that this was one of the few places to which she had had continual access, and which had not changed over a long period during which she had been moved between various foster placements, was very important to her. Channel explained the significance of the room in this photo in very sensory terms therefore that seemed to reflect May's idea of haptic belonging. At the same time, the photo itself may be interpreted as a means of 'displaying' family connections to the interviewer (and beyond). This idea of 'display' will be explored in the following section.

### 'Displaying' family at home, on the move and in the interview

Finch's work on the importance of everyday and routine 'display' as 'an activity which characterizes contemporary families' (2007, pp. 65–66) was also useful in interpreting the items photographed and ideal places drawn and discussed by the participants. Finch's emphasis on the importance of 'display' in empirical and conceptual terms draws on Morgan's work on 'family practices' (1996). The latter shifted understandings of 'family' away from particular structures to focus on the way family and other relationships are 'done' in everyday activity or routines; '[t]he focus is on the quality of relationships, and how they are expressed in practical actions therefore' (Finch, 2007, p. 70). Drawing on these arguments, Finch (2007, p. 66 emphasis in the original) contends that '*families need to be "displayed" as well as "done"*' and further (2007, p. 66) that 'the meaning of one's actions has to be both conveyed to and understood by relevant others if those actions are to be understood as constituting "family practices"'. She provides several examples of 'display' including non-resident fathers' activities with their children post-parental separation, relationship narratives and 'keepsakes' such as 'photographs or domestic artefacts' (2007, p. 77). In the context of this study, photographs of keepsakes and the participants' narratives about them proved particularly important.

Finch (2007, p. 77) also refers to particular circumstances, where 'relationships move further away from those which are readily recognisable as constituting family relationships', in which display may be particularly important. In particular, she mentions same-sex and other 'chosen' families, separated households post-divorce and transnational family relationships in which 'family' and 'household' do not (easily) coincide. Crucially, she also argues that 'the process of seeking legitimacy entails displaying one's chosen family relationships to relevant others and having them accepted' (2007, p. 71) and that '[b]eing *recognized* as having 'a family' just like anyone else is an essential part of this agenda' (2007, p. 74: emphasis in original). For Illouz (2007), being able to make such a claim and to have it recognised by others, is crucial to the prevalent 'psychoanalytic imagination' of the construction of self and identity. In this way, she argues that in contemporary 'Western' society there has been an increasing ideological emphasis on the centrality of the nuclear family to healthy child development, and that those who cannot lay claim to such a family, may be seen as 'damaged'. For 'looked after' young people who cannot live with their families of origin and/or have very fragile or non-existent relationships with parents who could not care for them as expected, the importance of being able to 'display' some kind of family might be seen as particularly heightened.

However, 'displaying' family is often more difficult for young people than for co-resident adults who tend to have greater control over what is displayed on the semi- public walls of living rooms. Photographs of important people were displayed by participants where they could, and were discussed in their interviews. This display took various forms. Part of the significance of mobile phones, for example, was that photos could be taken and stored on them, transported between different locations and shown to different people there. Several participants also discussed photographs of loved ones that they kept in their bedrooms. Jodie (15, residential care) discussed the photo of her former foster parents and their dog displayed in her room. Through her prominent presentation of this photo in a conventional frame, and through her identification of it as one of her most important items and discussion of it in the interview, Jodie may be seen as asserting her claim to a more conventional family set-up than the one in which she now lived. For example, in her interview she also emphasised that she would be spending her imminent birthday with these foster parents:

> EJ: That's good, that's good. So why have you taken this photo for me?
>
> JODIE: It was just to show you who they [foster parents] were and that was kinda like a good memory, like a memory of them.
>
> EJ: Uh huh, so one of your important objects.
>
> JODIE: Cause I've not got a picture of them on my computer so I thought I'd take a picture of that so I can put it on my computer.
>
> EJ: And is this a photograph?
>
> JODIE: Yeah it's a photograph, it's a photograph in a frame.
>
> EJ: Where does it ... where d'you keep it?
>
> JODIE: In my room ...
>
> EJ: ... Who gave this to you?
>
> JODIE: [Foster parents], they gave me it.
>
> EJ: How did you feel when they gave it to you?
>
> JODIE: Happy!
>
> EJ: Yeah, so it was nice that you had a photo of them?
>
> JODIE: Yeah.
>
> EJ: That's really nice. So they'll be coming for your birthday, doing a big celebration?
>
> JODIE: Yeah, we're going to have a party in the house and after that we're going to go to the cinema.

Several other participants also presented pictures of former foster parents in this way, thus asserting the familial nature of these connections.

An interview with PENFOLD (14, foster care) suggested that items might be displayed for other reasons too. He took a photograph of a guitar hanging on his bedroom wall. His explanation of its significance seemed to relate to maintaining a sense of consistent self from before he could remember and in spite of multiple moves, and of having a talent somewhat separate from his new foster family and from all the many others with whom he had lived. The guitar seemed therefore to

provide a means of displaying a comfortable sense of non- or ambivalent belonging:

> SW: So why did you take a picture of this guitar? Is it specifically this
> guitar or guitars in general?
> PENFOLD: It's just special. I've had that since I was so young
> and...even if it breaks I'll still keep it, it's just an amazing guitar.
> SW: Why is it so amazing?
> PENFOLD: Just cause it's a good memory when I was younger and I
> remember when I used to play it.
> SW: Did you used to play it on your own or did somebody teach you
> to play?
> PENFOLD: On my own.
> SW: Wow! So did you teach yourself to play guitar?
> PENFOLD: Mm hmm, since I was the age of four I taught myself.
> SW: And how did you get hold of this guitar?
> PENFOLD: I don't know.
> SW: It's just always been there?
> PENFOLD: Aye.
> SW: Laughter] and everywhere you've lived you've taken this guitar
> with you?
> PENFOLD: Mm hmm.
> SW: D'you play it much anymore?
> PENFOLD: Mm hmm, I still play it all the time.

Not all such keepsakes referred back to the past or previous living
arrangements. Tiger (10, foster care) had few things from before his
current placement but had taken up his 'adoptive' brother's hobby of
collecting animal ornaments:

> TIGER: I just like lions, I like big cats as well, but I really like all
> animals really.
> EJ: So how long have you been collecting these for?
> TIGER: Started 2010 or something.
> EJ: Is that when you moved here?
> TIGER: No, moved here in about 2008.
> EJ: Okay, so you took a while to see what [your adopted brother] was
> collecting and just see what was what and then you started doing
> it, and d'you think you're gonna carry on collecting?
> TIGER: Yeah.

Tiger presented photos of these items as some of his most important objects in his interview. In this way perhaps, as Finch speculates in relation to 'chosen' families, he seemed to assert his current, non-biological adoptive family as his 'real' and future family, as well as his desire to disassociate himself from a difficult past and to emphasise how happy he was in his current circumstances. Dylan (18, living independently) had fewer such resources with which to assert a past or current family since he had little contact with either his birth family or his former foster mother. However, he did take a picture of an item associated with the latter. He also spoke at some length about nametags, inspired by the television series '24', which he had sent for online emphasising that several of his friends had also ordered them. It is argued that his emphasis on these nametags may be seen as another attempt to display connection into the future, however fragile.

In addition to merely representing the keepsakes the young people displayed primarily in bedrooms, the interviews themselves seemed to provide a further opportunity to display family relationships and to have these recognised or at least recorded. Certain photos, drawings and discussions illustrated this observation particularly well. Mackenzie (14, foster care), for example, insisted on taking a photograph of boxes of birthday presents she was going to send to a brother she saw several times a year. It seemed that she wanted this ephemeral event that illustrated her relationship with him to be recorded in some way. Where the participants were in secure care, everyday display, and indeed taking photos for the project, was more difficult, if not impossible. However, the interviews provided these participants with other activities through which to imagine the possibility of such display and to bring them into existence through discussion and sometimes drawing. For example, Thomas (14, secure unit) could not display pictures of the inherited swords and clan shield that he spoke of as so important to him, but he could discuss them in his interview and identify a space for them imaginatively in his second interview drawings of his ideal home. It may be therefore that in such instances where the resources to affirm family were particularly limited, the interview process provided a rare and valuable opportunity to display family connection.

### Haunting including in the research process

Such findings illustrate then the profound importance of particular items or keepsakes to the participants in terms of both 'haptic' belonging (May, 2013) and the possibility these items provided to 'display' (Finch, 2007) family connections and have them accepted by others. It also seemed that the research process of taking pictures for, and their discussion in, the interview provided important possibilities for display in difficult circumstances. At the same time, the interview discussions pointed to circumstances where holding onto such items and their display might be very difficult, if not impossible. Further, the emotional significance of some of the items portrayed in photos or discussed in interviews could also be double-edged conveying loss and sometimes feelings of emptiness in particular places of residence, as well as connection to past relationships and to good memories, as discussed in the two sections above. In the following section, the capacity of such visual artefacts, produced through research, to draw the attention of viewers- researchers and potentially a broader public- to the lived experience of structural disadvantage is explored. At the same time, the potentially negative effects of this capacity of photos and drawings to 'stay with' participants and viewers beyond the interviews will also be discussed.

In her important book 'Ghostly Matters', Avery Gordon (2008, p. 4) urges sociologists to pay greater attention to the 'complexity' of ordinary experience and to the importance of 'haunting' or (2008, p. 196) 'see[ing] the things and the people who are primarily unseen and banished to the periphery of our social graciousness'. She further argues that it is important that sociologists, through their methods, register some of the aspects and effects of power and disadvantage that do not fit easily into 'neat' sociological categories. Employing characteristically poetic language, she (2008, p. 3) points to the way that power: *can drown you in the present..., cause bodily injury,... harm you without ever seeming to touch you* [and] *arrives in forms that can range from... state terror to "furniture without memories"'* (emphasis added). In her view, 'ghosts', which can represent both loss but also the possibility of different future possibilities, may connect a researcher with such understandings. Drawing on Raymond Williams' (1977) idea of a 'structure of feeling', she also emphasises that a ghost 'articulates *presence*' (1977, p. 135) as the tangled exchange of noisy silences and seething absences. Such a tangle – as object and experience- is 'haunting' (2008, p. 200).

Several of the items photographed and discussed by participants, such as Thomas and Mackenzie for example, might be seen in this way, reflecting the 'seething absence' of the possibility of living with parents or siblings, as well as their attachment to family memories and relationships. Similarly, Dylan's photo of his cat wearing a bell to provide him with company, simultaneously pointed to his love of this cat, but also to his frustration and loneliness. Further, Reggie's (23, living independently) photos of objects tended to emphasise a very individual, solitary identity, rather than connection to, or display of, family or community. For example, in his discussion of a photo of his varnished nails he emphasised how he could not wear nail varnish (an 'important object') in the area in which he lived for fear of being 'gubbed' [beaten up] and how other members of his family had questioned his sexuality when he painted his nails within the home.

Similarly, Reggie included a photograph of a bag to emphasise that he was always on the move between different places, and specifically emphasised that he had few possessions since 'having too much just slows you down'. He also produced several images of his tattoos; uniquely portable mementoes of periods in his life etched on his skin. In his view, these tattoos, even those he no longer liked, were permanent visual representations of his life story. However, his love of tattoos, and the designs he drew for tattoos he could not afford, also seemed to reflect his searching, even a yearning, for an adult, masculine identity, drawing, for example, on Maori culture:

REGGIE: [Laughs] oh that erm started out as a tattoo idea, erm, it was meant to be tribal, erm, tattoos are quite a big thing for me...

SW: Yeah, why d'you like tattoos so much?

REGGIE: I dunno, like, when I was younger it started out as 'that's my way to show I'm a man!' [laughs]

SW: Uh huh, so it's to do with masculinity?

REGGIE: I don't think so anymore, but when it started it was, yeah...

SW: Yeah.

REGGIE: ... it was very much oh well that's your rite of passage so you get a tattoo, okay, and now I don't like my first one, so erm... it's kind of, I don't know... Like the Maoris and all that, they do their tattoos but that's very much a rite of passage, you need to get it or you are not a man, that type of thing.

It seemed that in his reading of them, such traditional cultures presented a more settled and positive sense of belonging and identity than he felt were available to him through his fragile relationship with his own family and 'community'. Indeed, his most positive representations of family were the imaginary or fictitious ones that appeared in the films, computer games and television programmes he discussed prominently among his most 'important things'.

The fragility of some participants' possibilities for display was also illustrated by the loss of important spaces over the course of the project. By the time of her second interview, Channel had lost access to the living room and the décor she loved after an argument with her aunt. She was convinced that she could no longer go back to her aunt/ grandfather's place and felt bereft as a result. She was pale and had self-harmed, and related that before leaving on the fateful night of the argument, she had ripped a piece of the wallpaper from the wall. This strip of prized wallpaper was now stored in a box at her boyfriend's place, out of sight.

This poignant story reinforces the importance to Channel both of her aunt/grandfather's living room and of the opportunity presented by the first interview to display this place and discuss its family connections. However, it also reflects the profound loss associated with losing access to this space and the consequent even greater fragility of her possibilities for displaying family, left as she was with a fragment of wallpaper she could not easily show to others. The photos she had presented happily and proudly in the first interview were now somewhat tainted in retrospect, now charged with a sense of loss. Although subsequent discussions revealed that Channel herself did not see it in this way, the researchers also worried that this sense of loss was reinforced by the second interview itself and potentially by the subsequent storage of the first interview photos in a research archive. Such reflections suggested the potential power, but also risks associated with the creation and storage of such emotionally-loaded visual artefacts in the absence of careful consideration and sufficient contextualisation for subsequent viewers.

For Gordon '[t]o be haunted is to be tied to historical and social effects' (2008, p. 190). In her view, hauntings are important in encouraging thoughts of the possibility of different futures. As part of this argument, she contends that hauntings may provide a further spur to consider how the social structural underpinnings of such experience might become more visible in a political context in which experiences are often not 'recognised as social but taken to be private, idiosyncratic, and even isolating' (2008, p. 132 citing Williams 1977, p. 128). It is cautiously argued that the sensory and imaginative methods used in this project produced data that can highlight such hauntings or the effects of social structural disadvantage, thus restoring some complexity to young lives that tend to be treated reductively and viewed in exclusively problematic terms. For example, both the photographs of Channel's aunt's living room and the wallpaper she later took from it point to important presences and absences over time and to how her own agency in trying to preserve such spaces was constrained not only by others, but also by her lack of material resources. When contextualised by surrounding discussion then, these photos lend not only to an appreciation of the warmth of many of her relationships, but also to an appreciation of their fragility, potentially prompting questions as to why this should be.

The context in which such data are presented is important however. The production of such visual artefacts allowed for the possibility of more innovative communication of results than often follows research reports. Attempts to mobilise such possibilities have included a multi-media installation used at the research launch, practice and policy conferences, and in practitioner training, and a website containing much audio and visual project data. These have been welcomed as 'hitting home' more forcefully than conventional presentations, or at least questioning perceptions of certain aspects of social work processes.[4] It seemed that such short-lived exhibitions, including drawings, films composed of the photos and music produced by participants as at the research launch, opened up conversations for and between the numerous participants present, and carers, practitioners, policymakers and researchers. It may be therefore that such installations have the potential to shift 'policies, politics and public imaginations' (Falconer and Taylor, 2014), in significant, but hard-to-measure, ways.

However, changing perceptions, and more ambitiously, challenging underlying cultures focused on individual behaviour and motivations rather than social structural circumstances, may require much further thought. Notably, the 'haunting' produced by such discussions and artefacts may be double-edged for the participants. As Miller (2008) argues, 'emptiness' within home spaces or lack of material possessions can be associated with a lack of integration into places or relationships. These methods identified such absences in a way that was generally un-intrusive and non-pathologising for the interviewees. Indeed, it was often reported to us that participants really enjoyed the project, and all wanted to complete the second interview, even if this proved impossible to organise in some remote areas. However, some discussions were emotional. One of the older interviewees was upset at the end of his first interview (although he was very happy to complete a second). While it is not argued that such upset can or should be completely avoided, one issue to be considered carefully is that the production of somehow more concrete, often visual artefacts for interviews may 'stay' with interviewees longer than some of their words, especially when stored in an archive. For example, such images, particularly if displayed alone, might in some way solidify or become reified into hard-to-diffuse or escape negative imagery of the interviewees' lives, reinforcing any sense they (and subsequent viewers) might have that things could never change in their lives, in contrast to the imagination of different futures envisaged by Gordon.

Participants' decisions not to comply with the 'running script' in taking or displaying images of places or things they were happy to talk about in their interviews may have reflected similar concerns. Notably, in interview discussion Reggie emphasised a lack of connection with the second hand items of furniture in his flat ('furniture without memories'?) but while he identified it as his 'least favourite place', did not take any photos of this poorly appointed and rather empty bedsit for the project. On reflection, Reggie's non-compliance when it came to providing pictures of the flat he so disliked may have related to a sense that the production of such images might only serve to somehow permanently associate him with it, or to deny his agency and the possibilities of change, however much he felt he had or could move on. Reggie also refused to respond when an agency with which he was involved asked him to provide an update of his circumstances in part to help the author with evidencing the measurable 'impact' of the project for an ESRC impact report.[5] Such a reflection recalls another respondent's feeling of being defined by old reports contained in social work files and read out at children's hearings long after the event. At the same time, Reggie was willing to participate in person at the research launch and produce and discuss drawings to communicate his loneliness later for a very specific project output aimed at convincing policy makers and practitioners to improve particular services. All of these experiences suggest the importance of taking this 'flipside' of 'haunting' into account when considering the 'places' in which to show such artefacts. In particular, they suggest that the anonymised and relatively uncontextualised storage of items in archives may raise different, and potentially more problematic, issues than their more ephemeral but explicated presentation in an exhibition. Notably, although this study cannot present any evidence to this effect, archiving may unintentionally confer a sense of permanence to the circumstances presented in terms both of individual trajectories and in relation to the broader representation and imagination of particular social groups.

## Conclusion

This chapter has focused on intimacies and consumption in a broad sense and among less privileged young people not living in conventional 'family' circumstances. It builds on critical approaches to consumption in its focus on the less affluent, and its exploration of the importance of items with little or no monetary value. Consumption here also includes the use of objects and places belonging to others, a more collective notion of consumption perhaps than often employed. This chapter has highlighted the worth of such consumption to young people in negotiating more difficult emotional and sometimes material circumstances. It illustrates for example how access to certain décors and the presence, feel and smell of such keepsakes, such as teddies, can provide a sense of 'haptic' belonging across many years, retaining a sense of presence, however imaginary, in the face of important absences. It also identifies how the 'display' of such items, including through the medium of the interview process, may further contribute to a sense of belonging by indicating the young person's inclusion within some sort of viable family history, future or place. In addition, this chapter points to the research process itself as providing a further opportunity for the display of important relationships and of comfortable or more ambivalent sense of non-belonging through photos and drawings of important things and places. The importance of this opportunity was accentuated in particularly constrained and difficult circumstances such as secure care from which participants could not access much loved people, places and things to take photographs of them, but could draw them.

The chapter also raises issues connected to the production and 'consumption' of images by researchers, practitioners, policymakers and ultimately, the general public, pointing to how these artefacts may feed into public imaginations of particular issues and groups within society. Notably, it suggests that the visual artefacts produced in such research may 'haunt' the viewer in a different way to conventional research reports. It is argued that it is important for researchers, research councils, and other funders to consider the potential effects of their work on participants in somehow 'freezing' the social and individual imaginary of their potential trajectories. It is possible, for example, that the production of such photos, or their long-term storage in archives, that do not sufficiently contextualise this material, or link easily between the diverse types of data deposited for a participant, might lead to the coagulation of a sense of helpless vulnerability. This possibility that recalls similar critiques of famine photography, of representations of AIDS orphans (Meintjes and Geise, 2006) or 'damaged' children (O'Dell, 2008). In other words, archiving processes may have a reductive effect, removing complexity from the representation of participants' circumstances and denying them the possibility of a more open-ended future. As such, the current focus on the anonymisation of images and transcripts may need to be revised at least in part, to allow for the provision of greater context in relation to individual artefacts, and better linkages between different types of data from a project provided. These concerns have weighed heavily on the author and have made their consideration of research council requirements to archive all material from projects, and the claim of such organisations to be best placed to make decisions as to the sensitivity of data particularly difficult to negotiate. Such concerns also raise questions as to the ways research councils' need to 'evidence' impact in conventionally measurable ways may focus attention away from other options. The experience of this project pointed particularly to the possibilities opened up by more ephemeral exhibitions highlighting the haunting effects of 'seething absences' and structural conditions underlying the participants' complex lives in the way Gordon (2008) argues. It is hoped that further similar discussions and thought will develop ethically sensitive and effective ways of doing so.

## Acknowledgements

The author would like to thank Dr. EJ Milne, the Research Fellow on the project on which this chapter draws, as well as all of the project participants and the workers who helped us with recruitment. The project *Young People Creating Belonging: Spaces, Sounds and Sights* was funded by the Economic and Social Research Council (UK) (RES-061-25-0501).

## Notes

1. To explore data from the project including participant-produced photos, sound recordings, drawings, music and a film, please go to: http://www.researchunbound.org.uk/young-people-creating-belonging/.
2. The advisory group also included representatives of national children's organisations including the SCRA and Children 1st as well as social work and sociology academics with expertise in visual methodologies and theories of personal relationships.
3. Pseudonyms, as chosen and spelt by the respondents, are used throughout this chapter.
4. For a generous account of the research launch/ exhibition installation please see: http://blogs.iriss.org.uk/apmusings.
5. The ESRC has recently introduced a requirement that funded researchers file an impact report 12 months after the end of the funded period of a project. Researchers must evidence ways in which their project has had 'impact' beyond academia, for example through influencing policy and practice in measurable ways and are generally required to archive their data – including photos for the use of future researchers and others. These reports are then used by the research councils to justify their own activity to government.

# References

Allett, N. (2010) *Sounding Out: Using Music Elicitation in Qualitative Research* (Realities Working Paper 14). Manchester: National Centre for Research Methods.

Baynes, P. (2008) 'Untold Stories: A Discussion of Life Story Work', *Adoption and Fostering*, 32(2), 43–49.

Brodzinsky, D., Smith, D. and Brodzinsky, A. (1998) *Children's Adjustment to Adoption: Developmental and Clinical Issues*. Thousand Oaks: Sage.

Bull, M. (2007) *iPod Culture and Urban Experience*. London: Routledge.

DeNora, T. (2000) *Music in Everyday Life*. Cambridge: Cambridge University Press.

Falconer, E. and Taylor, Y. (2014) 'Making Space for Religion, Youth and Sexuality? Implications for Policies, Politics and Public Imaginations', www://weekscentreforsocialandpolicyresearch.wordpress.com/2014/09/02/making-space-for-religion-youth-and-sexuality-implications-for-policies-politics-and-public-imaginations/

Finch, J. (2007) 'Displaying Families', *Sociology*, 41(1), 65–81.

Gordon, A. (2008) *Ghostly Matters: Haunting and the Sociological Imagination*. London: University of Minneapolis Press.

Illouz, E. (2007) *Cold Intimacies: The Making of Emotional Capitalism*. Cambridge: Polity Press.

Livingstone, S. and Haddon, L. (2008) 'Risky Experiences for Children Online: Charting European Research on Children and the Internet', *Children and Society*, 24, 75–83.

Livingstone, S., Haddon, L. and Görzig, A. (2012) *Children Risk and Safety on the Internet: Research and Policy Challenges in Comparative Perspective*. Bristol: Policy Press.

May, V. (2013) *Connecting Self to Society*. Basingstoke: Palgrave Macmillan.

Meintjes, H. and Giese, S. (2006) 'Spinning the Epidemic: The Making of Mythologies of Orphanhood in the Context of AIDS', *Childhood*, 13(3), 407–30.

Miller, D. (2008) *The Comfort of Things*. Cambridge: Polity.

Miller, D. (2010) *Stuff*. Cambridge: Polity.

Milne, E.J., Mitchelland, C. and De Lange, N. (2012) *The Handbook of Participatory Video*. Lanham, MD: AltaMira Press.

Morgan, D. (1996) *Family Connections: An Introduction to Family Studies*. Bristol: Policy Press.

Morrow, V. (2001) 'Using Qualitative Methods to Elicit Young People's Perspectives on Their Environments: Some Ideas for Community Health Initiatives', *Health Education Research* 16, 3, 255–68.

O'Dell, L. (2008) 'Representations of the 'Damaged' Child: 'Child Saving' in a British Children's Charity Ad Campaign', *Children and Society*, 22, 383–392.

Osvaldsson, K. (2011) 'Bullying in Context: Stories of Bullying on an Internet Discussion Board', *Children and Society*, 25(4), 317–327.

Pink, S. (2009) *Doing Sensory Ethnography*. London: Sage.

Rasmussen, K. (2004) 'Places for Children – Children's Places', *Childhood*, 11(2), 155–174.

Rose, G. (2007) *Visual Methodologies*, 2nd edn. London: Sage.

Williams, R. (1977) *Marxism and Literature*. Oxford: Oxford University Press.

Wilson, S. (2014) 'Using Secondary Analysis to Maintain a Critically Reflexive Approach to Qualitative Research', *Sociological Research Online*, 19(3), 21. http://www.socresonline.org.uk/19/3/21.html.

Wilson, S. (2015) *Digital Technologies, Children and Young People's Relationships and Self-Care*. EPub ahead of print May 2015, In Children's Geographies.

Wilson, S., Cunningham-Burley, S., Bancroft, A. and Backett-Milburn, K. (2012a) 'The Consequences of Love: Young People and Family Practices in Difficult Circumstances', *Sociological Review*, 60(1), 110–128.

Wilson, S., Houmøllerand, K., Bernays, S. (2012b) 'It Just Feels Nice to Go Home to a Nice Home, and Not, Some House': Taking Account of the Sensory Construction of Difficult Family Relationships in Domestic Spaces', *Children's Geographies*, 12(1), 101–113.

# 7
# 'You're Not Going Out Dressed Like That!': Lessons in Fashion Consumption, Taste and Class

*Katherine Appleford*

As previous academic work suggests, there is an important relationship between motherhood and fashion. As Corrigan argues, 'clothing is a way of displaying family links' and mothers in particular play a significant role in the clothing choices and consumer socialisation of their children (Cook, 2008; McNeal, 2007; Pilcher, 2011; Rawlins, 2006). Though some suggest that this relationship can be tested during teenage years (Corrigan, 1989; Klepp and Storm-Mathisen, 2005), as daughter's friends become increasingly influential in decision making, as adults, it seems that mothers and daughter often look to each other as a source of advice and support (Clarke and Miller, 2002; Woodward, 2007). As Simmel (2004 [1901], p. 209) suggests, fashion affords individuals the 'satisfaction of not standing alone' and by shopping together and sharing clothing, accessories and fashion knowledge, mothers and daughters are able to lessen the burden of deciding what to wear.

Moreover, becoming and being a mother, can also have significant effects on the way that women feel about their bodies, particularly how they feel they look and consequently, how they dress (Gregson and Beale, 2004; Johnson, Borrows and Williamson, 2004; Longhurst, 2008). While for some women being seen as a mum allows for a relaxation of their normal boundaries and expectations of dress, for others, it is important not to 'let yourself go', in terms of one's identity or standards of attire.

In my research, the significance of motherhood concerning fashion tastes and fashion practices was too great to ignore. Nearly all of the participants discussed how their mothers had influenced their thoughts and attitudes on fashion as they were growing up. There was a general

sense that mothers, daughters, and sisters were preferred shopping partners as they better understood each other's body shape, their likes and
dislikes, and tended to offer more open and honest fashion advice than
friends.

Mothers, it seemed, played an important role in the cultivation of
consumption practices. But, more importantly, my research shows that
the practices, dispositions and tastes which mothers encouraged, such
as using catalogues, or prioritising quality or cost, depended upon their
class location and perhaps more significantly, the *way* in which mother's
taught their daughters about fashion and taste also differed with class.
So, while middle class mothers tended to operate as gatekeepers, vetoing
particular items that they perceived to be working class markers, working
class mothers appeared to make more 'collective decisions' with their
daughters about what to wear or what to buy. Indeed, several working
class mothers in this project shared clothing and accessories with their
daughters and regularly shopped together, whilst middle class women
tended to discuss their distaste for particular fashion items based on the
lessons their mothers had taught them.

The aim of this chapter, then, is to demonstrate the different classed
attitudes and fashion practices mothers help to cultivate amongst their
daughters, and to focus on the ways in which these lessons are 'taught'.
In doing so, the chapter highlights the investment mothers make in
their daughter's dress, and ways in which they foster a fashion habitus,
which can remain long into adulthood.

The chapter is divided into four parts, the first of which outlines the
context of study, on which this chapter is based. This section explains
how class was attributed, and the methods used to collect the data. The
second section looks more closely at the mother-daughter relationship. It discusses the sense of responsibility mother's often feel towards
daughter's and the way they dress, and how children's dress is often used
in evaluations of 'good' mothering. Here the chapter highlights the relevance of Goffman's (1990 [1959]: 1968) impression management, and
the way in which children's dress is seen as representative of parent's
taste. As such, it can work to not only enhance a mother's reputation
as a good parent, but their notions of taste and thus class status, which
perhaps is why middle class mothers are so keen for their daughters to
maintain standards or avoid specific items.

The importance of maintaining standards for the middle classes is
an argument developed further in third section, which concerns the
different ways mothers educate their daughters about fashion tastes
and consumption practices. Here, I argue that, while the middle class

mothers in this study had a greater tendency to 'gate-keep' their daughter's consumption by vetoing particular items, working class mothers instead looked to collaborate with their daughters, by shopping together, sharing catalogues and making more collective decisions about what looked good.

As explored in the fourth and final section, however, whether it is through vetoing or collaboration mothers are able to effectively cultivate shared attitudes and practices with their daughters, and thus a shared habitus. Mothers play a key role in cultivating particular views on fashion and an understanding of what suits them or what looks good. Consequently, it is perhaps unsurprising that mothers and daughters so often appear to share tastes or consider each other to be an important source of advice (Barnes and Eicher, 1998 [1992]; Clarke and Miller, 2002; Grove-White, 2001; Miller, 1997; Woodward, 2007).

## The context of the research

The focus of the study was the relationship between fashion and class, in the context of contemporary British women's dress. The project focused on women, rather than men, for two reasons. Firstly, women have traditionally been more closely associated with fashion and consumption (De Grazia and Furlough, 1996), and secondly much of literature around fashion and class tends to sit within the context of subcultures (e.g. Hebdige, 2006 [1979]), and as such, focuses more heavily on the practices of men. The specific aim of the project was to explore the ways in which class was mobilised through fashion discourse and fashion practice, and to examine how fashion was used in class evaluations. This involved researching how women shopped, where they shopped, what they thought looked good, their practices of dressing up, and significantly their thoughts and evaluations of others' dress.

Though the salience of class in western societies has been heavily questioned, particularly between 1980–1990 (Smith, 2000), over the last fifteen years a body of social theorists, including Rosemary Crompton (1998; 2008) Tony Bennett (2011) Steph Lawler (2005) Fiona Devine and Mike Savage (2004) and Beverley Skeggs (2004a, b) have strongly argued for its continued relevance in the UK today. Adopting a Bourdieuian (2005 [1984]) model of class, which attributes class on the basis of economic, cultural and social capital, and habitus, these theorists suggest that it is through our consumption habits and cultural tastes that class distinctions are now drawn. 'Taste is a marker of class' (2005 [1984], p. 12), and class, then, is something we enact and embody (McDowell,

2008; Skeggs, 2004a), made evident through the food we eat and the way we eat it, the books we read, the music we listen to, and moreover, by the clothes that we wear.

Though the nature of fashion today means that our clothing choices are more polycentric and pluralised than traditional theories maintain (Crane, 1999; Davis, 1994 [1992]; Slater 1997), evidence still suggests that fashion is used to evaluate individual's class locations, along with other aspects of social identity, both in America and in the UK (Barrett, 2011; Appleford, 2012). Fashion today is widely available and much more accessible to individuals then it has been in the past. The 'e-tailing' world and fashion media has expanded enormously (Church-Gibson and Bruzzi, 2013), enabling fashion trends to emanate from a great many sectors of society, and the advent of 'fast-fashion' has certainly helped many more people to engage in fashionable consumption. Indeed, contemporary fashion, is an important factor in communicating many different aspects of identity, including religion, gender, sexuality, political affiliations, and subcultures, and our tastes in clothing are therefore not only concerned with class. At the same time however, class is still often mobilised in fashion discourse and fashion practice and to an extent then, taste is still evaluated in class terms (Appleford, 2012; Hollingworth and Williams, 2010; Rafferty, 2011; Sanchez Taylor, 2012).

Certainly, throughout this study, fashion was used by participants to distinguish between class groups, and markers of taste were often read as markers of class. So, for instance, the wearing of tracksuits and trainers in spaces other than the gym, was commonly given as an indicators of working-classness by middle class participants, whereas for working class participants 'smart dress' including business suits, expensive coats and designer accessories were associated with being 'rich' and/or 'posh'. As Lisa, aged 26, told me: 'you can tell rich women, from the poor ones' as their clothes 'are all designer, it's not off the high-street, they're more quality'.

However, it was not just in their discussions of class that the links between fashion and class were apparent. In the women's understanding and attitude towards fashion, their shopping habits and tastes, the ways in which they perceived public and social spaces, their thoughts on looking good and, as this chapter demonstrates, in the ways their mothers taught them about fashion and encouraged particular fashion practices, class differences were evident.

In total 53 women took part in the research. Participants were aged between 18 and 70, the average age being 38; 8 were from Black and Minority Ethnic backgrounds; 35 were middle class, 18 were working class. As the main objective was to examine the attitudes, values and practices of British women, the research took a qualitative approach using semi-structured interviews and observations. The class location of the participants was determined on the basis of self-definition and demographic information including: housing, occupation, education, and partner's and parents' occupations – factors which have been traditionally used by sociologists to assess socio-economic status (e.g. Lawler, 2000; Skeggs et al., 2008; Walkerdine et al., 2001). Though self-classification is a subjective measure which can result in participants mostly defining themselves as middle class (Tan, 2004), in this project there was generally a good fit between the women's classification and their forms of capital. Indeed, the majority of participants classified themselves on the basis of their education, income and/or housing and although there were more middle class women in the project, this was mainly due to participants not being asked about their class status before they were recruited to the research.

Though most of the participants' self-classifications were fairly definite, as Skeggs' et al. (2008, p. 8) found, some working class participants, three in this instance, 'struggled to easily locate a class position' opting to instead dis-identify from being middle class as they did not considered themselves 'posh' or 'rich'. There was also less clarity for three women who felt they had come from 'working class backgrounds' (due to their parents' occupations or housing tenure) but who now consider themselves to be middle class, based on their occupations and home ownership.

Moreover, across the participants there was use of 'moderating terms' (Savage et al., 2001) such as 'I guess' or 'I suppose'. This was expected, for as Sayer argues questions of class can raise 'issues of relative worth' (2002, p. 163), and participants can often be ambivalent or uneasy with questions around their own class location. In fact, Savage (2003, p. 37) argues that individuals are much more likely to discuss class as a political issue 'out there' (Savage, 2000, p. 37) rather than in terms of their own class location, and although in this study self-classification was generally successful, the women still tended to discuss class in relation to others, situating themselves through a process of distancing. So, for example, participants would often explain what fashions, styles or practices they did not like, would not wear, or would not engage in, rather than focusing discussions on what they would do, in a bid to set themselves apart. Chloe, for instance, was very clear that she would not wear tracksuits and trainers because of the working class connotations and equally Valerie was very keen to explain what she would not wear.

> **Valerie:**  Well you see the chavs in ... always very tight fitting clothes,
> fake tan, but a nicer person would wear something I don't know,
> more conservative. I wouldn't ever want to look too tarty, and I
> wouldn't want to come across as something lower class ... I wear
> what I like, I wouldn't follow fashion for fashion's sake, I wouldn't
> want to look tarty, but I would want to look dressed up, but not
> too conservative.

This 'distancing' would seem to reaffirm Bourdieu's argument, that more
often than not, taste is concern with, or established through, 'distaste'.
Rather than asserting what our tastes are, Bourdieu argues that individuals,
especially those from the middle class, are much more likely to express
their taste through rejections, indignations or pitying remarks such as, 'I
can't understand how anyone can like that' (2005 [1984], p. 61). Similarly
Bennett et al. (2010, p. 211) identify a 'hostility' or 'resentment' around
particular tastes from working class participants who worked to distance
the individual from those practices and preferences. By setting out one's
dislikes or distastes, individuals work to create symbolic distance between
themselves and others in the social space, giving a sense of their place in
the social hierarchy (Bourdieu, 1989).

## A mother's role

In talking about their mothers, or their experience of motherhood, many
participants, both middle and working class, discussed the responsibility
they felt mothers had for children's appearance. As Ruth explained,

> I do see youngsters in ... short skirts, or leggings and they are far too
> big for that style. And ... I wish their mum would have said to them,
> 'Don't do that, that's not a good look for you'. I will tell Melissa ... I'll
> tell her that, 'That's not her colour', or 'it doesn't show off her shape'.
> [Aged 45, PA]

Academic work suggests that mothers are a significant influence over children's consumption habits (Cook, 2008; Martens et. al, 2004; Martens,
2014 [2010]; Ward, 1974]), not only as infants but pre-teens too (Arcana,
1979; Carlson et al., 1990; Harper et al., 2003), and they are often considered 'ultimately responsible for the way their children turn out' (Collet,
2005, p. 328) and thus, 'accountable for the clothes their children wear'
(Rawlins, 2006, p. 360). In fact, despite their increasing employment,
women continue to be the chief 'carers' within families (De Vault, 1991;

Jenkins, 2004; Bond and Sales, 2001; Walkerdine et al., 2001), and the food and clothing of the household still tends to be viewed as a mother's responsibility. Although they may have less autonomy over their children's clothes as they move into adolescence (Ganetz, 1995; Simpson and Douglas, 1998), they are still seen as an important source of fashion guidance and advice.

### Good mothers

One of the implications of this responsibility is that children's dress is often used to judge whether a mother is 'good' or 'bad'. Clarke (2004) argues that the consumption of food, clothing and toys is a fundamental aspect both in the construction of motherhood and the politics of mothering. Material items are used to create social identities, for both the mother and child, and mothers are judged in relation to each other based on their children's commodities and dress. Being perceived as a 'good mother' relies on having 'the "right" baby monitor, an "ethical" toy' or indeed 'a "pretty" dress' (2004, p. 71), and as Jane comments demonstrated, children's clothes are used to judge mothers' care for their children.

> Jane: ...you see little kids, they haven't got a pair of shoes they've only got a pair of trainers. Little girls in...trainers and dresses. I think if you're going to put her in a little dress...then go to Clarks, get her feet properly measured. I mean, we had three pairs of Clarks shoes every year...My mum was such a terrible snob, she'd see the mothers buying the shoes off the shelf and trying them on their children and saying 'that'll do'. She'd say, 'they're going to have bunions, they're going to have terrible feet when they're older'. And actually she was probably right. And again I associate it with a fairly middle class upbringing that certain people make sure that their kids, I suppose it's about looking after [yourself/ your children]. And that's what I think about class and fashion...The [middle class] people that look at whether it's actually doing your body any harm. [Aged 29, Lecturer & Yoga Instructor]

As well as emphasising the common association made between wearing trainers and working-classness, Jane's remarks highlight two key issues. Firstly, they demonstrate how children's clothing is seen as the responsibility of the mother, and deemed representative of her wider attitudes and practices in regard to mothering. By purchasing Clarks shoes for her and her sister, Jane felt that her mother demonstrated she was a 'good' parent, who cared for her children's long-term health and looked after their needs, unlike working class mothers who in purchasing shoes 'off the shelf' posed a risk to their children's wellbeing, in terms of suffering 'terrible feet' and bunions later in life. Secondly, they indicate that notions of mothering are classed, and while middle class practices are seen as 'right' and legitimate, working class practices are deemed 'abject' and 'wrong'.

Writing about class and 'good' mothering, Lawler (2000) argues that 'whether it is read as "democratic", as "sensitive" or as "natural", the type of mothering associated with white, middle class, women is marked as "normal", with any deviation from this norm constructed as pathological' (2000, p. 80). So although good mothering is said to be determined simply on the basis of a child's needs, 'which suggests a rather minimal level of adequacy', it is more typically the practice of the middle class which 'becomes the norm against which others are measured; ... the norm to which working class people are supposed to aspire' (2000, p. 79). It is the middle class notions of mothering which are deemed to be legitimate, and while middle class attitudes and practices towards mothering and consumption are seen to satisfy children's needs, working class practices such as buying shoes 'off the shelf' or letting their children wear trainers is deemed indicative of 'carelessness, irresponsibility and selfishness' (Gillies, 2007, p. 27).

**What is good mothering?**

In this research most mothers, again both middle- and working class, were aware of the way in which children's dress is viewed as representative of their status as a 'good' or 'bad' parent, and even during the interviews some mothers had concerns over how they might appear to me. In the interview with middle class participants Jessica and Lucy, for instance, both felt they had to explain that their children were in baby-grows rather than 'proper clothes' only 'for practicality,' as they had been swimming earlier in the day. The type of clothing believed to communicate good parenting however, appears to differ to some extent with social class. While middle class participants were keen to ensure that their children's clothes met the 'proper' (middle class) standards, the concern for working class interviewees was more that their children's dress protected them from the stigma of working-classness, and was clearly given higher priority than their own attire.

As others note, working class women often view personal sacrifices for the sake of the children and the household as part of their role as a 'good' parent (Skeggs et al., 2008), and as Casey (2008), Charles and

Kerr (1988) and Lawler (2000) argue. Many of the working class women in this project seemed to consider selflessness, putting the needs of the family first (Lawler, 2000, p. 153) as key to 'good mothering'. While some forfeited fashion purchases for themselves for the benefit of their children, others viewed purchases for their children as equally, if not more, important than those made for themselves. Joy, for instance, used clothing vouchers given to her for a Christmas present to buy clothes for her son, whilst Kim said that she would always buy something for her children, even if she did not purchase anything for herself. Although this may mean, as Joy says, that she 'looks bad' while her son 'looks good', it was important to her that her son was well dressed and thus demonstrated, in her mind, that she was a 'good mother', as sentiment echoed in Louisa's comments too.

> **Louisa:** I go to Next and Debenhams because I can kit the kids out so cheaply in the sale and it's really nice quality stuff. I don't like buying shit...I like to put the kids in stuff that's nice...I want to people to look at my kids and think they are really nicely, taste-fully dressed you know? [Aged 38, Nursery Nurse]
>
> **Joy:** I'll look bad...but he'll look good...But don't you find that you take much more pleasure in picking clothes for them [their chil-dren], rather than you? I love his [her son's] clothes, but mine I don't bother with...I asked for Next vouchers and GAP vouchers for Christmas and I was determined to spend them on myself and I spent them all on him. [Aged 19, Fast Food Restaurant Worker]

Moreover, while the working class women in this research, like that of Casey's (2008, p. 65), did not present a strong 'desire to "escape" their class position' when discussing their own dress or class location, they did have a greater desire for their children to be seen as respectable, and not to be seen as working class. Louisa remarked that she wants others to think that her children look 'tasteful', while Diane said that she did not want others to look at her daughters and 'think we were poor'. And so, by buying 'better quality' or designer items, these mothers hope to 'protect' their children from the 'pathological and worthless' conno-tations of working-classness (Skeggs, 1997, p. 86) and subsequently 'improve their lives' (p. 82).

> **Liz:** ...because I didn't have much money...it meant that I went to Quality Seconds and whatever was cheap. And I used to get some lovely things, because at the same time that I might buy

clothes from the cheaper shops, but I will get the good quality clothes...You can look and see, 'Well actually that doesn't look as if it's come from a cheap shop' so that's alright, you know?...So I could still be well dressed, but via cheap shops and the same with the girls. [Aged 41, Book-Keeper]

Like Louisa and Diane, Liz too had looked to find ways to buy clothing, which was affordable but did not look 'cheap', so that her children could pass as respectable and thus middle class. Moreover, it interesting that Liz's comments also suggest that quality is one of the characteristics of dress which conveys class and status, and that good quality clothing is an indication of respectability, as this was an association which several of the middle class women also made, as discussed later.

### Just like her mother

However, as well as shielding their children from the judgements of others, these working class women may also feel that ensuring their children are well dressed affords them some degree of protection too. Using Goffman's (1990 [1963]) work, which maintains that an individual tends to be judged 'socially by the company he is in' (1990 [1963], p. 104), Collett (2005) argues that children can be used as 'props' or 'associates' to 'influence the perception of the adults associated with them' (2005, p. 331). Mothers may view their children's clothes as a 'reflection on them' (2005, p. 337), and therefore, ensuring that their children are well dressed helps to 'verify their identities as "good mothers"' (2005, p. 332), who are providing their children with the 'proper care' (Kuhn, 1995, p. 54). Moreover, if greater attention is placed on the child, these mothers, like Joy, may also feel that it lessens the obligation upon them to dress up and 'look good', in order to establish respectability in their everyday lives.

The relationship between children's dress and parental status is not only evident in the discussions with working class women, however. Amongst middle class women too, there is evidence to suggest that mothers view their children as a form of 'associate'. As Lucy and Jessica's concerns over their infant's baby-grows demonstrated, these mothers can also feel that their child's appearance has some bearing on others' perception of them as Carol explained.

> **Carol:** I remember as a small child...we had a private dentist then, we weren't top notch, we were sort of middle class but for some reason we went to this private dentist and my mother made me

wear white gloves and my posh coat to go to this dentist ... I had to dress up to go to the dentist ... it's that sort of appropriate behaviour. [Aged 56, Hospital Manager]

Carol's comments again acknowledged some degree of 'impression management' on the part of her mother. As a private, rather than NHS, practice, it seems Carol's mother considered the dentist to be a middle class space, and it was important to her mother that Carol was dressed 'appropriately' in order to assert that their family were of the right class and status for that service.

Consequently, it seems that for these middle class women, children's dress is not only used to affirm mothers as good parents, as Collett (2005) argues, but to establish the social status of the parent and the child. Moreover, it is this anxiety over perceptions of class status which also appeared in middle class discussions around mothers' advice.

## Sanctioning and sharing

In his discussion of parental values, Kohn (1959) claims that while working class parents tend to emphasise notions of respectability, middle class parents are more focused on encouraging 'internalised standards of conduct' (1959, p. 337), particularly, the importance of 'maintaining standards'. Although Kohn's (1959) work is now quite dated and not at all concerned with fashion, his arguments still offer an interesting explanation for some of the attitudes and practices found in this study. This is not only because he identifies the importance of mothers in teaching children attitudes and practices, but also because he implies that middle class mothers are eager for their children to recognise class distinctions in practices and tastes, and to maintain 'middle class' standards as a result.

Indeed, maintaining respectability in a bid to distance themselves, and their families, from working class connotations was a common theme in discussions with middle class participants. As Jane and Carol's comments have already shown, these women were very much aware of the 'symbolic capital' that sartorial choices have (Bourdieu, 1990) and by encouraging their daughters to make the same links between fashion and class, middle class mothers work to secure and protect their own class status as well as that of their daughters. As Miller (1997) notes, middle class mothers have 'considerable concern that the material culture associated with their children should represent' their own tastes and 'stylistic aspirations' (1997, p. 36), not least because they 'act as symbolic representations of their parent's cultural orientations and attitudes' (Martens et. al., 2004, p. 164). Children, even as adolescents, can operate as 'associates' (Goffman, 1963) and their clothes are therefore just as important as their own, in terms of 'presentation of self' (Goffman, 1990 [1959]) and the potential profit (Bourdieu, 2005 [1984]).

## Gatekeeping

The desire for their children to distance themselves from working-classness, and to 'maintain standards' seems to inform the ways in which middle class mothers teach their daughters about fashion, and more specifically what *not* to wear. In interviews, middle class women often talked about their mothers operating as gatekeepers, controlling what they could wear as girls, and as teenagers, and discouraging them from wearing particular types of dress or specific items.

> **Chloe:** Whatever I wore, it was because she'd [her mother] chosen it or she'd help me choose it, and she'll always be the one to say, 'oh you can't wear that, you can't do this, you can't do that', and I think I've kind of learnt from her. [Aged 18, Student]

The idea that mothers exercise control over their daughter's consumption practices is not unexpected. As already discussed, the literature on gender and consumer research often cites mothers as household's the primary consumers (Miller, 1998) but significantly, it seemed that this gatekeeping was used to encourage distancing and distinctions from working classes and continued well into adolescence.

In middle class participants' interviews, for example, stories of mothers' gatekeeping were often accompanied by class references, with participants' mothers vetoing items considered be indicative of working class status. So for example, Jane and Rosie noted that their mothers would not allow them to wear tracksuits, trainers, or gold-hooped earrings, because of the working class associations. Elizabeth, again in a discussion of shoes, explained how her mother would not allow her to wear white stilettos, because of the 'Essex girl' connotation, and Hannah recalls that her mother had always stressed to her that wearing stilettos and short skirts would give the impression that she was not respectable.

> **Elizabeth:** White stilettos might have been deemed Essex girl... There are certain things that my mother would absolutely not let us have, like my mother would never ever let me have a pair of white stilettos and so still to this day I've never owned a pair. [Aged 42, Designer]

**Hannah:** It's the way you present yourself...in a pair of stilettos, and a short skirt...like my mother will say 'you should look nice and presentable', you know? There is a line of looking good and looking like a bit of a tart, especially on like a Saturday night,...you can show that you've been brought up well. [Aged 25, Legal Secretary]

The 'Essex Girl' 'portrayed as loud, stupid, coarse and sometimes menacing' (Gillies, 2007, p. 26), was, in many ways, the stereotype of working class woman throughout the 1980s (Skeggs, 2005; Lawler, 2005a) and was typically identified by her white stiletto shoes. Hence why Elizabeth, who comes from an 'upper-middle class' family, was not allowed to wear them. Today the term 'chavette' is perhaps more commonly used to describe working class women who are considered to 'drink too much alcohol, wear vulgar and revealing clothes and have little self-control' (Gillies, 2007, p. 26). They are more typically associated with wearing trainers, counterfeit design labels and large gold hoop earrings (Tyler, 2008), which perhaps explains the common veto-ing of tracksuits and trainers.

This type of class-centred gatekeeping is not only apparent when women talked about their own childhood however, it is also evident in the way some of them 'help' their daughters with their choice of outfit. Valerie, for instance, told me that she gives her daughter a bit more autonomy over clothing choices, but at the same time maintains some degree of control, and will not let her daughter wear anything 'too raunchy', because it displays the wrong type of femininity.

**Valerie:** In the last eight months she has wanted to choose her own clothes. Sometimes I help, but generally, as I've tended to choose stuff for her, she [her daughter] has quite good taste...But I don't want the girls to wear things that are too old for them, you know, they are still quite girly, I don't want them in anything too raunchy. [Aged 32, Legal Secretary]

By not allowing their daughters to wear items considered too 'raunchy', or using terms like 'Essex Girl', middle class mothers are educating their daughters about the relationship between fashion and class. They are teaching their daughters about the links society makes between particular items of clothing, styles of dress and class status, and they are also arguably cultivating class evaluations of dress and fashion practices in relation to other women, which can remain with them long into their adulthood. As Elizabeth says, she has 'never' owned a pair of white stilettos, because of the Essex Girl connotations, despite the fact that 'three years ago that Christian Louboutin was doing white patent stilettos and every A-lister was trying to get a pair'.

Not only do Elizabeth's comment demonstrate the links made between fashion and class, and the role of mothers in cultivating these associations, however, they also raise an interesting attitude towards designer goods. For although the Louboutin shoes may have been heralded as up to the minute fashion at that time, for Elizabeth they still did not connote good taste. Throughout this research, middle class participants were keen to stress that their consumption was not lead by fashion trends or brands, and that rather being 'fashionably' dressed they were keen to adopt a classic style. Indeed, those considered to be very trend-led or brand-led consumers were often described as 'fashion victims': obsessed with designer goods and media promotions, 'ready to adopt their every style, regardless of taste or appropriateness' (Arnold, 2001, p. 10). Instead, these middle class participants viewed their purchases as more considered, choosing styles which personally suited them, rather than those which were marketed as 'on-trend'. Wearing designer items did not necessarily connote good taste, and if anything, these women, and their mothers, encouraged a sceptical attitude towards fashion brands.

### Lessons in clothes shopping

Gatekeeping is not the only way in which middle class mothers ensure that their children are dressed in an appropriate middle class fashion, however. As Pilcher (2011) and Martens et al. (2004, p. 166) suggest, parents influence their children's consumption by actively 'cultivating ways of consuming'. Parents are constantly involved in teaching their children lesson about consumption, and this has 'significant implications for how children develop an everyday understanding of the process of shopping, purchase and consumption of goods' (2004, p. 166).

In this research, there was clear evidence in interviews and observations of middle class mothers actively teaching their daughters ways of consuming. When out shopping, mothers instructed their daughters about what to look for in terms of style and they clearly outlined priorities or criteria for making purchases, such the need for longevity, quality and cut.

> **Sarah:** It's all to do with fabric, I mean I could feel one piece of fabric and say, 'that's not bad' and then I could feel something else and feel 'that's definitely good cotton in there'...And I say to my girls, 'that

won't wash and it'll come up like a scrumpled mess...a nice good thick cotton...will wash and wash'. [Aged 52, former Police Officer]

As others have identified, quality tends to be high priority for middle class women (Miller, 1998; Solomon and Rabolt, 2009), and as Entwistle (2004 [2000], p. 50) notes, it is reflected in not only the amount spent, but also the fabrics used. Sarah's remarks indicated how fabric is a key aspect of middle class mothers' teachings about fashion, and she made sure to show her daughters how to compare the quality of the fabric and garments. Another participant, Carly, explained that she learned how to assess the quality of clothes by watching her mother check a garment's stitching, labels and fabric. As Kestler (2010) found, mothers appeared to be a valuable source of practical fashion information for daughters, especially with regard to making fashion purchases. However, in doing so, they were also generating classed practices and attitudes which, as Margaret said, 'stick' with women long into their adulthood.

> **Margaret:** My mother always insisted on buying clothes of good quality and that has stuck with me...you can feel the quality in the material. [Aged 45, Learning Support Assistant PT]

### Collective consumption and collaboration

The idea that mothers cultivate classed practices through actively engaging in their children's consumer purchases and fashion tastes is even more evident amongst the working class participants, however. Like 'dressing up' which takes place 'collectively' (Skeggs, 1997, p. 105), buying clothes and learning about fashion is also something which these working class participants looked forward to and tended to do together (1997, pp. 101–102).

> **Angie:** Oh we're shopping mad!...we love to shop...She used to live by East Croydon train station, so...I'd meet her in the mornings and we'd shop all day long. [Aged 54, full-time Mother]

Although shopping may have been considered a mostly middle class leisure pursuit in the nineteenth century (Rappaport, 2000), it has arguably become a much more typical cultural practice since the 1980s (Abbott and Sapsford, 2003 [2001], p. 24) and nearly all the working class women in this research talked about shopping with mothers, daughters and/or sister on a regular basis. Rather than mothers acting as gatekeepers, vetoing their daughters' choice of items or providing instruction on what to buy on these trips, these women placed much greater emphasis on *encouraging* their daughters to look good and letting their daughters lead the decision making.

> **Trisha:** I say, [to her daughter] 'come on let's go shopping' ... so she's in training, I try to encourage her about what would look good and what wouldn't look good. [Aged 43, full-time Mother]
>
> **Ruth:** I'll tell her that, 'That's not your colour' or 'it doesn't show off your shape' ... She's got a skirt, it's denim but it's got stars on the back, and so she said 'What colours will go with my skirt?' she's already started to say 'oh does that match?' [Aged 45, PA]

In Lawler's (2000) discussion of 'girls growing up', she explores the relationship between regulation and autonomy, and the idea that mothers are keen to let their daughters 'be themselves' (2000, p. 76). While Kellmer-Pringle (1986) argues that working class mothers are 'authoritarian' and tend to provide 'non-verbal forms of prohibition and punishment' rather than communicate with their children (1986, p. 50), Lawler argues that in her research both working and middle class mothers were eager to provide their daughters with some level of autonomy and the freedom of 'self-regulation' (2000, p. 82). Though none of the participants in this research used the phrase 'letting her be herself', working class mothers did appear keen to let their daughters lead the decision making in relation to the colour and style, adopting a more 'democratic' approach to their children's dress, contradicting Kellmer-Pringle's (1986) arguments, and encouraging their daughters to engage in discussion and collective decisions what to wear or what to buy.

### Sharing clothes, jewellery and catalogues

This shared practice or 'collective' consumption between mothers, daughters and sisters does not only exist in relation to shopping, however. Working class mothers were implicitly involved in their daughters' understanding of fashion in many different ways: they shared clothes and jewellery; they watched fashion programmes together and they read each-others' fashion magazines.

> **Becky:** I use my mum's catalogues, she gets the Next Directory and I get Littlewoods and we both just swap. [Aged 29, Nurse]
>
> **Jazz:** Sometimes I will see something and I really like it and I buy it. And then I might get it home and say 'Jade, do you want this?' [Aged 36, Cleaner]

For working class daughters, mothers are crucial in cultivating attitudes about how to dress and how to go about buying clothes. Daughters learn practices and attitudes from shopping or consuming images or media together with their mothers, and as a result generate a shared notion as to what looks good. In her discussion of femininity Skeggs (1997) argues that working class women's 'knowledge of femininity' is an 'amalgamation' of textual sources such as magazines and advertisements and 'local knowledge' from friends (1997, p. 103), but it may be that for younger women it is mothers who provide more local knowledge, and who help their daughters to decode media images and texts.

This is demonstrated by Yvonne, her ten-year-old daughter Keisha, and their use of catalogues. Catalogues were commonly used by working class women as a way of learning about fashion trends and buying clothes, and their credit schemes provided them with a way means of affording new items. As Casey (2014, p. 2) notes, part of the draw of catalogues is that they 'offer credit deals,' to those who historically have tended to 'have difficulties in getting credit,' and 'they present a collection of images and ideals' which consumers then 'have the opportunity to buy into'. Yvonne bought a large proportion of her clothes from catalogues and Keisha was obviously very involved in her mothers' purchase. Keisha knew the names of all catalogues that her mother received, they looked through the catalogue together, with Keisha helping Yvonne to select items, as well as choosing items for herself, and the two of them would discuss the merits of various looks together.

**Yvonne:** Most of the time I'm browsing…but if I see something and I put it by for that perfect time…just in case I've got somewhere to go…

**Keisha:** She's got this beautiful dress out of here, [shows me a dress in Fiftyplus]

**Yvonne:** It's from this one, FiftyPlus.

**Keisha:** With polka dots…Mummy, I was looking in this catalogue, and they had these [points to a coat].

**Yvonne:** Yeah I get ideas from the catalogue, mainly from the catalogue.

**Keisha:** She [Yvonne] gets Fiftyplus, Littlewoods, Ambrose Wilson…and this is my catalogue [La Redoute]…This is one of her dresses, and you've got 18 but you thought it looked big…[Aged 47, Care worker]

Yvonne has taught her daughter about the benefit of catalogues through her own shopping practice and by encouraging Keisha to use the catalogues too. Using her catalogue, La Redoute, Keisha now carries out the same practices that she sees her mother perform, browsing it for ideas and looking for special offers. Perhaps, as Oakley's (1979 [1972]) work would suggest, in a bid to be like her mother, Keisha is motivated to act like her and 'imitate' the relevant items of behaviour (1985 [1972], p. 179), whilst simultaneously helping her mother find suitable garments which will make her 'look good'.

## Shared habitus and shared tastes

Whether middle class or working class then, it seems that mothers are highly significant in cultivating knowledge, perceptions around fashion, and fashion practices amongst their daughters, and are central figures in the development of their fashion habitus. Bourdieu defines habitus as 'a system of durable, transposable dispositions ... which generate and organise practices and representations' (1990, p. 52), as well as schemes of perceptions (2005 [1984], p. 171). Thus, it is our habitus which enables us to produce tastes and 'classifiable practices and works' (2005 [1984], p. 170) that then operate as 'distinctive signs' of class positions (pp. 174–175), and further enables us 'to differentiate and appreciate these practices and products' in relation to others (p. 170). As a result, the habitus is a 'structuring structure' and a 'structured structure' (p. 170), which orientates individual practice and at the same time provides a means of classification and differentiation between class groups.

In addition to this, Entwistle (2009) and Entwistle and Rocamora (2006) argue that within certain fields such as dance, acting and fashion our knowledge or 'capital' is actually 'worn on the body' and articulated through a 'bodily habitus' (Entwistle and Rocamora, 2006, p .746). Exhibited through the clothes we wear and the way we move, our 'fashion habitus' (Entwistle, 2009, p. 114) is a physical and aesthetic practice, which makes our tastes instantly apparent and which therefore allows others to evaluate and place us, as Veblen suggests, 'at first glance' (1994 [1899], p. 103). Our 'fashion habitus' is therefore about displaying the 'right' kind of fashion knowledge and tastes, and making sure that our 'body actually looks like it belongs' (Entwistle and Rocamora, 2006, p. 746) within the social context.

A 'product of history', Bourdieu argues that our habitus is developed or 'acquired' (1990, p. 54) through our past experiences and early learning (2005 [1984], p. 78), which suggests that it is somewhat reliant upon the teaching of practices and attitudes that come from our parents. Indeed, Bourdieu himself identifies the transmission of cultural capital as specifically dependent upon a mother's free time (1986, p. 253). Mothers are the parents who spend most time on childcare, and thus the parent who is 'most directly involved in the generation of cultural capital' (Reay, 2004, p. 59), and arguably it is these cultural practices and tastes, learnt as infants, which are the 'most indelible' (2005 [1984], p. 79).

The long-term influence of mothers' practices, and the cultivation of habitus through maternal teachings is evident when the participants discuss the practices and perceptions that have stayed within them since childhood, and the long-term effect and influence their mothers have had on their understandings of dressing up and looking good. As Liz's comment below demonstrate, perceptions of good taste and good purchases, body image and appropriate dress appear to pass down the generations, and those lessons learnt in early childhood, as Bourdieu suggests, appear difficult to erase

> Liz: I've always been very conscious of not wanting to be fat, I grew up with my mum...always having a problem with her weight, she was constantly on a diet, and moaning about how big she was,...and I suppose with Kelly [her daughter] she's got her own style, but on saying that she's normally pinching my clothes or she'll buy stuff, and I think, 'oh I like that,' you know?...she had the same problem as me, she put on a lot and she went really fat...So, I know exactly how Kerry felt and that was why it was so difficult for both of us.

Although authors have explored mothers' influences in terms of body image and dieting (Benedikt et al., 1998; Pike, 1991; Waterhouse, 1998; Weiner, 2007), very few authors have employed Bourdieu's theory of habitus to help explain maternal influences around fashion consumption or consumer socialisation (see for example Martens et al., 2004; Pilcher, 2011 or Cook, 2008). Because of this fact, the way in which intergenerational transfer of habitus takes place has generally been overlooked. However, both psychologists and sociologists have recognised an important relationship between mothers and daughters for some time (see for example, Boyd, 1989; Chodorow, 1978; Dally, 1976; De Beauvoir, 1996 [1949]; Eichenbaum and Orbach, 1982; 1993; Fischer, 1981), and in doing so have noted the 'unconscious internalization of maternal values and behaviours' (Boyd, 1989, p. 291). This internalisation leads daughters 'to mother, and to be like their mothers', through a process of imitation, praise and reward (1989, p. 291).

Moreover, within the literature on fashion several authors have suggested that mothers and daughters share fashion and clothing tastes (Clarke and Miller, 2002; Grove-White, 2001; Miller, 1997; Woodward, 2007), and research has also shown that women commonly shop with their mothers and/or daughters, rather than friends as a result (Klepp and Storm-Mathisen, 2005; Rawlins, 2006). But while the significance of mothers in terms of women's values, consumer behaviours and fashion practices seems to have been acknowledged (Clarke and Miller, 2002; Miller, 1996; Woodward, 2007), the importance of mothers in passing on and reproducing *classed* practice and tastes appears to have been largely overlooked.

Even so, Bourdieu (2005 [1984]) claims that 'nothing perhaps more directly depends on early learning... than the dispositions and knowledge that are invested in clothing, furnishing cooking and more precisely the way in which clothes, furniture and food are bought' (2005 [1984], p. 78). As Martens et al. (2004) argue, the 'parent–child relationship must take centre stage in accounts of why children consume in the way that they do' (2004, p. 163). Parents, particularly mothers, 'clearly represent a young child's most significant influence' (, p. 166) in terms of consumption, and more importantly their role in cultivated class disposition 'may offer fundamental insights into the reproduction of structural differences' (p. 167).

That is not to suggest that the habitus is utterly determined by parental input. As Lawler (2004) notes, the habitus is not a 'straightforward reproduction' of history; it is a 'generative' process, which adapts to the changes and developments in the social world (2004, p. 112). It is something which can be 'disrupted' and shifted by social mobility and personal experiences. But at the same time, and in regard to fashion consumption, it seems that the notion that 'what we learn is what our mothers do' (Arcana, 1979, p. 13) is particularly prevalent. Whether it is through gatekeeping or through lessons in buying criteria or collective discussions over purchases and fashion media, mothers orientate their daughters' practices. They cultivate dispositions which structure their individual practice, and act as means of classification within the wider social context.

## Lessons that last

The extent of mothers' influence, and their involvement in cultivating women's fashion habitus is clearly demonstrated when participants talked about the practices that had 'stayed with them' since their childhood. Bourdieu argues that one of the characteristics of classed dispositions is that they are difficult to change, in part because those dispositions which develop during the 'early years of life' are so 'deeply rooted within us' (Jenkins, 1992, p. 72). In addition, like Louisa and Diane, several of the women in this study commented on the way they continued with practices that their mothers taught them as children, long into their adult lives.

**Louisa:** I tend to wear flat pumps out and I do like my ankle straps, but I think that's a childhood thing. My mum always used to put me in black patent ankle straps, and that has stayed with me. [Aged 38, Nursery Nurse]

**Diane:** It's taken me a long time to grow up when it comes to clothes, I was pretty much one of those who … my mother used to dress me and I carried on wearing those sorts of things even after I left home, … it was only when my older daughter said, 'Mum you shouldn't wear things like that' … and thought, 'I've been wearing this shape since I was about 14' [Aged 41, Receptionist]

Both Louisa and Diane seemed to suggest that their mothers were a significant and long-term influence on their fashion practices and tastes, and they are not the only participants to so. In the course of a discussion with a group of participants, all aged in their 60s, attention turned to the practice of 'keeping for best'. This was the idea that newly bought items should not be worn immediately, but initially should be kept for special occasions. Though this idea had been frustrating as a child, it was still something which some of them have 'never changed', and continued with even today.

**Bridget:** Do you remember 'best'? … You'd buy clothes … and they would stay in the wardrobe … When I was growing up, my mother would say 'I should keep it for best'.

**Geraldine:** You had something and you'd keep it apart, you'd only wear it on certain days.

**Bridget:** Yes, like Sunday best.

**Anne:** Sometimes I feel like a child because I've bought new clothes and then not worn them. Some things never change!

[Bridget: Aged 65, Retired; Geraldine Aged 65, Retired; Anne Aged 63, Retired]

Just as the comments from Louisa and Diane demonstrate, the remarks from these ladies highlighted the way in which childhood practices were continue into adulthood, and were even passed down to their daughters too. They suggest, as Bourdieu argues, that there is a 'durability' to our habitus, particularly in regard to practices learnt within the home and from an early age, and thus again indicate that mother's play a key role in cultivating practices and tastes around fashion, and in the intergenerational transfer of fashion habitus. Which perhaps may explain why mothers and daughters all too often find themselves sharing tastes, sharing advice, and swapping clothes.

> **Anne:** My daughter will show me something she's bought and she really looks good in and then she puts it on and says, 'I look like you. You can have it mum' [Aged 63, Retired]

## Conclusion

In conclusion, though academics have argued for the importance of the mother-daughter relationship in gender and consumer socialisation, and several have noted the way in which mothers and daughters share tastes, few have actually explored the way in mothers help cultivate classed practices in terms of fashion and dress, or how lessons in fashion differ with class position. Yet this research suggests that mothers play a significant role in cultivating a fashion habitus amongst their daughters encouraging particular fashion practices, tastes and attitudes from childhood and despite the impact of media or friends, continue to be a persuasive influence over women's fashion choices well into their adult lives.

As a result mothers appear to cultivate particular practices or tastes which operate as 'markers of class' (Bourdieu, 2005 [1984], p. 6), and more importantly the way in which they 'teach' their daughters about fashion seems also subject to class distinctions. While middle class mothers are keen to educate their daughters through gatekeeping and 'lessons' in fashion buying, working class women teach their daughters through collective practice, and by engaging with their children's fashion consumption. Indeed, for the working class women in this study, shopping together, sharing catalogues, and consuming fashion and fashion media together was typical, and closely linked to their collective performance of femininity.

For all mothers though, whether working or middle class, it seemed that making sure their children are dressed appropriately was highly important, as children's dress was seen primarily as a mother's responsibility and considered as a reflection on them. Read as a measure of 'good parenting' whether that is considered putting the needs of their child first or 'maintaining standards', ensuring that children are well dress is important as it helps to confirm the respectability and symbolic capital of the parent. And even, as adults, mother's are still greatly influential, as mothers and daughters come together to support one another and affirm each other's fashion practices and fashion tastes, and their lessons live on.

## References

Abbott, P. and Sapsford, F. (2003) [2001] 'Young Women and Their Wardrobes' in *Through the Wardrobe: Women's Relationships with their Clothes*, A. Guy, M. Banim and E. Green (eds). Oxford: Berg.

Appleford, K. (2012) Classifying Fashion and Fashioning Class. PhD Thesis, London College of Fashion, University of the Arts London.

Arcana, J. (1979) *Our Mother's Daughter*. Berkeley, CA: Shameless Hussy Press.

Barrett, W. (2011) *Social Class on Campus: Theories and Manifestations*. Virginia: Stylus.

Benedikt, R., Wertheim, E. H. and Love, A. (1998) 'Eating Attitudes and Weight-Loss Attempts in Female Adolescents and Their Mothers', *Journal of Youth and Adolescence*, 27(1), 43–57.

Bennett, T. (2011) 'Culture, Choice, Necessity: A Political Critique of Bourdieu's Aesthetic', *Poetics*, 39(6), 530–546.

Bennett, T., Savage, M., Silva, M., Warde A. Gayo-Cal, M. and Wright, D. (2010) *Culture, Class, Distinction*. London: Routledge

Bond, S. and Sales, J. (2001) 'Household Work in the UK: An Analysis of the British Household Panel Survey, 1994', *Work, Employment and Society*, 15(2), 233–250.

Bourdieu, P. (1990) *The Logic of Practice*. Cambridge: Polity.

Bourdieu, P. (2005) [1984] *Distinction: A Social Critique of the Judgement of Taste*. London: Routledge & Kegan Paul.

Boyd, C. T. (1989) 'Mothers and Daughters: A Discussion of Theory and Research', *Journal of Marriage and Family*, 51(2), 291–301.

Carlson, L., Grossbart, S. and Walsh, A. (1990) 'Mothers' Communication Orientation and Consumer-Socialisation Tendencies', *Journal of Advertising*, 19(3), 27–38.

Casey, E. (2008) *Women, Pleasure and the Gambling Experience*. Aldershot: Ashgate.

Casey, E. (March 2014) 'Catalogue Communities: Work and Consumption in the Catalogue Industry', *Journal of Consumer Culture*, DOI: 10.1177/1469540514528199

Charles, N. and Kerr, M. (1988) *Women, Food and Families*. Manchester: Manchester University Press

Chodorow, N. (1978) *The Reproduction of Mothering: Psychoanalysis and the Sociology of Gender*. Berkeley, CA: University of California Press.

Church-Gibson, P. and Bruzzi, S. (2013) 'Introduction' in *Fashion Cultures Revisited*, P. Church-Gibson and S. Bruzzi (eds). London: Routledge

Clarke, A. (2004) 'Maternity and Materiality: Becoming a Mother in Consumer Culture' in *Consuming Motherhood*, J. S. Taylor, L. L. Layne and D. F. Wozniak (eds). New Jersey: Rutgers.

Clarke, A. and Miller, D. (2002) 'Fashion and Anxiety', *Fashion Theory: The Journal of Dress, Body & Culture*, 6(2), 191–213

Collett, J. L. (2005) 'What Kind of Mother Am I? Impression Management and the Social Construction of Motherhood', *Symbolic Interaction*, 28(3), 327–347.

Cook, D. T. (2008) 'The Missing Child in Consumption Theory', *Journal of Consumer Culture*, 8(2), 219–243.

Corrigan, P. (1989) 'Gender and the Gift: The Case of the Family Clothing Economy', *Sociology*, 23(4), 513–534.

Crane, D. (1999) 'Gender and Hegemony in Fashion Magazines: Women's Interpretations of Fashion Photographs', *Sociological Quarterly*, 40(4), 531–563.

Crompton, R. (1998) *Class and Stratification: An Introduction to Current Debates* (2nd edn). Cambridge: Polity Press.

Crompton, R. (2008) *Class and Stratification* (3rd edn). Cambridge; Malden, MA: Polity.

Dally, A. (1976) *Their Power and Influence*. London: Weidenfeld and Nicolson.

Davis, F. (1994) [1992] *Fashion, Culture and Identity*. Chicago: Chicago University Press.

De Beauvoir, S. (1997) [1949] *The Second Sex*. London: Vintage.

De Grazia, V. (1996) 'Introduction' in *The Sex of Things: Gender and Consumption in Historical Perspective*, De Grazia, V. and Furlough, E. (eds). London: University of California Press.

De Vault, M. (1991) *Feeding the Family: The Social Organisation of Caring as Gendered Work*. London: University of Chicago Press.

Devine, F. and Savage, M. (2004) 'The Cultural Turn, Sociology and Class Analysis' in *Rethinking Class: Culture, Identities and Lifestyles*, F. Devine, M. Savage, J. Scott and R. Crompton (eds). Basingstoke; New York: Palgrave.

Eichenbaum, L. and Orbach, S. (1982) *Understanding Women*. New York: Basic Books.

Entwistle, J. (2004) [2000] *The Fashioned Body*. Cambridge: Polity.

Entwistle, J. and Rocamora, A. (2006) 'Field of Fashion Materialised: A Study of London Fashion Week', *Sociology*, 40(4), 735–751.

Fischer, L. (1981) 'Transitions in the Mother-Daughter Relationship', *Journal of Marriage and the Family*, 45, 613–622.

Ganetz, H. (1995) 'The Shop, the Home and Femininity as a Masquerade' in *Youth Culture in Late Modernity*, J. Fornas and G. Bolin (eds). London: Sage.

Gillies, V. (2007) *Marginalised Mothers: Exploring Working Class Experiences of Parenting*. Abingdon: Routledge.

Goffman, E. (1990) [1959] *The Presentation of Self In Everyday Life*. London: Penguin.

Goffman, E. (1990) [1968] *Stigma: Notes on the Management of Spoiled Identity*. London: Penguin.

Gregson, N. and Beale, V. (2004) 'Wardrobe Matters: The Sorting, Displacement and Circulation of Women's Clothing', *Geoforum*, 35(6), 689–700.

Grove-White, A. (2001) 'No Rules, Only Choices? Repositioning the Self within the Fashion System: A Case Study of Colour and Image Consultancy', *Journal of Material Culture*, 6, 193–211.

Harper, S. J. A., Dewar, P., and Diack, B. A. (2003) 'The Purchase of Children's Clothing – Who has the Upper Hand?' *Journal of Fashion Marketing and Management,* 7(2), 196–206.

Hebdige, D. (2006) [1979] *Subculture: The meaning of Style.* London: Routledge.

Hollingworth, S. and Williams, K. (2010) 'Construction of the Working Class "Chav" amongst Urban, White, Middle-class Youth: "Chavs", Subculture and the Value of Education' in *Young People, Class and Place,* R. McDonald, T. Shidrick and S. Blackman (eds). London: Routledge.

Jenkins, R. (1992) *Pierre Bourdieu.* London: Routledge.

Jenkins, S. (2004) *Gender, Place and the Labour Market.* Aldershot: Ashgate.

Johnson, S., Borrows, A., and Williamson, I. (2004) 'Does My Bump Look Big In This? The Meaning of Bodily Changes for First-time Mothers-to-be', *Journal of Health Psychology,* 9(3), 361–374.

Kellmer-Pringle, M. (1986) *The Needs of Children.* London: Hutchinson.

Kestler, J. (2010) *Intergenerational Fashion Influences: Mother-Daughter Relationships and Fashion Involvement, Fashion Leadership, Opinion Leadership and Information Seeking from One Another.* MA Thesis, Ohio University; available at: http://etd.ohiolink.edu/sendpdf.cgi/Kestler%20Jessica%20L.pdf?ohiou1261402077

Klepp, I. and Storm-Mathisen, A. (2005) 'Reading Fashion as Age: Teenage Girls and Grown Up Women's Accounts of Clothing as Body and Social Status', *Fashion Theory: The Journal of Dress, Body & Culture,* 9(3), 323–342.

Kohn, M. L. (1959) 'Social Class and Parental Values', *The American Journal of Sociology,* 64(4), 337–351.

Kuhn, A. (1995) *Family Secrets: Acts of Memory and Imagination.* London: Verso.

Lawler, S. (2000) *Mothering the Self: Mothers, Daughters, Subjects.* London; New York: Routledge.

Lawler, S. (2004) 'Rules of Engagement: Habitus, Power and Resistance' in *Feminism after Bourdieu,* L. Adkins (ed.). Oxford: Blackwell Publishing.

Lawler, S. (2005) 'Introduction: Class Culture and Identity', *Sociology,* 39(1), 797–806.

Lawler, S. (2005a) 'Disgusted Subjects: The Making of Middle Class Identities', *The Editorial Board of the Sociological Review,* 429–446.

Longhurst, R. (2008) *Maternities: Gender, Bodies and Space.* Oxford: Routledge.

Martens, L. (2014) [2010] 'The Cute, the Spectacle and the Practical: Narratives of New Parents and Babies at the Baby Show' in *Childhood and Consumer Culture,* V. Tingstad and D. Buckingham (eds). London: Palgrave McMillia.

Martens, L., Southerton, D. and Scott, S. (2004) 'Bringing Children (and Parents) into the Sociology of Consumption', *Journal of Consumer Culture,* 4(2), 155–182.

McDowell, L. (2008) 'Thinking Through Class and Gender in the Context of Working Class Studies', *Antipode,* 40(1), 20–24.

McNeal, J. U. (2007) *On Becoming a Consumer: The Development of Consumer Behaviour Patterns in Childhood.* Oxford: Elsevier.

Miller, D. (1998) *A Theory of Shopping.* Oxford: Polity.

Miller, D. (1997) 'How Infants Grow Mothers in North London', *Theory, Culture and Society,* 14(4), 67–88.

Oakley, A. (1979) *Becoming a Mother.* Oxford: Martin Robertson.

Pilcher, J. (2011) 'No Logo? Children's Consumption of Fashion', *Childhood,* 18 (1), 128–141.

Rappaport, E. (2000) *Shopping for Pleasure: Women in the Making of London's West End*. Woodstock: Princeton University Press.

Rafferty(2011)Class-BasedEmotionsandtheAllureofFashionConsumption.*Journal of Consumer Culture*, July 11 (2), 239–260 doi: 10.1177/1469540511403398

Rawlins, E. (2006) 'Mothers Know Best? Intergenerational Notions of Fashion and Identity', *Children's Geographies*, 4(3), 359–377.

Reay, D. (2004) 'Gendering Bourdieu's concept of Capitals? Emotional Capital, Women and Social Class' in *Feminism After Bourdieu*, L. Adkins (ed.). Oxford: Blackwell Publishing.

Sanchez Taylor, J. (2012) 'The Power of Breasts: Gender, Class and Cosmetic Surgery', *Women's Studies International Forum*, 35(6), 458–466.

Savage, M., Bagnall, G. and Longhurst, B. (2001) 'Ordinary, Ambivalent and Defensive', *Sociology* 35(4), 875–892.

Sayer, A. (2002) '"What are you worth?" Why Class is an Embarrassing Subject', *Sociology Research Online*, 7(3). Available at http://www.socresonline.org.uk/7/3/sayer.html.

Simmel, G. (2004) [1901] 'Fashion' in *The Rise of Fashion: A Reader*, D. L. Purdy (ed.). Minnesota: University of Minnesota Press.

Simpson, L. and Douglas, S. (1998) 'Adolescents' Purchasing Role Structure When Shopping by Catalogue for Clothing', *Clothing and Textile Research Journal*, 16(2), 98–104.

Skeggs, B. (2004a) *Class, Self and Culture*. London: Routledge.

Skeggs, B. (2004b) 'Context and Background: Pierre Bourdieu's Analysis of Class, Gender and Sexuality', *The Sociological Review*, 52(s2),19–33.

Skeggs, B. (2005) 'The Making of Class and Gender through Visualizing Moral Subject Formation', *Sociology*, 39(5), 965–982.

Skeggs, B., Thumim, N. and Wood, H. (2008) 'Oh Goodness I am watching Reality TV: How Methods Make Class in Audience Research', *European Journal of Cultural Studies*, 11(1), 5–24.

Slater, D. (1997) *Consumer Culture and Modernity*. Oxford: Blackwell.

Smith, N. (2000) 'What Happened to Class?' *Environment and Planning*, 32, 1011–1032.

Solomon, M. and Rabolt, N.R. (2009) [2004] *Consumer Behaviour in Fashion*. New Jersey: Pearson/Prentice Hall.

Tan, E. S. (2004) *Does Class Matter?* Singapore: World Scientific Publishing.

Tyler, I. (2008) '"Chav Mum, Chav Scum" Class Disgust in Contemporary Britain', *Feminist Media Studies*, 8(1), 17–34.

Veblen, T. (1994) [1899] *Theory of the Leisure Class*. London: Dove Publications.

Walkerdine, V., Lucey, H., and Melody, J. (2001) *Growing Up Girl: Psychosocial Explorations of Gender and Class*. London: Palgrave.

Ward, S. (1974) 'Consumer Socialisation', *Journal of Consumer Research*, 1(September), 1–14.

Woodward, S. (2007) *Why Women Wear What They Wear*. Oxford: Berg.

# Part III

# The Intimate Social Life of Commodities

# 8
# Pretty Pants and Office Pants: Making Home, Identity and Belonging in a Workplace

*Rachel Hurdley*

> *Purity is the enemy of change, of ambiguity and compromise. Most of us would indeed feel safer if our experience could be hard-set and fixed in form.*
>
> (Mary Douglas, 1966, p. 163)

This chapter is based on an ongoing ethnography of a British university campus. The principal research focus is on rethinking and diversifying notions of openness, space and organisation, in terms of how formal and informal social spaces make, and is made by organisational culture. Themes of homely/personal spaces and intimacies emerged during the study. Production and consumption are not separate practices, nor are these monolithic terms helpful in understanding the processual, contingent character of relations and interactions between people and things. The ways in which people shape work, place, and time around them using varieties of materials to make, maintain and perform identities are probably infinite – since they can be the work of a moment. Rather than provide a summary, therefore, the chapter offers four accounts of making home, identity and intimacy at work. And as the research materials include field notes, lists, photographs, film, drawings, audio recordings (and later transcriptions) of interviews in offices, on walks and in 'smokers' corner', the chapter also reflects these variations, rather than following a uniform pattern.

Since the ethnography is ongoing, this writing skirts the literature cited, rather than settling within it. In particular, Bourdieu's cultural analytic concepts (1977; 1986; 1990) and Goffman's social dramaturgy

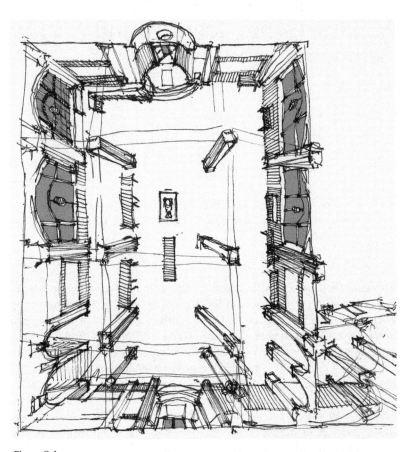

*Figure 8.1a*

*Figure 8.1b*

(1959; 1971; 1983) shaped how I thought about ephemera, developing from earlier work on 'the power of corridors' (Hurdley, 2010). In the first account, *Archaeology of a Desk*, the chapter examines fixed personal space through the archaeology of Margaret's desk drawer, shelving, and pin-boards in the office she shares with two colleagues. Famous for the sheer quantity of stuff she stores and displays, Margaret uses this space and the stuff in it to both accomplish belonging, and distinguish herself, things and practices from the pollutant effect of the workplace. She has also inherited goods from the previous occupant. Next, in *The Birthday Party*, temporally bounded shared spaces such as a seating area where students meet between lectures are the focus. They possess that space, for that time, making a nest of intimacy by casting down bags, coats, moving furniture, lolling their bodies, making a noise and leaving rubbish. Third, *Brand New Office* is an inhabitant's account of a new building, completed in 2013. Finally, *The Cupboard and the Statue* is a poetics of space: the literal edge of this large workplace, where tiny, precarious homes and moments are made.

The chapter engages critically with mainstream social theory on consumption and identity, particularly the grand narratives of Giddens and Beck. By exploring the small and large spaces of work, I show how both the individualisation thesis and emphasis on risk fail to engage with differing concepts of value and intimacy found in contemporary empirical research (for example, Smart, 2007; Gabb, 2008; Taylor, 2013; Skeggs and Wood, 2012). 'Home', like identity and belonging, is relational and intersectional, tempering and tempered by the workplace through nuanced appropriation of things, spaces and times.

## Background: homing from work

This campus ethnography stems in part from an earlier study (Hurdley, 2013). This considered the ways in which people engage with small domestic spaces and everyday materials to make and maintain identities, belonging and 'home'. While identities doing gendered/gendering, classed/classing and family hierarchy work materialised in the home, these were contingent upon, and also maintained dominant values of the 'universal particular' (Savage, 2003, p. 536). Whereas the blurring of boundaries between work and home has entered the vernacular as 'working from home', the parallel practice of 'homing from work' remains understated. For example, one participant in the study asked to be interviewed in his university office, where he displayed family photographs and other 'homely' artefacts.

  Bourdieu laid the foundation stone for cultural analysis in late twentieth and early twenty-first century Anglo-American sociologies of consumption (Heinich, 2010). However, there is no space in this poststructural structure for alternate practices and identities outside dominant circuits of value and property (see Strathern, 1996). This closed circuit depended upon constant forgetting, silencing, and devaluing 'the rest'. 'But what people and places fall off this map being relegated to or indeed choosing to reside, in distant and decentred peripheries?' ask Sanger and Taylor (2013, p. 3). Those who cannot account for themselves as legitimate members of the circuit do not count. *What* matters – cultural materials, such as texts, things, routines – and *who* matters are eternally bound. Other post-Bourdieusian scholars are extending, rebuilding and re-rendering this architecture (for example, Skeggs, 1997; 2004; Adkins and Skeggs, 2005; Lawler, 2008; Bennett et al., 2009; Casey, 2008; Atkinson, 2012; Taylor, 2013).

  Nevertheless, leading theorists continue to plot the social in eras, allowing endless rediscovery of 'the new' through modernity or post/ late/liquid modernity, filled with fragmented/ atomised/ globular/ globalised/ mobilised/ individualised neo-liberal persons (Giddens, 1991; Beck, 1992; Rose, 1998; Bauman 2001, 2013). In particular, consumption has been theorised as a defining late modern practice, together with a transformation in intimate social relations (Giddens, 1992; Beck and Beck-Gernsheim, 1995, 2002, 2013; Bauman, 2003). Pondering the world might be valuable for theory-building, but these stories became grand narratives, underpinning economic, political and social monolithic 'truths'. 'Genesis amnesia' (Bourdieu, 1977, 1990) besets such theories – as if 'the social' can periodically be cleaved stone-like; a paradox for purveyors of fluidity. The four accounts will show how de Certeau's (1984) concepts of 'delinquent narratives' in a micropolitics of resistance are similarly overwrought (or overthought). Such desk work, the charting and building of sociological citadels like 'the "geometry inspired" hierarchical list of what or who counts' (Weston, 1996: cited in Taylor, 2011, p. 212), however, is disrupted by practices of everyday life both in the family and other networks.

  This chapter looks at different kinds of ordinary 'desk work', such as the warming of water for an unapproved cup of tea, the care for colleagues, and the dilapidations and inefficiencies that fuzz the cold clear lines of the 'official imprint' of 'institutional authority' (Goffman, 1983, p. 17). Goffman's (1961) 'hospital underlife', where patients enjoy greater control through either tacit permission or insubordination, was a constant theoretical thread throughout the ethnography, although universities and asylums have some different institutional attributes (Scott 2010; 2011). The 'free places', 'group territories' and 'personal territories' that patients used through either insubordination or tacit permission shadow the following accounts. The 'official imprint' of 'institutional authority' is stamped into the campus, through practices and materials, such as lecture timetables and the performative architectures of culturally valuable old buildings and prestigious new developments. Scott's recent rethinking of Goffman's (1961) Total Institutions is a critique of what she terms 'Reinventive Institutions', including universities, whose 'greedy practices' (Scott, 2010, p. 226) 'are accepted by their subjects as fair, objective and morally benign' (p. 220). Rather than Foucault's (1975/91) theorisation of Bentham's panopticon she suggests that horizontal surveillance by peers leads to 'performative regulation' through the 'discipline of interaction order' (Scott, 2010, pp. 226–227).

The effects and mediations of human bodies in social space, itself an ambiguous concept, are concerns for Bourdieu, Goffman and those who have extended their ideas. Yet, concepts of consumption and production or reproduction persist, and are only strengthened by sociologies of space (Lefebvre 1974 [1991]). For example, the visual impact of large public or corporate buildings has been, and remains a dominant socio-spatial concern, as does the control of bodies moving through space (Dovey, 1999; Dale and Burrell, 2008; Bennett REF). These buildings are there to be consumed visually, while the institution surveys and swallows up its subjects. Moreover, synoptic surveillance by peers is as much a constraint as the eye of the 'university' – whatever that may be. How can empirical and theoretical sociological writing on consumption, embodiment and interaction interpret the architecture of social organisation, beyond existing work on organisational behaviour (for which, see Hurdley, 2010)?

The sites of the following accounts are all on a university campus, which is sometimes, and in some places, homely, messy, friendly, and even familial. I saw something happening that was neither the 'production of space', nor 'delinquent narratives', strategies of resistance or disciplinary regimes. Something is happening in the social monoliths of the twenty-first century, which narratives of power cannot quite relate.

Neither 'statement' buildings nor other capital accumulations invested with value by those who possess and profit from them can shape such processes. No longer have capitals, but inflections mattered: the intimate intricacies of everyday life.

## A note on presentation

Since this book engages critically with mainstream theories of consumption, the chapter is not formulaic in presentation of empirical materials. As any method of representation is interpretive, the four accounts are practices in different forms of turning research into text and image. Different organisational cultures shape and are shaped by anyone interacting with the materials and spaces of organisation. Similarly, the ordering of research materials through interpretation, and of these on the page, are not simply 'products' for consumption, but are 'relational materials' (Law 1994, p. 23), in processes of meaning-making with the reader. Ways of representing research are always under methodological discussion (see Hammersley and Atkinson, 2007; Law, 2007; Denzin and Lincoln, 2011). Particularly salient to this study are the ethical dilemmas of writing organisational ethnography, and the associated aesthetics of representation (Rinehart, 1998; Hammersley, 2008; Ellis, 2009; Ybema et al., 2009; Hurdley, 2010). 'Synthetic sociology' (Hurdley, 2014) separates the properties of mess and lumpiness from research materials, to achieve elegant architectural orders of knowledge (see Foucault, 1966/89, pp. xvi– xviii).

As Bourdieu, drawing on Marx, cautioned reflexive sociologists to take care, lest they mistake 'the things of logic for the logic of things' (1990, p. 61), so a smooth rendering of research materials that vary in their qualities would, however legitimate, be an act of misordering. First, the stuff of Margaret's desk spills out in an increasingly disordered list. Then students celebrate a birthday within the common time of the lecture schedule, observed in (edited) field notes, with a counterpoint of semi-fictionalised doings within and between legitimate practices. A senior academic takes the long view on a new building, his words cut and collated from a long interview transcript. As a quiet ending, 'unofficial' adaptations of campus materials suggest other ways of doing things, originally assembled in photographs and field notes. These four written accounts are interspersed with images from the project, which do not illustrate the text, but offer other ways of knowing, the aim of ethnography (Hurdley, 2007; Atkinson, 2014).

*Figure 8.2a*

*Figure 8.2b*

## Four accounts

*Archaeology of a desk: Margaret's list of things (compiled by the researcher)*
This is my little home:

**On the desk**: bacon baps (Sean always gets them on Fridays).
Bootees and a shawl for my daughter's baby (from Beth's bottom drawer; things her mother & grandmother made).

**On top in the drawer:**
*Disaster Button 'just-in-case' bag containing:*
Spare tights; brand new spare tights (for the girls – not my minging ones). Pretty pants & not so pretty plain pants – office pants just in case – functional pants (looking a bit bedraggled); skin balm (*Mother & Baby*, must have bought it cheap); another moisturiser (gone lumpy); every size of toothpaste, every make of toothpaste; flannel, (a leftover from hospital); deodorant; Strepsils for sore throat; bandage just in case.
Also: a sewing kit (temporarily lost); my own French dressing; a proper soup spoon (from my set at home); foil & Clingfilm; breakfast cereals. My own glass; pegs; *Power Surge* cuddly toy from my son (he knows that I'm failing), a *Little Miss Giggle* McDonalds toy from my daughter; a stressball 'hen' ~~from my daughter~~ from my sister who worked in Ministry of Agriculture
*plus*
gloves just in case.

**Underneath**:
Marriott shoe polish & shoe mitt, (I don't know when I stayed in the Marriott but obviously a long time ago)
Stuff that goes on forever: a ~~spare belt~~ handbag strap (to carry heavy things home).
University t-shirt made 2004! (Never been worn but just in case I dribble – low enough to wear as a dress).
I don't know where my sewing kit's gone.
Always teabags.

**At the bottom**:
*A box of office-y things inherited from Anne who was here before, in the type-writer days*:
Keyboard cleaner; anti-static screen wipe – mine so must be more recent; solvent cleaner. Never used any of it. Toothbrush cover (broken); potato peeler & bone-handled butter knife made in Sheffield (when the hell did I bring those in? Why? Maybe to peel pears).

**On the corner of the desk:**
Tin opener; the red-handled butter knife from Heather. Daily essentials to lend out – 'Can I borrow your knife?' 'Can I borrow your spoon?' Special cutlery I know is mine (I'll donate these to somebody). Plastic spoons (never used) and bits & bobs; random things to pick out Chinese sweets someone brought back. Might be useful. Bowl of fruit; cup and saucer that doubles as soup bowl; raffle ticket (didn't win).

**On the shelf:**
My name in Chinese because I'm learning Chinese (Is it the right way round? must laminate it). Cat on cushion (which Michelle wants when I leave); a book by an author with the same name as me someone found when they tidied their office; a beautiful little box (from a Chinese student); a panda from one of the girls; a plaque from one of the boys, with the leaflet in English that tells you all about it & the box it came in.

Behind the plant, a beautiful box (empty) with a butterfly clasp from a Korean visitor. Tree of Life from a Mexican visitor, made of clay typical for the region (pushed to the back because Michelle hates it. Must keep at home in case she ever visits again); my little lady; Teddy hiding a bottle of Spanish liqueur (not allowed in the office but one of the visitors gave me that).

**On the low cabinet:**
The teapot my daughter found in a charity shop (made by someone with my name!); espresso cup; Nespresso machine from the ex-Head of Department (we all love it).

**On the pinboard**
My *Race for Life* medal – we all did it together; Christmas card with crocheted flower (made by a colleague for each of us); big poster made by a colleague for me as a reminder of our field trip to Berlin; a very intricate fan (too pretty to leave flat); a card from a student who's gone now; photo of my mother; photos of my children; the date thing (from my daughter) that I haven't changed; photo of my daughter's Dalmatian (which suddenly died so I can't bear to take it down).

**Essential Daily Box**
Cereals, cereal bowl, my spoon & my spare Weetabix (sugar by the coffee machine); Dalmatian mug from Michelle (doubles as a cereal bowl as I have to drink tea out of a bone china cup); hand cream from a girl who used to work here; my own squeegee thing (the one in the kitchen is always minging wet).

Emergency rations: Penguin biscuit; packet of crisps; little bit of mouthwash. Glass used as a storage container. Spare Sainsbury's carrier bag I've had for years … a hole in it so it's no use.

Office tea towels – not mine – a set I bought for the office to replace the minging old one no one washed (I wash them at home every week so someone will have to do that now).

I did have a sewing kit in here, there's a sewing kit and people come to me for the sewing kit, don't know what I've done with it now.

### The narrow top drawer:
My homage to Anne, almost unchanged since I inherited it, except to top up supplies: little boxes with different size staples in, miniature bulldog clips (so cute in different colours).

My bit: pencils and a few tissues – the economy version in the office – not posh tissues. Also *The Philosophy of Office Life* notepad; Big Mistakes eraser; 'Mr Wonderful' toy, now lost – think the dogs ate him (all from the shoe box Mich made up years ago for our Christmas Bran Tub)

(I shall leave those random things here that Anne left here)

### Left hand drawer
Files; a gap to keep my handbag in.

## The birthday party: observations

10.44 am, a science department in an old building: large three-sided seating area, bounded by wooden trellises, with one small low round table in the centre, one in the corner where I am sitting, on which I've put my bags, and a third at the other corner. A bin adjacent to the corridor: sign 'Throw your rubbish away. No drinks'. A female student has sat down and put her coffee on the middle table. She is texting. Three female students sit down near me, one says, 'I don't want to sit in a line, it's strange'. I guess I have stolen the corner. In the other corner, the table has been pulled out for a birthday cake with candles. I can hear cries of 'Happy Birthday' etc. It is clearly prearranged as a girl says, "We all just said we'll meet in the foyer." The group next to me are discussing lab work and a story about a lecturer not helping or understanding. Chairs are moved out around the middle table where four boys sit and eat, two stand to talk.

*Happy Birthday* is sung. Three separate groups: the three girls next to me, the four boys on chairs with one now on the floor and the sixth now seated, the birthday group of ten or so standing and seated. The girl is texting, with a magazine on her lap. Bag on seat next to her. Seat between me and girls unoccupied. Boy standing with them has just sat down. The lone girl has left – time for lectures. The girl who was telling the story is still telling stories about experiments and making them entertaining, joking about someone not understanding: 'She is definitely retarded'. Another relates a similar one. The six boys are now all seated, discussing work. Some eating, some holding yellow sheets: coursework? Seem settled. Birthday group there with balloons, squeakers etc.

*In the toilets, two young women are chatting in front of the sinks. Their bags are on their shoulders as there is nowhere to put them down (except the floor) or hang them up. One rummages in her bag for mascara which she applies, leaning over the sinks to look in the mirror. The other takes off her wet coat, swapping her bag from hand to hand, before removing her jumper to stuff in her bag and put her coat back on. She then gets out a small make-up bag and starts putting on lip gloss. A toilet flushes, and a woman comes out wanting to wash her hands. The students break off their talk, stepping back from their make-shift dressing table until the woman moves to the hand-dryer, which temporarily interrupts their conversation. She leaves, as the young women drink from water bottles and make their way to the next lecture.*

It is 11.10 [lecture start time] so all three groups seem settled. The boy with the three girls left a few minutes ago. Girl's bag on chair between us now. One empty chair where the lone girl was. One girl leaves birthday group waving, hugging another girl. Boy gets lone girl's chair to join the large male group. He bats away a balloon from the birthday group. The boys discuss football. The one who just joined them hasn't spoken. He was sorting some papers and has left. Birthday group is mixed boys and girls, playing with balloons and squeakers. Talking quietly. Girl comes and sits next to me, puts her bag down, does not seem to be part of the group. Boy with papers has returned, talking with neighbour and reading free student paper [which is passed round, as is another paper]. Balloon thrown on floor to float around. Boy playing with lighter. Birthday group a bit smaller now, two boys standing, two girls sitting. Balloon still floating.

*A research student, living with his family in university accommodation, comes in for a long day's work at the computer. In his bag is a sandwich box, an apple, an old squash bottle full of water, a flask of coffee and rolling tobacco. The food and drink saves him from the expense of campus food outlets, although, without access to a microwave, he misses having hot food at lunchtime. Every hour or so, he takes a cigarette break, packing his bag up and locking the computer, but leaving a note book on the desk and a scarf on the back of the chair, to ensure no one takes his place. The signs around campus are constant reminders that smoking is not permitted on university grounds, but he prefers to risk censure than stand in the rain on the pavement. Joining the small group under the trees, he waves to a friend who comes to join in the gossip. The Research Director, on his way back from a quick coffee up the road, stops by to catch up with a colleague. An undergraduate walks past into the university refectory, carrying his Costa cappuccino. On his way back into the computer room, the student notices that someone has plugged a kettle into a well-hidden socket. Steam rises.*

11.30: Lighter returned by birthday group to a member of the boy group. One of them is reading the paper and asks if the others have seen 'the law student story' – seems to be about a drinking disaster. Girls group talking about work. Birthday girl still there in birthday sash. Several empty seats there now. Boy group discussing football. Girl next to me silent and looking at a diary. Boy in corridor through double doors opposite, leaning on windowsill, drinking from can. Waiting? Girl next to me seems to be reading blurb at start of diary, so not really reading. Is she waiting here? Boy group telling experiment stories. Another boy leaning on other side of corridor, now the two of them walk towards entrance together. Birthday girls and male group get up to leave. Play a trick by hiding absent friend's coat above a pushed up ceiling tile. They all know each other. They leave the balloons. The male group leaves free papers, an empty coke can and other rubbish on the table. They do not return the chairs. They rescue the coat after some discussion.

*Meanwhile, a student cycles towards the car park at high speed. She passes the vents blasting warm air from a science department. The student locks her bike and hurries into the building, a large rucksack on her back. She gets into the lift alone. As it rattles up the building, she finds her deodorant in a side pocket, sprays under her top and tucks the can back into her bag. Just in time for a tutorial, she leaves the scent of sweat and chemical flowers in the lift.*

11.50 a.m., they have all left. The girl group is leaving. They must all have been here for an hour break between lectures. Someone has left a coat on chairs where the birthday group were, not the coat they hid. They feel this is a safe place to leave stuff? Girl next to me leaves, throwing rubbish in the bin.

12.01 – the rush starts [after lectures].

## Brand new office: in Simon's words

'The pictures are wondering if they'll ever get hung. Not because of a lack of will but because it looks like you're not allowed to bang nails in the walls, or any other fixtures. So in other words I haven't got round to deciding whether to take the risk of banging a nail in the wall. [The blinds are] between two bits of glass so they're operated electronically, only they don't work. Yet. But if I could make them work and shut the door I have total privacy and or I can choose to have partial privacy or I can choose to have no privacy whereas Steve [the IT technician] can't choose any of those things. I'm embarrassed about leading a very democratic team and all parts of that team are really important. If you wanted to reflect that in terms of physical geography, layout and buildings, ideally they should be four sides of the same space. But they're not. They're in a situation which means two of them have private space offices and two don't. So that physical fact makes it more difficult for me to underline the parts we all play which are essential. They're like jigsaw pieces you know; take one of them away and the whole thing is not a picture any more. There are always hierarchies and categories, it's just that they become starker, become rewritten in a less arbitrary manner. In this situation it's a pretty neat division in all.

There is a sense in which the surroundings kind of diminish things; it would be very difficult to have anything but a desk between two chairs. It's that thing about a building and the way it's equipped really, furnished. Being, being very task-focused only, you know, perfunctory, yeah. So maybe it takes a while for other compensatory habits or alternative ways of using a space to emerge. You know, if there were rules about banging nails in the wall, people will have forgotten them, eventually. Or you know, if there were arrangements where you could only have [desk space] for six months they will unravel eventually. Now what people do [in the older campus buildings] is partly a function of original design, but it's also a function of a great deal of adaptation over a great deal of time. [But you] have to weigh up the cultural capital of old buildings with the vast cost of maintaining them. And all we've got here is the front-end [of] someone's pretty strong, actually powerful conception of what a workspace should be like. Another driver is being seen to develop buildings, capital projects, bring a different kind of capital to the institution. They surround it with evidence of growth, of success. It reminds me of an ocean liner ... or a prison.'

## The cupboard and the statue: poetics of things

Tucked under one of the grander statues and almost the same shade of grey, is a duvet. A syringe. Beneath a balustraded balcony, cardboard boxes lie flattened and spread along the stone, the length of a man. Contractors loading furniture into skips pause to make a few chairs into a circle for their coffee break. Above cushioned chairs and dismantled desks, a kitchen sink juts from the skip. In a staff room fridge, cartons of milk proliferate, many labelled with people's names, some turning to cheese. On the tables lie the remains of a buffet with a sign, 'Help Yourself'. A student pauses for some minutes to tap at his laptop on a broad oak windowsill. Down a corridor is a tall cupboard recessed into the wall, an original feature. It is stacked to the ceiling with boxes of weekly donations for a Foodbank scheme: cereals, pasta, meat, beans, sauces, long-life milk and honey. No Smoking signs uselessly guard bins greying with ash and pockmarked by cigarette burns. Noisy hot air vents interrupt phone calls of coffee gulpers, hurrying to another meeting. Tucked against the vents, a blanket, damp cigarette butts, an ageing Sainsbury's holding a sandwich box, crisp packet and crushed can. The curve of a wall, sweeping under the main body of the building, is scarred by skateboard wheels; fine sport at the weekends.

Up the road looms the new building; its innards a white cathedral of learning, its walls clean of art or Blu-tack, for the time being. But soon, Stephen's pictures will hang on adhesive hooks, making one small corner a different place. The same signs that proliferate on and in older buildings on campus will start to appear: *Put Hot Drinks Here to Avoid Spillages*; *Use Other Door* and other marks of everyday use. Staff will hesitate at the doorway, remembering the quality of the coffee, the inhuman scale of the space, and turn towards the sofa and teapots of a nearby café. They will walk past the supermarket, soon to be demolished to make way for more university development. In an old building, female toilet is refurbished, with more cubicles and a long shelf below a mirror, separate from the sinks and new hand dryers. When the door opens from the busy entrance hall, women's faces stare back from the mirror. Margaret takes early retirement, leaving Michelle with the cat ornament but moving the Tree of Life to her living room windowsill.

Despite hints, Sean does not inherit her soup spoon. Stuck to the office pinboard is a photograph of Margaret in her kitchen, drinking coffee from the Nespresso machine on the worktop: her retirement present. She is wearing the 2004 University t-shirt as a nightie.

All these things: boxes and furniture discarded as rubbish; rubbish transformed into beds and common rooms; boxes storing food for those who sleep in the shelter and warmth of university property; food made waste. A Sainsbury's bag kept so long 'just in case' in Margaret's drawer, it rots and has to be thrown away; a similar bag left by someone who leaves his bed there too: will either or both be in a bin when or if he returns? She imagines future needs; he faces need now, and a precarious future where 'just in case' is too vast to be imagined. Signs multiply on campus, many added as *post hoc* correctives to errors and disobediences by its 'users'. There are never enough signs for the multiple imagined, possible and practised transgressions. Signs accentuate the many inefficiencies, lack of control and unplanned failures of the organisation. A door is not fixed for many weeks; rubbish is left in a seating area; people drink Costa coffee in the refectory. As 'the university' (and what constitutes that is always unclear) continues to pursue economic and cultural capital through the acquisition and development of property, little things and small events rub and knock at its material grandeur. A toilet is refurbished to adapt to users' needs, but another problem (of unwanted visibility) is produced. Are broken doors and planned iconic buildings emblematic of an organisational capital that is never quite (good) enough? Provision is made (by individuals using university email systems, paper signs and storage) to nurture the bodies of those who lack economic (and social) capital via Foodbanks. A single desk space is a home in miniature, while others who have no space to call their own use what is available: a bag, a plug socket, a wall. Is this resistance, individual autonomy, or making do?

## Some conclusions

To return to the central theme of the book, dominant theories of the neo-liberal, or individualised, or globular/globalised individual consumer cannot be sustained by empirical research. Although Bourdieu's (1986) cultural analysis was empirically thorough, introducing a new theoretical paradigm, the system of value he constructed rests on a 'universal particular' (Savage 2003, p. 536) that excludes so many and so much. While more recent cultural theorists have designed their theses of post or late modernity around notions of mobility, consumption and access to circuits or networks of power, these are as ungrounded as the mobile worlds they postulate (Giddens 1991, 1992; Beck, 1992; Beck and Beck-Gernsheim, 1995, 2002, 2013; Rose, 1998; Bauman, 2001; 2003; 2013). Paradoxically, however, these lie heavy on sociologies of identity. The chapter shows how, regardless of the validity of such readings of power and value in the twenty-first century, other ways of doing identity, home (or homeliness) and belonging are at work. Designing the social in eras, building blocks of time, space and people anew with each sociological demolition of what went before certainly produces neat horizons. But 'the horizon is not the joining of earth and sky' (Pallasmaa, 2005, p. 34).

There are parallels between what this sociology is doing, and what participants do in this research project. Just as sociologists can write of 'the individual', so participants spoke of 'the university'. These absent monoliths may shape identity and belonging practices, but not entirely. So, radical sociologies of everyday practices are formed partly by that dominant architecture. However, precisely because they are 'radical', rooted in the mundane, they play in a different key. There is no harmony, except as an accidental effect.

Making and maintaining group membership through impression management and interaction order (Goffman, 1959; 1983) are highly visible accomplishments in the accounts, framed within institutional times and spaces. Scott's revision of the 'total institution' to theorise how 'reinventive institutions' and their inhabitants/employees maintain a 'disciplinary regime' (2010, p. 226) further explicates mundane interactions. However, there is something else going on. This is highlighted by the materials left behind on the peripheries of campus buildings: blankets, boxes and drugs paraphernalia. These were little homes, and might be again, but any accomplishment of identity or belonging runs parallel to the circuits of value established through legitimated practices (Bourdieu, 1986). Passers-by have no interaction with the people who leave these fragments, who inhabit the same space, yet make them utterly different: dwelling places, rather than for walking through or past. Statues and vents metamorphose in this 'other' world. They are skeuomorphs, used quite differently from their intended purpose, and valued for quite different properties: bodily warmth and shelter, perhaps camouflage, rather than heat disposal and visual cultural capital. The things themselves offer a multitude of meanings and possibilities, yet attending only to dominant circuits of value *de*means them. Similarly, there can be no 'performative regulation' (Scott, 2010), if this is a different drama.

Within the buildings, things that people do everyday are not tactics of resistance, nor always regulated through institutional/interactional regimes. Simon's 'brand new' office is designed 'for a work purpose', and he is separated off from his team through an architecture of hierarchy (Lefebvre, 1974 [1991]; Dovey, 1999) branding work with the stamp of clean-cut efficiency However, this attempt at organisational geometry is disrupted because his office is not a fit space for meetings. It becomes effectively useless for one of its designated purposes. Purpose transforms into purposelessness through everyday practice. Margaret's drawer, designed for files, has a gap for her handbag. The other large drawer becomes a little home, where her identity – as someone who uses a soup spoon for soup and can drink tea only from a bone china cup – is forged over years, supported by her workplace colleagues who in turn reshape the workplace into somewhere familial and intimate.

Although such practices are often disturbed by organisational 'reorganizing;...a wonderful method...for creating the illusion of progress while producing confusion, inefficiency and demoralization' (Ogburn, 1957, pp. 32–33), there is nevertheless hope in these peripheral doings, miniature 'architectures of decency' (Oppenheimer and Hursley, 2002; see also Harvey, 2000). As an ending, I will return to the Douglas's (1966) epigraph on purity that opened the chapter. Attempts at organisational 'purity' fail: signs go up, toilets are refurbished, and the endless quest for solidity in big buildings and properly implemented practices goes on. But there is another culture, of hands, feet, skateboards, kettle steam and balloon-blowing breath that wears away at the hard edges of the stone and warms the concrete. This culture is not, then about the production or consumption of space, bodies, and things in the 'hard-set and fixed' certainty of nouns such as modernity, individual or consumption, which deny process, ambiguity and mess. In their solid states, they are powerful monoliths celebrating or mourning how the 'late modern' or 'postmodern' world works. They overshadow the slip-sliding ephemera happening around and about them. However, this is all still happening, regardless of what programmatic statements are made, in built or written form, And perhaps this is the conclusion, for the time being: something else is happening, that does not engage with dominant sociological discourses and counter-discourses for which power remains the central trope. Working towards a 'minor sociology' of making, doubting, losing, trying, even failing, may offer another way of understanding what is happening here.

*Figure 8.3a*

*Figure 8.3b*

# References

Adkins, L. and Skeggs, B. (2005) *Feminism After Bourdieu*. Oxford: Wiley Blackwell.

Atkinson, P. (2014) *For Ethnography*. London: Sage.

Atkinson, W. (2012) 'Review Essay: "Where Now for Bourdieu-inspired Sociology?"' *Sociology*, 46, 167–173.

Bauman Z. (2001) *The Individualized Society*. Cambridge: Polity.

Bauman Z. (2003) *Liquid Love: On the Frailty of Human Bond*. Cambridge: Polity.

Bauman Z. (2013) *Liquid Modernity*. Cambridge: Polity.

Beck, U. (1992) *Risk Society*. London: Sage.

Beck, U. and Beck-Gernsheim, E. (1995) *The Normal Chaos of Love*. Cambridge: Polity.

Beck, U. and Beck-Gernsheim, E. (2002) *Individualization: Institutionalized Individualism and its Social and Political Consequences*. London: Sage.

Beck, U. and Beck-Gernsheim, E. (2013) *Distant Love*. Cambridge: Polity.

Bennett, T., Savage, M., Silva, E., Warde, A., Gayo-Cal, M and Wright, D. (2009) *Culture, Class, Distinction*. London: Routledge.

Bourdieu, P. (1977) *Outline of a Theory of Practice*. Cambridge: Cambridge University Press.

Bourdieu, P. (1986) *Distinction: A Social Critique of the Judgment of Taste* [trans. R. Nice]. London: Routledge.

Bourdieu, P. (1990) *In Other Words: Essays Towards a Reflexive Sociology*. Cambridge: Polity.

Casey, E. (2008) *Women, Pleasure and the Gambling Experience*. Aldershot: Ashgate.

Dale K. and Burrell G. (2008), *The Spaces of Organisation & the Organisation of Space*. Basingstoke: Palgrave Macmillan.

De Certeau, M. (1984) *The Practice of Everyday Life* [trans. S. Rendall]. Berkeley: University of California Press.

Denzin, N. and Lincoln, Y. (2011) 'Introduction: The Discipline and Practice of Qualitative Research'in N. Denzin & Y. Lincoln (eds), *Sage Handbook of Qualitative Research*, pp. 1–20. London: Sage.

Douglas, M. (1966 [2002]) *Purity and Danger: An Analysis of Concept of Pollution and Taboo*. London: Routledge.

Dovey, K. (1999) *Framing Places: Mediating power in built form*. London: Routledge

Foucault, M. (1989 [1966]) *The Order of Things*. London: Routledge.

Foucault, M. (1975 [1991]) *Discipline and Punish*. Harmondsworth: Penguin.

Gabb, J. (2008) *Researching Intimacy in Families*. Basingstoke: Palgrave Macmillan.

Giddens, A. (1991) *Modernity and Self-Identity*. Cambridge: Polity.

Giddens, A. (1992) *The Transformation of Intimacy*. Cambridge: Polity.

Goffman, E. (1959) *The Presentation of Self in Everyday Life*. Harmondsworth: Penguin.

Goffman E. (1961) *Asylums: Essays on the Social Situation of Mental Patients and Other Inmates*. Harmondsworth: Penguin.

Goffman, E. (1971) *Relations in Public*. New York: Harper and Row.

Goffman, E. (1983) 'The Interaction Order', *American Sociological Review*, 48, 1–17

Hammersley, M. (2008) *Questioning Qualitative Inquiry: Critical Essays*. London: Sage.

Hammersley, M. and Atkinson, P. (2007) *Ethnography: Principles in Practice*. New York: Routledge.

Harvey, D. (2000) *Spaces of Hope*. Edinburgh: Edinburgh University Press.

Heinich, N. (2010) 'What Does "Sociology of Culture" Mean? Notes on a Few Trans-Cultural Misunderstandings', *Cultural Sociology*, 4(2), 257–265.

Hurdley, R. (2007) 'Focal Points: Framing Material Culture and Visual Data', *Qualitative Research*, 7, 355–374.

Hurdley, R. (2010) 'The Power of Corridors: Connecting Doors, Mobilising Materials, Plotting Openness', *The Sociological Review*, 58(1), 45–64.

Hurdley, R. (2013) *Home, Materiality, Memory and Belonging: Keeping Culture*. Basingstoke: Palgrave Macmillan.

Hurdley, R. (2014) 'Synthetic Sociology and the "Long Workshop": How Mass Observation Ruined Meta-methodology', *Sociological Research Online*, 19(3) http://www.socresonline.org.uk/19/3/contents.htm.

Law, J. (1994) *Organising Modernity*. Oxford: Blackwell.

Law, J. (2007) 'Making a Mess with Method'in *The Sage Handbook of Social Science Methodology*, W. Outhwaite and S. Turner (eds), pp. 595–606. London: Sage.

Lawler, S. (2008) *Identity; Sociological Perspectives*. Cambridge: Polity.

Lefebvre, H. (1974 [1991]) *The Production of Space* [trans. D. Nicholson Smith]. Oxford: Blackwell.

Ogburn, C. G. 'Merrill's Marauders' (Harper's Magazine, 1957, pp 29–46) Available at https://archive.org/stream/harpersmagazine214alde#page/n47/mode/2up [accessed August 13, 2014].

Oppenheimer, A. and Hursley, T. (2002) *Rural Studio: Samuel Mockbee and an Architecture of Decency*. Princeton: Princeton University Press.

Pallasmaa, J. (2005) *The Eyes of the Skin: Architecture and the Senses*. Chichester: Wiley.

Rose N. (1998) *Inventing Ourselves: Psychology, Power and Personhood*. Cambridge: Cambridge University Press.

Sanger, T. and Taylor, Y. (ed.) (2013) *Mapping Intimacies: Relations, Exchanges, Affects*. Basingstoke: Palgrave Macmillan.

Scott, S. (2010) 'Revisiting the Total Institution: Performative Regulation in the Reinventive Institution', *Sociology*, 44, 213–231.

Scott, S. (2011) *Total Institutions and Reinvented Identities. Identity studies in the Social Sciences*. Basingstoke: Palgrave Macmillan

Skeggs, B. (1997) *Formations of Class and Gender*. London: Sage.

Skeggs, B. (2004) *Class, Self, Culture*. London: Routledge.

Skeggs, B. (2011) 'Imagining Personhood Differently: Person Value and Autonomist Working-class Value Practices', *The Sociological Review* 59(3), 496–513.

Skeggs, B. and Wood, H. (2012) *Reacting to Reality Television: Performance, Audience and Value*. London: Routledge.

Smart, C. (2007) *Personal Life*. Cambridge: Cambridge University Press.

Strathern, M. (1996) 'Cutting the Network', *The Journal of the Royal Anthropological Institute*, 2(3), 517–535.

Strathern, M. (2000) *Audit Cultures: Anthropological Studies in Accountability, Ethics and the Academy*. London: Routledge.

Taylor, Y. (2011) 'Intersectional Dialogues – a Politics of Possibility?' *Feminism & Psychology,* 21(2), 211–217.

Taylor, Y. (2013) *Fitting into Place?: Class and Gender Geographies and Temporalities.* London: Ashgate.

Ybema, S., Yanow, D., Wels, H. and Kamsteeg, F. H. (2009) *Organizational Ethnography: Studying the Complexity of Everyday Life.* London: Sage.

Weston, K. (1996) *Render Me, Gender Me. Lesbians Talk Sex, Class, Color, Studmuffins...* New York: Columbia University Press.

# 9
# Buying for Baby: How Middle-Class Mothers Negotiate Risk with Second-Hand Goods

*Emma Waight*

The passing on of used or otherwise second-hand baby and children's goods is nothing new. Clothing, as well as toys and equipment, can barely be used by one child before growing out of them; that item now redundant for one family yet with plenty of useful life left in it for another (Gregson and Crewe, 1998). Such goods may be passed on to family or friends as 'hand-me-downs' or entered into semi-formalised systems of exchange including charity shops, car boot sales or online sale sites. The term 'second-hand' is used here to describe goods which have not been purchased brand new from conventional retail outlets but rather have already been owned and/or used by another. Whilst second-hand is the term commonly used in the UK and adopted by key authors including Gregson and Crewe (1997; 2003), in the US and other parts of the world 'thrift' is often appropriated and mirrored in the originating literature (Arnould and Bardhi, 2005; Medvedev, 2012).

This chapter draws on a broader UK-based study on the second-hand consumption practices of parents, namely mothers consuming used baby and children's clothes, toys and equipment at nearly new sales. The study explored the role of social networks in structuring attendance to the sale, as well as the social role of the sales themselves as a site facilitating bonding, learning and information flows. In addition, it included an investigation of the multiple ways in which mothers negotiate and moderate the risks entailed in consuming previously used goods through social practice, adherence to safety conventions and domestic divestment rituals. The final point provides the focus of this chapter and considers the ways in which middle-class mothers negotiate risk and enact intimacy through the material in order to benefit from the enhanced affordably of second-hand goods. Whilst conventional shopping practices have been studied extensively to date, the shift from a concern with formal retail sites to a more holistic view of consumption as an everyday practice has only occurred in the last decade or so and even then is still under-researched. Focusing on the mother as consumer as well as carer, this research addresses a gap in the knowledge of mother's co-consuming practices related to second-hand goods (Cook, 2013).

The life of an object, as well as the relationship between an individual and the object, does not begin and/or end at point of purchase. Whilst there is an increasing awareness and interest in the journey of commodities prior to retail, primarily linked to ethical concerns of worker exploitation and environmental degradation (Vitell and Muncy, 1992; Humphery, 2011) new products purchased in mainstream retail outlets are generally still not considered by consumers for their pre-purchase lifecycle. Instead, they are thought to 'begin' at the point of purchase, any history prior to that readily disregarded. As such, consumers are able to mobilise the symbolic value of commodities through the way they are appropriated post-purchase, providing a material form in which to construct and display their identities. This then means that second-hand goods, already used by another, may be seen to be tainted, contaminated or otherwise influenced by their past.

Current research into the second-hand consumer has only just touched upon how actors may edit, rationalise and justify this inscribed material biography (Gregson and Crewe, 1997; Horne and Maddrell, 2002). Instead the main focus of enquiry has been on categorising the second-hand consumer – the financially and socially excluded (Williams and Windebank, 2002; James et al., 2010), the politically/sustainably motivated (Franklin, 2011; Waight, 2013) and the vintage identifier (Palmer, 2004; DeLong et al., 2005). Such work would benefit from a greater consideration of both gender and class, particularly in light of the middle-class consumer and the multiple reasons leading such a group to second-hand economies when they are not otherwise excluded from conventional retail. Indeed Gregson (2007) calls for a broader conceptualisation of consumption research; an approach that does more than simply relate consumption to production but considers the social lives of things – the sorting, divesting and disposal. In her book 'Living with Things: Ridding, Accommodation, Dwelling', Gregson (2007, p. 20) states,

Where this takes us is in the direction of approaches which refuse a separation between the human and the non-human and which insist on the object-ions and object-edness of things, but which position such cohabitations within the dwelling structure itself.

Consumption in the home becomes a broader practice shaped by sorting, mending and cleaning. Intimately moulded by familial structures, domestic ideals and habitual routines, consumption then, according to Warde (2005, p. 137) is, 'not itself a practice but is, rather, a moment in almost every practice'. This sentiment is mirrored in Miller's (1999; 2004) work as he positions consumption as a practice of care, something we do as an act of devotion or even sacrifice when faced with the responsibility for shopping on behalf of the household. This is the approach taken for my own research which positions the consumption practices of mothers within the broader practices of care embedded in the parenting role. Mothers consume on behalf of their children in order to provide such care, love and provisioning, the act of consumption itself situated as a social practice. Cook (2008) describes this motherly consumption as 'co-consuming', as women consume on behalf of another, negotiating and prioritising the needs of both her child and herself. In this manner motherly consumption cannot be regarded as a subjective, singular practice but as bound within a complex web of social norms, expectations, anxieties and desires. Second-hand shopping, as an intimate and 'risky' practice, offers a wealth of opportunity for investigating such norms and anxieties.

In the UK societal changes have influenced these norms and expectations with increased emphasis on the professionalisation of parenting and the boundaries constituting that of the 'good' parent (Holloway and Pimlott-Wilson, 2014). The scope for new parents' support networks have also altered as the middle-classes find themselves living further from established friends and family, having moved away for education and work (Edwards and Gillies, 2004). Indeed one in ten UK households move every year and our lives are increasingly dispersed both geographically and across networks (Cass et al., 2005). As such support networks too are more dispersed with less weight on the local community who traditionally provided a platform for localised shared provisioning. Not only have hand-me-downs long been part and parcel of family life, passing down clothes and toys from older to younger children both within and across family ties, in the more distant past used clothing of all types were a valuable commodity and commonly traded door-to-door (Lemire, 2005).

In contrast, second-hand retail sites are now generally considered unconventional and informal. Whilst some are situated within purpose-built shops, others are placed temporarily in alternative spaces – a playing field in the case of car boot sales, and school or village hall in the event of nearly new sales. Existing literature might chart these spaces as 'alternative' retail sites, but informal exchange networks are deeply embedded in the history of society itself, as previously described. Of course, rather than trading from door to door, those wishing to rid of redundant goods now have a number of options available for disposal. Some of these channels are hidden through informal exchange networks and social ties and increasingly, facilitated by online networks. Others are more visible, like the charity shops which have become increasingly professionalised, encroaching on the thoroughfare of the British high street (Horne and Maddrell, 2002). Studying mothers at nearly new sales, Clarke (2000) uses the term 'trafficking' to describe the movement of children's wear from one family to another, colloquially suggesting an 'underground' form of consumption. Indeed such term is loaded with precarity, connoting a form of provisioning that requires skill and labour, and is antithetical to conventional channels of consumption.

The precarious nature of second-hand goods is embedded in the unknown; we do not know where that item has been, who has been using it and whether it is fit for purpose. Risk is an inherent part of purchasing second-hand, and all second-hand consumers have to weigh-up this perceived risk. Second-hand goods by their very nature have a past, and are therefore inscribed with biographies that consumers must negotiate in different ways (Gregson and Crewe, 2003). These perceived risks are closely linked to cleanliness, both physical and envisioned, as well as a lack of product guarantee that the product is fit for purpose. In contemplating the intimacies of consuming charity shop clothes, cleanliness and indeed the threat of disease, is cited as a particular problem for potential consumers. A focus on bodily narratives relates to the way in which consumers view second-hand clothing as previously worn by another – the 'safest' clothes are those worn furthest from the body (Gregson et al., 2000). The theme of risk and anxiety is particularly pertinent when considering the practice of consuming on behalf of someone else, bringing to light further moral debates inscribed in the practice of consumption (Afflerback et al., 2013; Cairns et al., 2013).

With this in mind, this chapter focuses on the negotiations and risk reduction strategies practiced by middle-class mothers as they engage in consuming second-hand baby items, negotiating parental responsibilities and obligations with the desire to protect the 'pure' child (Clarke, 2007). Crudely put, existing literature situates the second-hand consumer in one of two camps; the 'excluded consumer', whose financial and/

or social restrictions lead to exclusion from conventional retail sites, and everyone else. The latter type, the agency-driven consumer, is led to alternative second-hand retail channels for a host of social, cultural, financial, political or ethical reasons (Williams and Windebank, 2002; Guiot and Roux, 2010). Whilst interesting, this chapter does not focus on why, if they can afford new goods, middle-class mothers purchase second-hand goods for their children. Rather, it focuses on how they negotiate bringing such goods into use within the domestic sphere. Consumption has long been considered in light of class (Lunt and Livingstone, 1992; Bourdieu, [1984] 2010) and so too has parenting (Klett-Davies, 2010). Class remained central to this study as the nearly new sales used to recruit interviewees were themselves organised largely by middle-class volunteers for middle-class parents. The notion then, of the interviewees not aligning to the 'excluded consumer' demographic but being rather more agency-driven remains central to the analysis of consumption-divestment practice within the sales and at home.

Whilst the sales are used by fathers as well as mothers, with many in attendance as a couple, mothers were selected for the interviews as they remain the primary consumer decision maker within the home, particularly with regard to caring for children. 30 mothers were interviewed, accessed through the nearly new sales aligned to the UK's largest parenting charity. Interviewees varied in age group from 20–24 to 40+ with nearly half being aged 30–34. Two were first time expectant mothers, the others all being mothers to one or two children up to the age of ten. Two thirds were educated to degree level, with six holding postgraduate qualifications, significantly higher than the UK national average of 38 per cent graduate attainment for working age adults (ONS, 2013). All interviewees were white British apart from one participant who was of Turkish origin.

## 'Good' second-hand stuff and 'good' mothering

The nearly new sales were organised by local branches of NCT (formerly National Childbirth Trust) and the three UK branches/sales sampled to recruit interviewees comprised a suburb of a large Midlands city, an affluent historical Southern city and a more socially diverse naval town on the South Coast of England. Alongside the interviews ran a broader ethnographic study where I conducted participant observation at fifteen nearly new sales over the course of eighteen months. Generally the nearly new sales are held bi-annually across the UK through local branches and held in schools, church halls or leisure centres on a Saturday or

Sunday. Whilst NCT members are offered early entry to shop, the sales are open to all, enabling members of the public to buy and sell maternity, baby and children's goods in what is considered by the attendees to be a highly efficient setting. Indeed in an age of increased geographic mobility for the middle-classes, the sales offer a useful route of exchange for parents within the community to pass on used children's goods (for a small charge). Whilst the nearly new sales provided a point of access, many of the mothers used the sales as one of a range of channels to acquire second-hand goods. The transcripts focus in part on the sales, but also on broader provisioning practices for acquiring goods through family and friends, at charity shops and car boot sales and through online classified advertisements.

Very little academic research has touched on nearly new sales, the most notable being Clarke's (2000) ethnographic study on a nearly new sale run by a North London mothers' group (not NCT). Clarke locates the sale as an 'ostensibly middle-class enterprise' even though the participants recruited are women living on low incomes (but who, according to Clarke, pursue middle-class values). Indeed the sales are positioned as the alternative to NCT, stating that 'whilst many mothers in the ethnographic study happily embrace the liberal endeavours of the NCT the legacy of formal mothering advice stands as an anathema to most women involved in the nearly new sales'. The discussion of NCT at all indicates the centrality of NCT in the lives of middle-class mothers, whether or not they partake in the services offered by NCT (such as antenatal classes, nearly new sales or breastfeeding support) or subscribe to membership. NCT nearly new sales offer a stand-alone service for the benefit of local parents (in addition to being a fundraising endeavour). In this regard the sales do attract a more diverse socio-demographic than the antenatal classes NCT are renowned for, but they are still a largely middle-class venture, a characteristic certainly shared and shaped by the volunteers. As many of my findings within the locale of the NCT sale support that of Clarke (2000) it would be superfluous to make much for the case that the sales used for this study differ to that studied by Clarke had it not been for the impact of the institutional association of NCT on pacifying parental anxiety.

Participation at the NCT nearly new sale is structured in large part by social networks, which in turn are situated in fixed networks established through NCT and subsequent parenting networks. Many parents become involved in other aspects of NCT as an expectant or new parent in order to establish a local support network. A trusted association to NCT is the first point I wish to make in suggesting ways in which mothers negotiate risk, whether it is safety or health risks to the child, or threats to the mother's self-identity. Mothers choose the nearly new sale over other forms of second-hand retail in order to minimise the risks invoked by consuming second-hand goods because they are engaging in such action as part of a group. Indeed Bourdieu ([1984] 2010) relays the claim that geographical space is never socially neutral, the sale is thus a field attracting a particular social group: in Bourdieu's terms, those sharing a similar habitus. This, I argue, leads to the notion that the used goods at the sale have come from a home similar to the home of the consumer, because the field itself is attracting a homophilious group, thus creating a greater degree of trust and familiarity with the goods. This is implied by Erin,

> I don't really buy clothes from charity shops, they look a bit more manky and dusty. The ones from NCT look like they've just come from somebody's bottom drawer, they've not been up in the loft and they don't look like they're at the end of their life. (Erin: married, 40+, full time mother)

Erin implies that because charity shop clothes look more 'manky and dusty' they are not suitable, as presumably they are deemed to be unclean or unhygienic. Despite this, she still recognises that clothes from the NCT sale have come ambiguously from 'somebody'. She does not know whom, but in her mind they are clothes that have been cared for. The generalised nature of the comment further suggests that she is drawing more on supposition and fixed personal beliefs because in actuality few charity shop clothes are 'manky and dusty' as they have become increasingly professionalised in recent years (Horne and Maddrell, 2002). Indeed other interviewees talked of positive charity shop experiences. Furthermore, having volunteered at the nearly new sales myself, unpacking, sorting and repacking the goods, the quality of items varies greatly. Rather than quality being consistently high, it seems more likely that good quality items can be found simply due to the sheer volume of goods available. The notion of quality then comes from a range of sources, not least the name itself 'nearly new sale' but also embedded in the association to NCT and its position as a trusted name working to support parents.

## Divestment and hygiene

An excluded consumer has little choice over the way in which he/she procures goods. Indeed a characteristic of the excluded consumer is a desire for new goods halted by an economic, and to a lesser extent social, exclusion from such first-cycle retail channels (Williams and Windebank, 2002). In contrast, the interviewees included in this study were all employed, on maternity leave or financially supported by their partner whilst they took a career break. They were well-educated and interviews were conducted in their nice, middle-class, homes. Their motives for consuming second-hand goods are therefore more complex, with more options and essentially a plethora of choice. These mothers are driven, but not restricted, by a thrift normativity (everyone is looking for a bargain). Therefore the advantages and disadvantages of consuming a previously used object must be negotiated on a case-by-case basis with mothers responsible for providing the best for the family whilst making resources go further. Rationalisations for consumption practices ranged from personal negotiations of risk using habitual divestment rituals, to compliance with wider norms and conventions. These negotiations centre on the fact that all used goods have an embedded previous history, a biography a new owner cannot access. A number of respondents recognised and commented on the fact that they were more comfortable in taking used goods from someone that they knew rather than a stranger. Tina, a first-time expectant mum, was one of those respondents, she said,

> Baby bedding I'm sceptical about. I've been given some by my friend but that's only because I know her. My mum bought me a second-hand Moses basket but it had only been used twice. (Tina: married, 20–24, dental nurse)

Tina tried to justify her acceptance of these items by saying that she knows where they have come from, or in the case of the Moses basket, that it had only been used twice by another family. Presumably this means it has not been used enough to be permanently tainted or contaminated by a previous owner. Tina was the most closely aligned to the 'excluded consumer' demographic of all of the interviewees. As a young first-time parent on a reasonably low salary her narrative was littered with the need to be 'resourceful'. She acquired many items second-hand but direct from family and friends rather than through unknown channels. Tina is an example of a mother's first tentative step into the vast second-hand economy of children's things and as such it is of little surprise that she lacks confidence. As Kehily and Martens (2014, p. 239) state,

> The new parent of today is confronted with a myriad of products that are designed to 'safeguard', 'guide' and 'monitor' the young child and ensure its well-being.

The rhetoric of parenting advice used by the commercial world in order to sell baby goods is one of a number of external stimuli eliciting anxiety in new parents. Mothers spoke openly about the anxiety they felt as a first time mum and how this manifest in wanting to buy everything new and in keeping the young baby away from dirt, germs and harm. Anxiety was found to reduce over time though, and parents on their second or third child were more likely to acquire far more items second-hand. Indeed, Tina had only attended one nearly new sale to date, buying just a couple of items for herself rather than her unborn baby, including an unworn maternity swimming costume. Having investigated what the sales were about, she expressed a desire to return after the baby was born, when we might expect her to then purchase objects for the child. Tina recognised the process of cleaning as a way to rid of any potential threat embedded in second-hand goods. She continued,

> I have bought second-hand bottles but I have bought brand new teats. The bottles were used by my godson and they've been sterilised. I'm a dental nurse so I know how the sterilisation works so I know that they are going to be clean but I wouldn't buy second-hand teats or second-hand dummies even though I know they're going to be sterilised but that's just something I wouldn't buy second-hand.

Tina goes on to say that she plans to breastfeed her baby so bottles will not be used regularly and as such there is no point buying new ones when second-hand ones were available so readily from a known source. Here we see Tina's wage-work role as a dental nurse shaping her mothering practices, however, despite understanding the scientific process of sterilisation, she still cites teats and dummies as unsuitable for second-hand consumption. We might suggest this is due to the physical bodily contact between the teat and the baby's mouth, embedded not just with notions of hygiene but also with the intimate relationship between the teat and the mother's breast. The bottle or dummy can be regarded as a direct extension of the mother. The unsuitaly of second-hand bottles was a common narrative of the interviewees; if the mother cannot feed her child directly herself then only the best (new) substitute will do.

Despite a suggestion in existing literature that second-hand clothes can be seen to harbour 'traces of disease, death, sex and other bodily functions' of previous owners (Horne and Maddrell, 2002, p. 50) all of the mothers interviewed had dressed their child/ren in second-hand clothes, thus implying that parents do not have an issue with dressing their child/ren in clothing previously worn by another. Clearly, the mothers interviewed had all participated in nearly new sales and as such we would assume they are intent on consuming at least some goods second-hand. There were however, varying limits to this practice, as described by Melissa,

> I think clothes wise. It's a daft way of differentiating but anything that's going directly onto his skin so sleep suits, vests. Two reasons, one I'd rather know that they're fresh, pristine, and also muslins as well are something I'd bought new, and also for what they cost brand new in the shops, supermarkets always do good deals on bundles of vests whatever. They are something I always buy first hand. (Melissa: married, 30–34, environmental consultant)

Melissa's comments match that of a number of interviewees for whom items like vests and sleep suits are so inexpensive to buy first-hand that the financial gains of buying second-hand does not justify the risk of clothing the child in something unknown or potentially contaminated. Her practice is not as 'daft' as she cites. As young babies are seen to be particularly messy, such intimate items are commonly disregarded as suitable for second-hand exchange, and often end up in the bin. One mother even described the practice of exchanging used undergarments as 'a bit gross'. This aligns with much of the work by Gregson and Crewe (2003) who found that the safest second-hand clothes are those worn furthest from the body. Mothers are therefore more likely to buy outer-wear as second-hand baby clothing rather than intimate wear.

Yet, whilst intimate clothing has more contact with the skin, outer-wear has more contact with the outside world. This is a characteristic recognised by mothers, but not as another challenge to negotiate in regards to risk and hygiene as we might expect. Instead, situations offering greater opportunity for external contamination are seen as the perfect place to utilise second-hand clothing. These situations include going to nursery school and playing in the garden, as described by Gina (co-habiting, 40+, civil servant) who believes that second-hand clothes are well-suited to dirty activities and help her to relax as a parent, 'If she's playing out in the garden and it gets stained, I don't start worrying about it'. This suggests that she buys clothing of little financial and/or symbolic value for such outdoors activities in order to avoid such value being diminished through contamination with dirt.

Textiles are commonly thought to harbour unfavourable histories more profoundly than other goods. This is not just evident through the participants' reluctance to buy second-hand vests and baby bedding, but also through what could be considered less intimate items like stuffed toys which were often cited as something mothers would not buy second-hand. Solid items like books and plastic toys could easily be wiped clean; their history literally erased in one swipe of an antibacterial wipe. For many, washing and cleaning goods once home is part of a ritual, a process of divesting each item of its previous owner before it is welcomed into a new home. Again this practice is changeable however, and is often directly correlated to years of motherhood,

> I used to get the antiseptic wipes out, put everything in the washing machine, clean everything. I think the last one, I got them home and thought, you know, they're going to play group two or three times a week with things that haven't been washed for three years. Generally I give things an antiseptic wipe over. (Erin: married, 40+, full-time mother)

Erin explained the way in which her divestment practices altered after her most recent trip to a nearly new sale. She reflects on the fact that she cannot control her child's experiences now that he spends time outside the domestic environment at play group. It is a sudden realisation and self-reflection which allows her to relinquish some of that control. She still prefers to clean goods once in the home, but more out of habit than anxiety. For some interviewees, it was the first time that they had reflected on their divestment practices. These were generally the mothers who did not have stringent divestment practices and had given little thought to the possibility of dirt or germs lurking on their new acquisitions. Therefore, in one or two cases, my questioning seemed to actually induce anxiety, a fear that perhaps they should be cleaning these goods before they are fully brought into the home. Indeed Pink (2007, p. 170) states,

> Individuals' actual practices of domestic consumption of laundry products, services and fresh air are processes through which they constitute their gendered identities and make moral statements about the 'right' way to be a woman.

Pink stresses the sensory experience of doing laundry, portraying it as a personal and intimate practice yet with the ability to be appropriated as a form of expression. Whilst some mothers practice divestment rituals as part of a habit to reduce anxiety, others did not see any risk attached to the second-hand object past that which is visible. For these mothers if it looks clean it is clean, and therefore poses little threat.

Laura (married, 30–35, non-disclosed occupation) finds comfort from that fact that she is 'buying something off a rack' at the nearly new sale. Here, Laura is aligning her nearly new sale consumption practices to conventional retail channels. This clearly puts her at ease, aware as she is that everything has been 'worn and washed'. Laura is putting her trust in an assumed practice of washing to eliminate any threat to her child, as she does not clean the items herself. Perhaps this says the most about her idea of where those goods have come from; putting her trust in the volunteers and sellers at the nearly new sale to ensure everything is clean and therefore safe.

For some then, the appearance and smell of an object as 'clean' is enough to justify its purchase and use, whilst for others a further cleansing process is required once the goods are in the home. The practice of cleaning goods could be regarded wholly unnecessary if items looked and smelt clean already. This was the echoed by a number of mothers but evidenced most strongly by Karen, a keen environmentalist and moderator of her local Freecycle group,

> [Once I get home] I bring them into this room and unpack the bags and just put them away. You can tell that they're all clean and ironed. They'll never be ironed again after that. You can tell that they are clean because they smell of the detergents that have been used, and the detergents I use tend to be pretty unfragranced so these smell much cleaner than our normal stuff and I don't iron so I certainly wouldn't wash them until they've been worn. I'll keep that washed and ironed smell as long as possible. (Karen: non-disclosed marital status, 40+, homemaker)

Karen argues that the second-hand things she buys from the sales are actually cleaner than her normal children's clothes and she feels no need to further divest them of their previous biography. Karen feels that she understands second-hand exchange networks and for her they are part of a normalised way of provisioning, not just for her children, but also for herself and her home. She is proud of this practice, and it constitutes just one of a range of ethically-motivated practices structuring her consumption habits (placing importance on locally sourced food for example, as well as ethical supply chains in the fashion industry). Her commitment to ethical consumption goes further than middle-class conspicuous consumption rather, Karen aims to minimise her ecological footprint through her everyday consumption practices by making use of second-hand economies and minimising the environmental impact of her laundry routines.

Differences in the rationalisations of mothers' second-hand consumption practices influence both what they buy and what they do with what they buy. The stark difference between Karen's narrative and that of the other mothers was her focus on being guardian of the Earth first and foremost, as opposed to guardian of her children. Mothers mediate and negotiate risk through learned-experience. Perhaps as Karen was so invested in consuming second-hand goods for her own use, the practice of co-consuming used children's goods was not such a leap. We learnt before how Tina's knowledge of the sterilisation process comforted her own hygiene practices, but the range of practices described in this chapter have attempted to show that mothers' consumption-divestment practices are not normalised.

Whilst the domestic labour entailed in care work is hidden from public view, the outcome of that labour is evidenced externally through cleanliness of the self, clothing and visible health. Laundry practices are a form of inconspicuous consumption shaped by very personal routines, but as Jack (2013, p. 418) so nicely states, 'not washing is hidden, but wearing dirty clothes is visible'. Such practices of cleanliness then, are one way in which 'good mothering' can be made visible. This has been found to be a particular concern of working-class parents, who feel the need to make visible their ability to keep a nice home and care adequately for their children. Indeed there is a symbolic and social significance of being clean, yet routines of cleanliness are rarely discussed outside the family and as such practices of cleanliness lack normative collective conventions (Shove, 2003; Shove et al., 2012). Instead, Pink (2007) asserts that laundry practices are intimately linked to personal identity and the sort of person one wishes to be. With this in mind this chapter has looked at three types of mother in relation to the cleansing/divestment practices of second-hand baby goods. The inexperienced young mother, keen to express her knowledge of sterilisation as a way of highlighting her understanding of the procedures of childcare; the more experienced middle-class mother, able to adjust her divestment practices over time as she becomes more confident in her agential skill to negotiate risk and; the politically-orientated mother, who with high levels of cultural capital and an ethically-motivated outlook does not construct laundry practices to be a central tenet of expressing visible notions of childcare. In this manner, consumption-divestment practices are seen as a way for mothers to construct an identity of the parent they wish to be, just as Pink posits with laundry practices more generally.

## Safety conventions and governance

It is clear that the practice of washing and cleaning alleviates concerns of hygiene and contamination in the co-consumption of used goods. Another concern of parents is that of safety, which has clear repercussions on second-hand consumption practice. Indeed Furedi (2001, p. 26) says, 'Parents are bombarded with advice that demands that they create a risk free world'. Such a notion suggests parents are unable to detach themselves from the wider social norms of care which are thrust upon them from a wide range of sources. Again, co-consumption becomes simultaneously a practice of care as parents seek to find the appropriate material objects to care for and protect their child/ren. During the interviews discussions on safety were overwhelmed by a narrative of governance, realised both through NCT guidelines of what can be sold at nearly new sales and through wider recommendations from authoritative bodies. You cannot sell car seats and mattresses through the NCT sales for example, in line with official parenting advice. Nearly new sale volunteers adhere to this, priding the sales on not just offering a retail platform for second-hand exchange but on providing a service to support parents. There are ways to get around this rule however, by advertising items on a notice board at the sale. This means that such items are not sold within the locale of the sale, but indeed the process of exchange could still be facilitated by the sale.

The rhetoric of safety governance took two main guises. For some, the notion of using second-hand car seats and mattresses was personally recognised as unsafe. Their views were no doubt influenced by formal recommendations (although it would be impossible to untangle such interventions), but they displayed a sense of personal agency in choosing to follow these guidelines rigorously. For others, the boundaries of acceptability were less pronounced. These mothers were aware of the recommendations and what they should say or do, but showed greater flexibility in negotiating the risks involved. Maggie, quoted below, highlights these rules of safety governance by discussing the 'guidelines' and 'safety advice' one should adhere to as a mother,

**Emma:** Is there anything particularly you wouldn't buy second-hand for your children?

**Maggie:** Well, I know the guidelines are you shouldn't reuse mattresses and car seats so I wouldn't buy those but as I said I bought the Moses basket, I'm just buying a new mattress for it. I think that's probably it, just anything that goes against safety advice I think really (Married, 30–34, full time mum).

For some mothers, these safety restrictions came to mind first when I asked what items they would not be comfortable acquiring second-hand, whilst others began by alluding to individualised practice, such as not buying soft toys or second-hand shoes. On the whole these safety restrictions were positioned as strict regulations, not offered for subjective negotiation. In this manner the idea of using second-hand mattresses or car seats was always positioned as something you should not do with little discussion or justification for why you should not do it. It was accepted as part of the responsibility of being a parent, but there was the odd contradiction in this practice. In response to being asked what she would not buy second-hand, Nicole immediately says that she would not buy a car seat, before realising that she actually nearly did,

> Car seats, I wouldn't buy a second-hand car seat. Although having said that we were looking into buying a car seat for my mother-in-law who has Katie one day a week. I called someone at the nearly new sale, because I don't think you can sell car seats there at the moment but they had written, privately call us and I did actually call a lady but it was the wrong size car seat, for a tiny baby, so actually I would have definitely considered buying that, I was going to have a look at it, so maybe I would have bought a second-hand car seat. Everyone says you can't buy a second-hand car seat! I think if you've got it from a trustworthy source, that's the thing. (Nicole: married, 20–25, research assistant)

Nicole recognises that convention dictates not to buy a second-hand car seat because 'everyone' says it, but she is clearly open to negotiating this risk and making the decision for herself based on whether she trusts the source. Her implication here is that a stranger she has been connected to through the nearly new sale is a trustworthy source. This correlates with the theory posited earlier in this chapter that the nearly new sale is a socially homophilious locale built on a trusted association to the NCT. Nicole further justified this act by explaining that the car seat would not be used very often, as it was a secondary seat for her parent's car.

All of the other mothers interviewed, said that they would only consider buying or taking a second-hand car seat from a friend or relative for whom they knew but of course, Nicole suggests that in practice this may not be the case. Whilst the overwhelming safety narrative from interviewees was an adherence to recognised safety guidelines, Nicole demonstrates that such rhetoric is pronounced through parenting practice to different degrees. Nicole was well-educated (to PhD level although not in social science), which could perhaps have played a role in her agential response to prescribed safety norms. Further research is required to entangle the full influence of class and education in the negotiations of risk concerned with second-hand goods. Her story is however a clear example of the way in which social norms structure many of the mothers' consumption practices whilst allowing for personal agency and reflexivity (both consciously and unconsciously).

## Conclusion

This chapter has explored the second-hand consumption practices of thirty mothers in relation to risk negotiation and reduction. It draws on the belief that the mothers interviewed are not 'excluded consumers' but rather participate in second-hand consumption channels for a range of other financial, social, political, cultural and/or ethical reasons in order to provision for their children. By focusing on a discourse of thrift in relation to care and nurture, I have explored the way in which material provisioning becomes part of broader parenting practices. I have also aimed to show that such co-consuming practices are shaped by class, enabling mothers to construct the identity of the parent they wish to be through their consumption and divestment practices.

The narrative of risk has focused on two main themes, namely hygiene and safety. Concerns over hygiene are particularly prevalent when consuming textiles which are seen to harbour traces of previous use – bodily fluid or dirt – which may contaminate the child. The intimate relationship between the material and the body is a three way process, linking mother, child and object within the practice of love and care. The focus in this regard is often on that which is visible, the practice of washing trusted to divest the object of harm. Whilst practices of cleanliness in the home are not normalised (but are influenced by social factors) the second theme, that of safety, is heavily structured by social norms and conventions. These conventions are shaped by external governance which is rarely questioned by the mothers in this study, except when they feel that they have the cultural capital to negotiate such risks on their own terms.

This chapter has focused on actual bodily risk, as mothers strive to protect and nurture the child. What it has not been able to do in much depth, however, is explore the relationship between the material and the identity of the women as mothers. Reliant on parental care, children are ideal carriers of vicarious consumption, indeed some studies have found that mothers conspicuously consume through their children (Bailey, 2001; Thomsen and Sorensen, 2006). As such, not only do mothers have to negotiate physical (or the perceived physical) risk when co-consuming second-hand goods but we could also extend this risk to a threat against maternal identity. Indeed external contamination through the mother's intimate relationship with the material may jeopardise her position within her peer group or threaten her identity as a mother which she may wish to display as 'good mothering'.

## Acknowledgements

I thank Kate Boyer (Cardiff University) and Nick Clarke (University of Southampton), as well as the editors of this collection for helping me to develop the ideas found in this chapter. This research was funded by the ESRC and NCT as part of a RIBEN doctoral studentship. I also thank NCT staff and volunteers for their support, and for giving me access to their nearly new sales.

## References

Afflerback, S., Carter, S. K., Anthony, A. and Grauerholz, L. (2013) 'Infant-feeding Consumerism in the Age of Intensive Mothering and Risk Society', *Journal of Consumer Culture*, 13(3), 387–405.

Arnould, E. J. and Bardhi, F. (2005) 'Thrift Shopping: Combining Utilitarian Thrift and Hedonic Treat Benefits', *Journal of Consumer Behaviour*, 4(4), 223–233.

Bailey, L. (2001) 'Gender Shows: First-Time Mothers and Embodied Selves', *Gender and Society*, 15(1), 110–129.

Bourdieu, P. ([1984] 2010) *Distinction: A Social Critique of the Judgement of Taste*. London: Routledge.

Cass, N., Shove, E. and Urry, J. (2005), 'Social Exclusion, Mobility and Access', *The Sociological Review*. 53(3), 539–555

Cairns, K., Johnston, J., MacKendrick, N., (2013) 'Feeding the "Organic Child": Mothering through Ethical Consumption', *Journal of Consumer Culture* ,13(2), 97–118.

Clarke, A. (2000) '"Mother Swapping" the Trafficking of Nearly New Children's Wear' in *Commercial Cultures, Economies, Practices and Spaces*, P. Jackson, M. Lowe, D. Miller and F. Mort (eds), pp. 85–100. Oxford: Berg Publishing.

Clarke, A. (2007) 'Making Sameness: Mothering, Commerce and the Culture of Children's Birthday Parties' in *Gender and Consumption: Domestic Culture and Commercialisation of Everyday Life*, E. Casey and L. Martens (eds), pp. 79–96. Abingdon: Ashgate.

Cook, D. T. (2008) 'The Missing Child in Consumption Theory', *Journal of Consumer Culture*, 8(2), 219–243.

Cook, D. T. (2013) 'Introduction: Specifying Mothers/Motherhood', *Journal of Consumer Culture*, 13(2), 75–78.

DeLong, M., Heinemann, B., Reiley, K. (2005) 'Hooked on Vintage', *Fashion Theory*, 9(1), 23–42.

Edwards, R. and Gillies, V. (2004) 'Support in Parenting: Values and Consensus Concerning Who to Turn To', *Journal of Social Policy*, 33(4), 627–647.

Franklin, A. (2011) 'The Ethics of Second Hand Consumption' in *Ethical Consumption: A Critical Introduction*, T. Lewis and E. Potter, pp. 156–168. Oxon: Routledge.

Furedi, F. (2001) *Paranoid Parenting*. London: Allen Lane.

Gregson, N. (2007) *Living with Things: Ridding, Accommodation, Dwelling*. Wantage: Sea Kingston Publishing.

Gregson, N. and Crewe, L. (1997) 'Performance and Possession: Rethinking the Act of Purchase in the Light of the Car Boot Sale', *Journal of Material Culture*, 2, 241–263.

Gregson, N. and Crewe, L. (1998) 'Dusting Down Second Hand Rose: Gendered Identities and the World of Second-hand Goods in the Space of the Car Boot Sale', *Gender, Place & Culture*, 5(1), 77–100.

Gregson, N., Brooks, K. and Crewe, L. (2000) 'Narratives of Consumption and the Body in the Space of the Charity Shop' in *Commercial Cultures, Economies, Practices and Spaces*, P. Jackson, M. Lowe, D. Miller and F. Mort (eds), pp. 101–123. Oxford: Berg Publishing.

Gregson, N. and Crewe, L. (2003) *Second Hand Cultures*. Oxford: Berg Publishing.

Guiot, D. and Roux, D. (2010) 'A Second-hand Shoppers' Motivation Scale: Antecedents, Consequences, and Implications for Retailers', *Journal of Retailing*, 86(4), 355–371.

Holloway, S. L. and H. Pimlott-Wilson (2014) 'Any Advice is Welcome isn't it? Neoliberal Parenting Education, Local Mothering Cultures, and Social Class', *Environment and Planning A*, 46(1), 94–111.

Horne, S. and Maddrell, A. (2002) *Charity Shops: Retailing, Consumption and Society*. London: Routledge.

Humphery, K. (2011) 'The Simple and the Good: Ethical Consumption as Anti-Consumerism' in *Ethical Consumption: A Critical Introduction.*, T. Lewis and E. Potter (eds), pp. 40–53. Oxon: Routledge.

Jack, T. (2013) 'Nobody was Dirty: Intervening in Inconspicuous Consumption of Laundry Routines', *Journal of Consumer Culture*, 13(3), 406–421.

James, S., Brown, R. B., Goodsell, T. L., Stovall, J. and Flaherty, J. (2010) 'Adapting to Hard Times: Family Participation Patterns in Local Thrift Economies', *Family Relations*, 59(4), 383–395.

Klett-Davies, M. (ed.) (2010) *Is Parenting a Class Issue?* London: Family and Planning Institute.

Lemire, B. (2005) 'Shifting Currency: The Culture and Economy of the Second Hand Trade in England, c.1600–1850' in *Old Clothes, New Looks: Second Hand Fashion*, A. Palmer and H. Clark, pp. 29–48. Oxford: Berg.

Lunt, P. K. and Livingstone, S. M. (1992) *Mass Consumption and Personal Identity*. Buckingham: Open University Press.

Medvedev, K. (2012) 'It Is a Garage Sale at Savers Every Day: An Ethnography of the Savers Thrift Department Store in Minneapolis'in *Exchanging Clothes: Habits of Being II*, C. Giorcelli and P. Rabinowitz (eds),, pp. 230–254. London: University of Minnesota press.

Miller, D. (1999) *A Theory of Shopping*. Cambridge: Polity Press.

Miller, D. (2004) 'How Infants Grow Mothers in North London' in *Consuming Motherhood*, J. S. Taylor, L. L. Layne and D. F. Wozniak (eds), pp. 31–54. London: Rutgers University Press.

ONS (2013) Graduates in the UK Labour Market. London, Office for National Statistics.

Palmer, A. (2004) 'Vintage Whores and Vintage Virgins: Second-hand fashion in the Twenty-first Century' in *Old Clothes, New Looks: Second-hand Fashion*, A. Palmer and H. Clark (eds), pp. 197–214. Oxford: Berg.

Pink, S. (2007) 'The Sensory Home as a Site of Consumption: Everyday Laundry Practices and the Production of Gender' in *Gender and Consumption: Domestic Cultures and the Commercialisation of Everyday Life*, E. Caset and L. Martens (eds), pp. 163–180. Aldershot: Ashgate Press.

Shove, E. (2003) *Comfort, Cleanliness and Convenience: The Social Organization of Normality*. Oxford: Berg.

Shove, E. and Pantzar, M. et al. (2012) *The Dynamics of Social Practice: Everyday Life and How it Changes*. London: Sage.

Silva, E. (2007) 'Gender, Class, Emotional Capital and Consumption in Everyday Life' in *Gender and Consumption: Domestic Culture and Commercialisation of Everyday Life*, E. Casey and L. Martens (eds), pp. 141–162. Hampshire: Ashgate Press.

Thomsen, T. U. and Sorensen, E. B. (2006) 'The First Four-Wheeled Status Symbol: Pram Consumption as a Vehicle for the Construction of Motherhood Identity', *Journal of Marketing Management*, 22(9–10), 907–927.

Vitell, S. and Muncy, J. (1992) 'Consumer Ethics: An Empirical Investigation of Factors Influencing Ethical Judgments of the Final Consumer', *Journal of Business Ethics*, 11(8), 585–597.

Waight, E. (2013) 'Eco Babies: Reducing a Parent's Ecological Footprint with Second-Hand Consumer Goods', *International Journal of Green Economics*, 7(2), 197–211.

Warde, A. (2005) 'Consumption and Theories of Practice', *Journal of Consumer Culture*, 5(2), 131–153

Williams, C. and Windebank, J. (2002) 'The Excluded Consumer: A Neglected Aspect of Social Exclusion?' *Policy and Politics*, 30(4), 501–513.

# 10
# The Hidden Lives of Domestic Things: Accumulations in Cupboards, Lofts, and Shelves

*Sophie Woodward*

This chapter seeks to challenge the assumption that the accumulation of things that are not currently in use in domestic spaces is a sign of the 'throwaway society' (Cooper, 2010), or a product of frivolous consumers' constant desire for the new. This assumption entails thinking about things predominantly in terms of use-value and also that consumption is a result of individuals' choices and preferences. In the current media fascination with clutter – seen in programmes such as Channel 4's *The Hoarder Next Door* – things that accumulate in domestic spaces, such as attics and cupboards, spill into whole rooms as a symptom of a psychological disorder. Having an excess of stuff that we do not use is seen as either wasteful or as a sign of an individual with a life that is out of control – an understanding that is mirrored in the multiple professional decluttering services. What is needed is a focus, not upon the extreme behaviour of hoarding that these programmes portray, nor individual consumers who continue to buy new stuff when they have an excess of things at home, but on what has been termed 'ordinary consumption' (Gronow and Warde, 2001). That is, the everyday patterns of use and storage of things within the home that is not spectacular but rather how people enact their everyday lives and relationships through things.

In focusing upon the things that have accumulated in domestic spaces as a form of everyday consumption practices, this chapter also develops two further challenges to the sustainability discourses around wastefulness and the popular representations of hoarding. Firstly, assumptions of the 'throwaway society' are based upon a flawed understanding of people and their things wherein an excess of things is seen as a sign of materialism. Instead, by adopting a material culture perspective, the interactions between people and things are central to the enactment and ordering of everyday life (Miller, 2005) and constitutive of the fabric of our social relations (Latour, 2000). They are the medium through which people construct their self-hood and biography, and their relationships to others and wider social worlds as people and things are mutually constituted. Things that are no longer used may still resonate with memories or associations of other people, as the process of ridding can become a problematic and emotionally charged experience (Lucas, 2002; Gregson, 2007).

Secondly, this chapter challenges the understanding that the focus should be upon an individual and their possessions, which an individual has chosen to buy and then keep. Not only is the notion of 'choice' problematic, but also, things are always relational, in the sense that they may have been owned by and used by many different people, they also may externalise aspects of a relationship – such as dependence upon a parent – or even an absence of a relationship through feelings of loss. Whilst the relationship between material culture and consumption briefly introduced above is one that is well established (arising from Miller, 1987) the one between consumption, material culture and how this constitutes everyday relationships has been less extensively researched (although there are exceptions such as Hurdley, 2006; Woodward, 2007). It is this which is the focus of this chapter, as it will outline planned research into the accumulations of things that are not currently being used within domestic spaces and the practices and relationalities that surround these. This chapter will develop an understanding of critical consumption through a focus on the intimate and relational facets of domestic goods. The values and meanings of things accumulate and disperse as everyday relationships are imagined and entrenched through things kept in domestic spaces. These things will be defined as 'dormant' in order to avoid reducing the domestic life of things to their use by people, as most things spend at least some time in storage, whether this is as a precursor to being disposed of or to being reused, it is therefore important to consider this phase of the life of things. The project that this chapter introduces aims to explore dormancy as a part of the material vitalities, which is not reduced to how things are moved by people (in the wake of Appadurai's account on the social life of things, 1996) or what people do with them. This empirical part of this project, which will take place within people's homes, has yet to be carried out (see Woodward, 2014, the project website) and therefore this chapter offers an account of why dormant things matter both theoretically and through the insights afforded through a pilot that has been carried out. In thinking through the pilot project, the focus has shifted from unused items to the accumulations of dormant things in the home – a shift that will be charted later in the chapter. Things that have accumulated include both the deliberately stored as well as items that 'end' up being pushed to the back of a cupboard, things have been forgotten about, or those which resonate with personal and relational meanings. The chapter aims to widen out the sociological understanding of consumption beyond what is currently being used, to items that are here understood as dormant and kept within the home as a means to explore the ways in which things allow us to enact, construct, or even dismantle our everyday relationships.

## Doing relationships through things

In developing an approach to dormant things, I will draw on a series of related literatures: families and relationships, consumption, temporalities and practices, and material culture. Although these can be considered distinct literatures, there are emerging connections between these fields, as is evident in recent developments in the study of relationships. David Morgan (1996) paved the way for the focus upon the *doing* of relationships as he argued that family is not an institution of a defined entity but rather a collection of practices. This has been developed by Finch (2007) through the related concept of 'display', as a potential route into thinking about how family practices are conveyed to others. She suggests that this process of display or conveying to others is necessary in order for people to be sure that they are 'doing family things' Finch, 2007, p. 67). In a context where the household does not equate to family and what constitutes family changes over the life course, people have to actively engage in defining what their significant relationships are. The implication of this is that family practices are *displayed* and that *display is a family practice*. This approach lends itself to the study of material culture within the home – and can clearly connect to studies such as Hurdley's work on mantelpieces (Hurdley, 2013) and Rose's study of family photography (Rose, 2010) – both of which foreground material practices in the doing of relationships.

Gillian Rose (2012) looks at the practices surrounding family snaps as 'visual objects' which form both subject positions and relationships. These practices range from taking, printing, dating, storing, and displaying to looking at and circulating. Display here is the putting on display of particular photos, yet similarly we can consider the showing of a family album and talking through this as an act of display. In the example of domestic photographic practices, this act of display happens in relationship to storage – photos are put in a box and out of view. Similarly in Hurdley's (2013) work on mantelpieces, although the focus is upon the items that are placed on the mantelpiece, these are understood by her participants, and in Hurdley's analysis, in relationship to things that are not there – often as things are in storage. Things that are made visible and are able to be put on display are always in relationship to that which is stored away – either as a deliberate act of concealment or through reasons of space. Often the choice of what is displayed is, in Finch's sense of display, an act of conveying to others which relationships matter. Yet this chapter will argue that the process of putting in storage, being out of view, is equally important as a relational practice. My own previous work with wardrobes (Woodward, 2007) challenged the over-emphasis upon the public presentation of the self at the expense of both clothing that is tried on in the bedroom and also things that never leave the wardrobe (see also Banim and Guy, 2001).

Hurdley's and Rose's case studies are useful as they prioritise everyday relational practices with things. There has been a transition in studies of consumption from the spectacular and focuses upon strategies of differentiation and identity construction through to what Gronow and Warde (2001) called 'ordinary consumption' which entails a focus upon everyday practices within the home. This had previously been a facet of feminist scholarship of the home (DeVault, 1991) with a focus upon domestic spaces and the activities that women carried out in the home which had been devalued and hidden from view. These accounts paved the way for a renewed focus upon consumption in the home as part of the enactment of everyday life. In line with these recent shifts, practice theory approaches to consumption have been developed which rethinks consumption as the use of things in the enactment of social practices (Warde, 2005). A key facet of the use of practice theory to explore consumption is through routines which highlight a temporal dimension to consumption practices as part of the rhythms of everyday life. Practice theory approaches have been important in situating consumption within everyday life, and as practices are seen as composed of multiple elements – including for example knowledges and things – it also places material culture as the heart of everyday acts of consumption. However, in centring social practices, Rose has noted that practice theory approaches can be reductive of the subjectivities of people, such as in Shove's work where Rose suggests that people are reduced to 'tool-users' (Rose, 2010). I would also add to this critique that these approaches do not give adequate account of the relationalities between people. Shove et al. (2012) foreground the relationalities between social practices, and between elements in practices and this usefully allows a move away from thinking about an individual and their possessions, yet what is lacking is a sense of how people's significant relationships are constituted through things. How this happens is a useful route into developing an understanding of the intimate and relationship means through which everyday values of things are negotiated and shift. My pilot and previous work into wardrobes encountered unwanted clothes sent by a mother to a daughter living overseas that filled a spare room, a loft full of old children's toys kept with the hope of future grandchildren. Things resonate with actual and imagined relationalities, and their entanglements in relations to others can be so powerful that people feel unable to dispose of things.

In several points in this chapter I have talked about relationalities; a relational focus is something that is present within numerous distinct literatures within which it is conceived very differently, such as actor network theory (which will henceforth be referred to as ANT), social networks, practice theory, and in work on personal relationships. In this chapter, relationalities are employed to signify a number of different relationships that can be explored when looking at dormant things: the relationships between things, between a person and their things, and relations between people through things. In practice theory, social practices are understood as the interaction – and thus relationship – between different elements such as knowledges, competences and things. Ingold (2007) has suggested that there should be a renewed focus upon materials, arguing that in studies of material culture and consumption there tends to be a neglect of the materials things are made of and an assumption that things are coherent (this latter comment is something that is shared by work in the fields of non-representational theory and also ANT). Although I would depart from this stance in several ways, it is useful in highlighting the relationalities at play between materials, form, and the environment (things such as dust that cause things to change). However, I would suggest that there is still virtue in thinking about things as things; for example even if a table is made from wood and other materials, it ultimately falls apart and will be broken down into constituent materials, it still has a significant life as a table. It is important to do justice to this life and the significance this has in the lives of people. Therefore even though this chapter will draw from writers such as Ingold in his emphasis upon needing to look at materials and upon the vitalities of these materials as things change through are interactions with the environment, it will still draw from material culture perspectives. These perspectives allow an understanding of the co-constitution of people and things and the ways in which the making, use and storing of things is central to the constitution of social relations.

## Wardrobes as a method: looking at accumulations and assemblages of things

Domestic spaces – such as shelves and cupboards – and the things that accumulate in them are the empirical focus of this proposed research. Yet here I would also like to propose that this is a kind of method. The interest in dormant things and the spaces in which they reside arises from previous work on women's wardrobes, which also explore the possibilities of wardrobe studies as a kind of method. I will here outline some of the wardrobe research in terms of this as a possible set of methods and approach and also what this allows us to understand. This will then be extended to consider wider spaces within the domestic. The research into women's wardrobes (see Woodward, 2007) arose out of a desire to redress the over-emphasis upon the public presentation of identity through clothing, and to situate clothing within household economies and provisioning. The emphasis then fell not only on what is worn out in public, but what is kept and never worn, what is tried on in the home, and maybe never be worn and things that used to be worn but may never be again. By looking at wardrobes – as a space for things that are worn all the time and things that are rarely worn if ever – allowed an understanding of the diversities of clothing practices. It is beyond the scope of this chapter to rehearse the findings of this research (see Woodward, 2007 for a full account) but here I will briefly outline the methods and the types of insights these elicited in order to explore how this could be extended to other storage spaces within the home.

The research was broadly ethnographic, taking place in London and Nottingham, in order to situate clothing practices within women's relationships and lives more broadly. The research started with a wardrobe inventory and interview, as I photographed each item women owned as they responded to the request to 'tell me about' each item. Subsequent to this, I got women to fill in wardrobe diaries in order to explore both the outfits that women wore and what occasion to and also things that were tried on and never actually worn out of the house. From this I constructed an understanding of clothing in the wardrobe as temporally dynamic ranging from items that are never worn (see also Banim and Guy, 2001), items that tried on but never worn, items that are worn rarely and items that are worn all the time. This was constructed as a typology of 'active', 'inactive' and 'dormant' – items that are not currently worn but are kept with the potential to be worn again. These dormant things are those that are of particular interest in the proposed research here. In the wardrobe research they were categorised at things that were not being currently worn but may be used again. However, as I developed this research into other storage spaces, I realised that this is reductive of things to possible future uses. Dormant will be expanded here to incorporate things where future possible uses may not have been considered – items that have accidentally ended up in a cupboard, or deliberately kept as they are replete with memories or associations of others.

The wardrobe as a method is one that has been explicitly formulated subsequent to the wardrobe ethnography by Klepp and Bjerk (2012) who have also developed it as method and employed through specific empirical projects (such as Van der Laan and Velthuis 2013). In each case it is explored as a method of moving towards a material culture understanding of clothing, as meanings are not reduced to what is said, and also as a critique of associating clothing with an explicit formulation of identity. The wardrobe is a space where clothes (and other things) accumulate and offers a means to explore consumption beyond display; it allows for an exploration of the practices through which things 'end up' accidentally accumulating as well as things that are deliberately stored and hidden. Things are considered in relationship to others – how the wardrobe is ordered – what things are submerged at the bottom, which things hang pristine in a clothing bag, and which others are crumpled and un-ironed on the floor. Exploring wardrobes methodologically incorporated all of these interrogations of the space of the wardrobe and its relationship to the things and the condition they are kept in within the wardrobe. As already mentioned in this chapter, the research explores the relationalities between things and between people through things. This approach is enabled through looking at accumulations of things in particular spaces, as meanings are not reduced to individual items. Exploring the relations between things in the wardrobe was also a means of understanding the relationships between people. Although the research involved looking at women and their individual wardrobes, the women selected for the research were predominantly those in relationship to each other (family networks, friendship groups, colleagues) as a means to explicitly explore the relationships between women. However, even within the specific wardrobes, when women talked about each item and when they acquired it, it is apparent that wardrobes are full of items handed-over or gifted to them by significant others. The positioning of these in storage spaces and the condition they are in also tells a lot about the ways in which the relationship or particular facet of it is preserved.

This project aims to extend this approach to other spaces where things rest within the house, and in turn to consider the relationships between these spaces. The specific focus upon the accumulations of things within domestic spaces, which is different to 'storage' which implies a deliberate and explicit act of separating out. As the wardrobe research highlighted – and also apparent in Hurdley's work on mantle-pieces things often just 'end up' (2013) – as people are unable to remember how something was positioned in the back of a drawer – or are surprised to find it there. There is a lack of existing research into things at rest, as work upon domestic consumption tends to focus upon things in use, or things in movement. This project will focus upon dormant things (see Woodward, 2014) which include the deliberately hidden away and concealed, the things which end up accidentally situated at the back of a drawer, and things which the provenance of has been forgotten or that do not mean very much to people through to things that are replete with personal and relational meanings. Dormant things of this order are not fully addressed in academic work; items 'at rest' are acknowledged as being a significant moment in the life of things, as they await reuse, repair or disposal (Schiffer et al., 1981; Gregson, 2007), yet have so far been considered as a background to processes of ridding (Gregson, 2007), through a specific temporal trajectory of an imagined future (Hochschild, 1996), as a specific genre of material culture (Woodward, 2007) or in terms of possible future uses (Fisher, 2009).

This research will focus explicitly upon spaces within the home where things 'pause', through looking at the accumulations of things. These accumulations can also be conceived of as assemblages; this idea has been expounded in the work of Jane Bennett (2010) as well as within work on actor network theory (such as Law, 1994). Thinking about the juxtapositions of things as assemblages in Law's sense (developed in Hurdley, 2013) allows an assemblage to be an assemblage of people stuff, moments, times, talk, architecture (amongst other things) which assemble to perform the social. By focusing on the assemblages and layers of things within domestic spaces (akin to archaeological approaches such as Harrison, 2011), this project will develop an original approach to a largely unnoticed but vital set of questions about our relationships with things.

## From unused things to spatial accumulations of things

The main empirical research for this project has not yet been carried out. However, as I have been developing the theoretical framework and the research design for the project, I found myself opening drawers in my house to think through the ideas of the project. I would read a bit from a book, write a bit on my computer, and find my eyes wandering up to the shelves around me. I found it impossible to think through the project and its possibilities without thinking through specific things, spaces and assemblages. Given that the project involves foregrounding things and their relationalities, this is perhaps hardly surprising. And as a consequence of this, I carried out a pilot project, which involved looking at different spaces for dormant things with each participant (3 in total). As is perhaps in the nature of a pilot, there was not any attempt to choose particular participants, or types of houses. I will in this final section of the chapter introduce some of these examples as a means to more concretely develop the possibilities and ideas of the project to start to develop the ideas of looking at spaces of accumulation and assemblages and what the consequences of this are.

## Kitchen drawers

When I first conceived of this project I was interested in things people did not use any more. The project has since developed into the idea of dormant things and looking at the accumulations of things. Each of the examples discussed here are ones which I first looked at as an example of an 'unused' thing in the home. As I started talking to people about them and think about them, I started to think about their meanings in relation to the things around them. As such, the examples will be presented as the movement from looking at the unused thing to thinking about assemblages. The first 'thing' that was explored was a now unused hand-blender. It belonged to a woman on the cusp of turning 40, who lives in a house with her partner, having previously lived alone. She owned the hand-blender for nearly 20 years, as her mother had bought it for her when she first went to university. It was an item that she had used regularly for making soup and other 'everyday meals'. She loved the item and it is something that made her a better cook as it 'saved' her a few times – such as when a cheese sauce was lumpy. The years of use are evident in its appearance, as the plastic Even once she has been given a new one by her sister,at the end has broken, so even though the motor still works, it is unusable as food spurts out of the bottom when it is used. The hand-blender has also aged through exposure to the sun and to foodstuffs as the plastic has gone a yellowish colour. Now that the item is broken, she has since asked for a new one for Christmas – an almost identical model but with more attachments. Even once she has been given a new one by her sister,I ask her why she still keeps it, and she tells me she will get rid of it, 'just not yet'.

The old hand-blender has always been kept in a drawer in the kitchen under the hobs for ease of access. Even though it is now broken, it still resides in the same place. The new one now sits next to it. The other things in the drawer include saucepans and frying pans; none of the other items are broken, and most are used regularly, with a few such as a spare frying pan being used less frequently. A year after first speaking to her about this, I got in touch with her again – she told me that the hand-blender is still there in the same drawer. In part she told me that both laziness and 'sentimentality' that kept her from getting rid of it. What is interesting about this example is that even though it is no longer useful, it is as if she can't end its life too abruptly. It may no longer have a useful life in her home, but it does still have a life. The item is allowed to pause in the drawer before it begins its journey to disposal. This raises interesting issues around the lives of things and how dormant things can be thought of as being vital. Developing on from Appadurai's work (1986) the lives of things have been considered predominantly in terms of the movement of things, and what people do with them. There has been a critique of this position as it has failed to attend to the materiality of things (Thomas, 1991); indeed dormant things form a necessary challenge to this, as their continued life cannot be reduced to movement as they rest in drawers and cupboards. They have a continued material vitality which emerges from the interaction of materials and the environment (Ingold, 2007) as things continue to change. Yet even this is not enough to explain the continued life of things that are not used, their ability to provoke responses, or their materiality that means people feel unable to dispose of them.

The unused item is placed back into the same cupboard after it is broken. In part this may be initially due to habit, it is where it usually goes, she may not be able to think about where to put it. Yet also, even when I talk to her about it, and she takes it out of the cupboard as we reflect upon it, it still returns to the cupboard. It has 'ended up' where it has always been, yet there is a sense that this is where it belongs for the last phase of the item's life in the home. Moreover, it is placed in an assemblage with a range of other things that are still being used all the time. In doing so, the thing is not being defined as waste, or rubbish, but instead is vitalised by being part of this assemblage. The space in which it rests is not one that is a 'storage space' but instead for 'kitchen things' and also 'things that are used all the time'. It is technically a space that is usefully positioned for things that are used on or next to the hob. The presence of a broken hand-blender does not totally disrupt this space, but rather allows the thing to transition to it being 'waste'. This illustrates how the meanings and uses of spaces are muddled by the things that are assembled in them.

## Rarely used rooms

The second example is in a different type of space – residing on the floor of a room that is rarely used. The 'unused thing' that this example started with was a large stainless steel rice cooker, which was owned by a man in his late 30s, who used to live alone but now lives with his partner. The rice cooker started off in the kitchen, but as it was never used, moved to a shelf in the room that is hardly used, to sitting on the floor at the edge of the room. The room is one that will be being redecorated, and as such in the interim has 'ended up' being a place where things are dumped. It is not a storage room, but by virtue of things being placed in there that are not often used, areas of it have taken on that function. There is space in the room where tools are kept which are organised on a separate shelf. The movement of the rice cooker to the floor shows that it is not a forgotten about room, but there have been clear attempts to order the room.

The rice cooker was purchased 6 years ago, by his sister – he had asked for it for Christmas as he had previously had a flat mate who had had one that cooked perfect rice easily and you didn't have to 'think about' cooking – you just put in the rice and water and it did the rest. In the first year he owned it he used it a few times while when he was sharing a house when the housemates were eating together. But the main problem was that it cooked rice for 6 people '[a one person rice cooker] was what I had in mind when I requested a rice cooker – not one suitable for opening a restaurant with'. As rice doesn't keep well, he found it wasteful. When he eats rice with his partner now, they cook it in the saucepan – even if they were cooking for several people – as she finds the idea of a rice cooker a hassle, preferring 'multi-functional' items such as saucepans.

When I ask him why he has not got rid of it already, he says in part he has not got round to it, but also as it was a present from his sister it stops him being able to offer it to family and it is also about the 'time distance away from being given it. When I know she [sister] has gone to the effort of buying it'. As it was gifted to him, he is forced to keep the thing for what is a 'suitable time'. There is a vast literature – predominantly anthropological – about the gift (ensuing from Mauss, 1992). This relates to examples from my work on wardrobes, where gifted clothing in one example took over almost an entire storage room, as a woman's mother continued to buy her clothing she did not want (Woodward, 2007). The gifts effectively externalise a relationship to others, and as such may not only be a cherished item but may also be a burden. Through several reorganisations of the house, the unused thing is moved about. When he moves in with his partner, she has no attachment to the thing or its history and it is evicted from the kitchen as he also comes to acknowledge that it will not be used. It joins the assemblages of other 'unused' things in various transitional spaces within the home, which in the case of the rice cooker ends up being placed with other things that belong to him. When it is moved to the floor, it has begun its journey out of the home.

In both this example and the hand-blender, there is a clear life beyond use. In part there is an issue of convenience or getting round to disposing of things, or even that unless space demands you dispose of something then there is no need to worry about this. In most cases, people do not want to get rid of things straight away – as though things cannot end their life too abruptly. Even if there are examples where people would be happy to get rid of something straight away – if they do not get round to doing it, as a consequence, things *have* a continued life. Things are animated by their own histories, uses and also relationalities (seen in the gifted items) and they are also animated by what they are placed with – seen in the example of the unused hand-blender as it is placed with things that are used all the time. The hand-blender doesn't move and as such its own vitality cannot be conceived of in terms of movements or even what it done with it. Even though the rice cooker is moved several times, it is not the movement that vitalises the rice cooker, but rather it is moved in an attempt to manage it and find a space for it because of its continued vitality as a gifted item.

## Under the bed

These two examples are both coming towards the end of their life in the home. But also, as I suggested other things that have accumulated are items that have the potential to be reactivated. The final example is of a mattress, which is something that resided within my own home for a while. Items as large as a mattress are interesting as often due to its size, they are much harder to store and often find themselves in garages, lofts or unused rooms. The mattress is one that lived in a flat I shared with my partner when we first moved in together in a rented flat. It was given to him by his brother, who had finished living in his shared student house. It was the only thing kept under the bed, which was one of the only spaces it would fit in the flat given its size. The mattress spent most of the year living in that flat under the bed, but it had the potential to be used when someone came to stay when it became a bed on the living room floor. It was stored under the bed, not only because there was enough space, but also because it had the effect of concealing the mattress. Deemed un-slightly, it was not something that could have been rested against the wall in the bedroom or living room, as that would make the house look like a temporary dwelling or student digs rather than a 'home'. The construction of 'home' as 'home' centres upon the ability to house friends/family who are staying; yet also for it to look like a 'home' the mattress has to be unseen and hidden to avoid looking like temporary accommodation. Even though the flat itself is rented and 'temporary' – as it is the first flat that is shared together it has to feel as though it is a 'home'. Returning to Finch's notion of display (Finch, 2007) – having the capacity to home other people matters to the construction of this as a serious relationship and as a home, yet this here happens also through what is concealed – the mattress has to be hidden in order for this same process of display to take place.

This year is only one phase in the life of the mattress, and it has since been passed onto another family member to make use of as this partic- ular thing has a continued life ahead of it that does not yet include being disposed of. There is a desire to prolong its useful life, and although the mattress is not 'special' in itself, nor would anyone know from looking at the mattress that it is the same one – its family continuities and move- ments seem to continue to propel it in this way such that it has a life of its own. The mattress has in fact moved 6 times in less than 5 years, given the size of the mattress this has required the mobilisation of other family members. The moving of stuff in part comes to constitute family connections (in a family where communal DIY weekends are common); 'helping out' in practical tasks is pivotal to the connections between the family living in different parts of the country. The mobilisation of family members that this requires is therefore pivotal to its journeys. The relationality of the mattress is multiple; firstly, it comes from its previous histories of use which propel it to be kept within the family and passed on. Secondly, the materiality of the mattress and its size propels the mattress to be moved by several family members, creating and rein- forcing relationships between family members. What matters is not just what people do with it, but also what it enables and directs people to do. The moving of the mattress is a way of 'doing' relationships (Morgan, 1996) and of showing to each other which relationships matter (Finch,

2007). The relationships which matter were always carried within the mattress when it was not being used. Through the size of the mattress and the ways in which it carried these possibilities, the act of exchange is a moment through which this doing and displaying of relationships is possible. Thirdly, the mattress can only be used by other people who are connected to the family through perceptions of cleanliness – the materiality of the mattress includes things like dust. When we focus not just upon 'things' but upon things as part of assemblages, the focus is then upon the mattress, dust and the traces of bodies that have slept there. In this instance, the mobility of the thing is important in how it enabled continued connections between others. In other instances, the size of things may mean that things have a state and remain dormant in a garage for longer due to the materiality and size of a thing.

## Conclusions

The example of the mattress is one that is very different to the others from the pilot, not only in terms of its size but also as it could be thought of instead in terms of something that is used occasionally. However, it is a useful example to include in relation to the others in part due to the issues it raises around space and the materiality and size of things. It also highlights a different type of dormancy — as a more shifting and temporary phase in the life of things. The dormancy here is of a cyclical nature as the mattress moves in and out of being kept under the bed, rather than just before the end of its life and before disposal which seems to imply a more linear trajectory (although of course it is never just linear as these time before disposal is a snapshot in the life of things). How we think about dormancy and the life of things is one that is constituted by the materiality of stuff, the lives of people and their practices. In this example dormancy is a phase that weaves in and out of the thing being used.

As this project has developed, it has entailed a shift from thinking about unused things to how dormant things 'accumulate' that entails looking at the assemblages of things in, for example, drawers. The broken hand-blender was vitalised by being assembled with things that are used all the time, kept next to the new hand-blender; the rice cooker was kept with other things that are not often used, or that people don't know what to do with. Things may be deliberately placed with particular types of things, yet in other examples they 'end up' somewhere, and the effects of assemblage are accidental. The mattress is an item kept alone, but can still be considered as an assemblage, as dust rests on its plastic cover, and the mattress itself includes the imprints and bodily matter of people who have slept on it. Assemblages are not just of discrete 'things' – even if the mattress is still same thing at the beginning and end of year resting under bed. Assemblages are also spatial, as these spaces are also material and exist in relationship to each other.

Running through this chapter has been the idea of the life of things – an issue which is touched upon in a range of different theoretical positions. The pilot study has provided some incipient ideas around how things that are dormant can be seen to be vital. By virtue of remaining in the house, even things kept accidentally have a life. But the accidental keeping is only a small part of the picture, as instead what emerges is that things have their own trajectory. Even if things are not necessarily cherished, they cannot be disposed of straight away. Things that are profoundly evocative of people that we may feel unable to dispose of, yet most of the things that reside in drawers and cupboards are not as explicitly cherished. They have formed part of the everyday enactment of people's relationships and lives and even when they are no longer used they still continue to do so. How things enact relationships is as much a question of what is displayed as that which accumulates in the hidden spaces of the home.

## References

Appadurai, A. (ed.) (1996) *The Social Life of Things: Commodities in Cultural Perspectives*. Cambridge: Cambridge University Press.
Banim, M. and Guy, A. (2001) 'Dis/continued selves: Why Do Women Keep Clothes They No Longer Wear' in *Through the Wardrobe: Women's Relationships with Their Clothes*, A. Guy, E. Green and M. Banim (eds), Oxford: Berg.
Bennett, Jane. (2010) *Vibrant matter: A political Ecology of Things*. Durham: Duke.
Cooper, T. (2010) *Longer Lasting Products*. Surry: Gower Publishing.
DeVault, M. (1991) *Feeding the Family: The Social Organization of Caring as Gendered Work*. Chicago: University of Chicago Press.
Finch, J. (2007) 'Displaying Families', *Sociology*, 41(1), 65–81.
Fisher, T. (2009) 'Hoarding, Reusing and Disposing: The Home as a Repository for Transient Objects'in *Studies in Contemporary and Historical Archaeology in Theory 8*, BAR International Series 2363, *Modern Materials: Proceedings of CHAT Oxford 2009*, Laura McAtackney and Brent Fortenberry (eds), pp. 51–59. Oxford: Archaeopress.
Gregson, N. (2007) *Living with Things: Ridding, Accommodation, Dwelling*. Oxford: Sean Kingston Publishing.
Gronow, J. and Warde, A. (eds) (2001) *Ordinary Consumption*. London: Routledge.
Harrison, R. (2011) 'Surface Assemblages', *Archaeological Dialogues*, 18(2), 141–161.
Hochschild, A. (1996) *The Time Bind*. New York: Henry Holt.

Hurdley, R. (2006) 'Dismantling Mantelpieces: Narrating Identities and Materialising Culture in the Home', *Sociology,* 40(4), 717–733.

Hurdley, R. (2013) *Home, Materiality, Memory and Belonging: Keeping Culture.* Basingstoke: Palgrave Macmillan.

Ingold, T. (2007) 'Materials against Materiality', *Archaeological Dialogues,* 14, 1–16.

Klepp, I. and Bjerk, M. (2012) 'A Methodological Approach to the Materiality of Clothing : Wardrobe Studies', *International Journal of Social Research Methodology,* 17(4).

Latour, B. (2000) 'When Things Strike Back: A Possible Contribution of "Science Studies" to the Social Sciences', *British Journal of Sociology,* 51(1), 107–123.

Law, J. (1994) *Organising Modernity.* Oxford: Blackwell.

Lucas, G. (2002) 'Disposability and Dispossession in the Twentieth Century', *Journal of Material Culture,* 7(1), 5–22.

Mauss, M. (1992) *The Gift.* London: Routledge.

Miller, D. (1987) *Material Culture and Mass Consumption.* Oxford: Basil Blackwell.

Miller, D. (ed.) (2005) *Materiality.* Durham: Duke University Press.

Morgan, D. (1996) *Family Connections.* London: Polity.

Rose, G. (2010) *Doing Family Photography: The Domestic, The Public and The Politics of Sentiment.* Hampshire: Ashgate

Schiffer, M., Downing, T. and McCarthy, M. (1981) 'Waste Not, Want Not: An Ethnoarchaeological Study of Reuse in Tuscon, Arizona' in *Modern Material Culture. The Archaeology of Us,* R. Gould and M. Schiffer (eds). New York: Academic Press.

Shove, E., Pantzar, M. and Watson, M. (2012) *The Dynamics of Social Practice. Everyday Life and How It Changes.* London: Sage.

Thomas, N. (1991) *Entangled Objects: Exchange, Material Culture and Colonialism in the Pacific.* Cambridge: Harvard University Press

Van der Laan, E. and Velthuis, O. (2013) 'Inconspicuous Dressing: A Critique of the Construction-through-Consumption Paradigm in the Sociology of Clothing', *Journal of Consumer Culture,* Epub ahead of print, October 2013.

Warde, A. (2005) 'Consumption and Theories of Practice', *Journal of Consumer Culture,* 5(2),131–153.

Woodward, S. (2007) *Why Women Wear What they Wear.* Oxford: Berg.

Woodward, S. (2014) Dormant things, University of Manchester. Available at http://projects.socialsciences.manchester.ac.uk/dormant-things (home page) [accessed November 28, 2014].

# Index

agency, 55, 62, 66, 80, 114, 140
  and consumption, 201, 210, 212
  gender, 55, 75
  and space, 138–9
appropriation, 78, 80, 176
austerity, 67

bedroom, 87–104, 109, 110–11,
  132–3, 135, 228
body, the, 52, 63, 92, 146, 212
  and capital, 162–3
  and consumerism, 67, 200
Bourdieu, Pierre, 147–8, 150, 162–6,
  173–4, 177–8, 179, 189, 203

capital, 16, 113, 147, 162
  cultural, 163, 187–8, 189, 190, 209,
    212
  economic, 43, 68, 69, 73, 179,
    189
  symbolic, 155, 167
capitalism, 30, 65, 67, 69–70, 72–3,
  79, 80–1
care, 51, 79, 127, 199
  of children, 19, 22, 25, 132, 198–9,
    209, 210, 212
  gendered, 30, 69, 150–2, 154, 163
carnivalesque, 108, 122
charity shops, 183, 197, 200, 203
children, 43, 95–6
  agency, 28, 90, 110, 114, 140, 160
  care of, 17, 19–20, 25, 27, 29, 151,
    201, 209
  and class, 16, 22, 25, 28, 151–60,
    166–7
  and consumption, 41–2, 45, 56,
    132, 145, 150–60, 164–7, 197–213
  domestic life, 18–19, 22–3
  and labour, 15–17, 20, 109, 112–15,
    117–18
class
  consumption, 37–56, 146–67,
    197–213

and family, 14, 17, 21, 27–8,
  146–67, 197–213
  and gender, 24–5, 30, 53–6
  governing, 39–44, 46, 49–50, 55
commercial homes, 107–22

difference, 16, 70
  classed, 46, 148, 164
  gendered, 75–6
discourse
  counter-discourse, 53, 55, 120–2,
    216
  family life, 22, 29–30, 109–11, 115,
    118–22
  fashion, 147–8
  of governing class, 40–1, 43, 46
  of the Ten Hours Movement, 17,
    21, 27–8
diversity, 50
  domestic/family, 98, 107, 121, 132
divorce, 40, 97–8
domestic, 90–1
  consumption, 21, 36–56, 107,
    109–10, 121–2, 199, 201, 216–30
  gendered labour, 20, 29–30, 55
  happiness/comfort, 17–19, 21–5
  norms, 22, 71, 122
  practices, 13–14, 20, 22, 28, 30–2,
    115–16
  storage/display, 216–30

embodiment, 64
empirical sociology, 108, 122, 131,
  178, 189, 217, 221
ethics, 62
  and consumption, 61, 81, 151, 198,
    201, 208, 212
  and labour, 26
  in research, 128, 179
ethnicity, 49, 72
ethnocentric, 68
ethnography, 89, 173–4, 176, 179,
  201–2, 221–2

everyday lives, 87, 128
  consumption, 36, 55, 66, 107, 198,
    208, 216–19, 230
  display, 112, 129–31, 135, 154
  practices, 108–9, 115, 120, 131, 177,
    190–1, 219
  space, 89–90, 216

family
  breakdown, 40–1, 97–102, 126–42
  display, 99, 108, 115–22, 126–7,
    130–42, 145, 157, 177, 218–19
  economics, 24, 26–8, 46, 51,
    107–22, 204
  and gender, 68–9, 74, 150
  geographies, 37, 50–1, 199, 228
  ideals, 21–6, 40, 109, 132, 153,
    199
  practices, 13, 28–30, 56, 108–22,
    131–2, 218
  pressures on, 14–21, 107–22
  relationships, 21, 25, 31
  space, 87–9, 93–4, 97–104, 109, 111,
    178, 191
fashion, 61–2, 70, 75–81
  appropriation of nature, 78–9
  class, 146–67
  consumerism, 61, 66, 70, 75, 147–8
  critiques of, 75–7, 79
  and gender, 75–7
  mothers and daughters, 145–7,
    150–1, 153, 155–67
feminism, 61–5, 70–7, 219
Finch, Janet, 109, 115–17, 119, 126–7,
    131–2, 135, 218–19, 228
friendship, 70–1

Gillies, Val, 27, 152, 157
global, 70, 75, 80
  economies, 65–6, 70, 72–3, 79, 81

heteronormativity, 70–1, 77, 79–80,
    118–19, 121
history, 27, 60–1, 76, 162–3
  family, 141, 164
  oral, 45–6, 108
  of used goods, 198, 200, 204, 207,
    227
housing, 14, 74, 88

identity, 49
  challenges to, 136–7, 177
  and consumption, 65–6, 80, 87–8,
    93–4, 96, 99, 103, 151, 176, 198,
    212, 219
  and fashion, 75, 154, 221–2
  formation, 87–9, 91, 93–4, 103, 137,
    190
  gender, 29–30, 207, 213
institutional analysis, 177–8, 190–1
intersectionality, 176

language, 60–1, 62–3
leisure, 22, 31, 39, 88, 90, 107–8, 111,
    116, 122, 159
lived experience, 63, 97, 121, 128, 136

marriage, 30–1, 40, 55–6, 97
masculinities, 62, 76, 137
methods/methodologies
  with children, 38, 108, 127–30
  diaries/drawings/music, 128, 221
  feminist, 61, 219
  interviewing, 91–2, 108, 126–9,
    135–6, 141, 149, 201, 221
  mixed, 139–40
  participant observation, 38–9, 149,
    184, 201
  participatory, 129
  photo elicitation, 128, 135–6
  qualitative, 127, 149
  recruitment, 127–8, 201
migration, 36, 53–4, 56
modernity, 45, 50, 73, 191
money, 20, 24, 41–4, 46, 48, 54, 71,
    114, 120, 153–4
Morgan, David, 115–16, 120, 122,
    131, 218
mothers, 68, 74, 95, 118–19, 145–8,
    150–67, 197–213
mundane, 64, 99, 100, 107, 108, 116,
    190

objects
  and belonging, 53, 99, 126, 141
  and identity, 47, 50, 54, 93, 129,
    136–7
  status/hierarchy, 46–7, 51, 212
  transitional, 130

objects – *continued*
  value and meaning of, 36–9, 43, 48, 56, 204
office, 176–7, 182–4, 187, 189, 191

performativity, 109, 112
positionality
  classed, 37–8, 149, 153, 162, 166, 213
  and consumption, 46–7, 122, 198–9, 202–3
  in the home, 55, 94, 97, 218, 222–3, 225–6
postmodern, 61, 62–3, 66, 68, 70
poststructuralist, 62, 177
poverty, 16–17, 28, 75
power, 136, 176, 178, 190
  and commodities, 47, 66
  lack of, 24–6, 28, 31
practices, 52, 129
  of consumption, 25–6, 38, 41–4, 52, 54–6, 70, 90, 94, 96, 104, 146–67, 177, 197–213, 216, 219
  cultural, 38, 50
  domestic/family, 13–14, 21–2, 26, 28–32, 108–22, 131–2, 218–20
  economic, 41, 81
  fashion, 49, 145–67, 221

reflexivity, 45, 179, 212
relationships
  interpersonal, 21, 26
  intimate, 13, 36, 37, 53–4, 56, 71–2, 75, 115, 177, 205, 212–13, 220
  personal, 220

second hand, 140, 197–213
sexism, 76
sexuality, 71, 77, 118, 137
shopping, 145–8, 158–62, 198–9
social inclusion, 141
stigma, 127, 152
storage, 101, 102, 216, 217, 219, 222–3, 225, 226–7
  cupboards, 95, 188, 218, 221–2, 225, 230
  of data, 138, 140, 141
  lofts, 220, 227
  shelves, 221, 224
structure, 89, 131, 136, 162, 164, 177, 199, 212
style, 50–1, 75–6, 149, 150, 157, 158, 160, 163

Ten Hours Movement, the, 14, 16–18, 21, 23, 25–32
transitions, 26, 87, 103, 119, 130, 226–7
transnational, 36–7, 40–1, 47, 51–3, 56

urban, 21, 60–1, 65, 69–70

violence, 72

welfare benefits, 67, 68, 88
workplace, 14, 26, 30, 116, 119, 176, 191

Printed and bound by CPI Group (UK) Ltd, Croydon, CR0 4YY